THE Telecaster GUITAR BOOK

Muddy Waters and trusty Telecaster

A COMPLETE HISTORY OF FENDER TELECASTER GUITARS

THE TELECASTER GUITAR BOOK
A COMPLETE HISTORY OF FENDER TELECASTER GUITARS
TONY BACON

A BACKBEAT BOOK
This new second edition 2012
First edition (as *Six Decades Of The Fender Telecaster*) 2005
Published by Backbeat Books
An Imprint of Hal Leonard Corporation
7777 West Bluemound Road,
Milwaukee, WI 53213
www.backbeatbooks.com

Devised and produced for Backbeat Books by
Outline Press Ltd
2A Union Court, 20-22 Union Road,
London SW4 6JP, England
www.jawbonepress.com

ISBN: 978-1-61713-105-9

A catalogue record for this book is available from the British Library.

DESIGN: Paul Cooper Design
EDITOR: Siobhan Pascoe

Printed by Regent Publishing Services Limited, China

12 13 14 15 16 5 4 3 2 1

CONTENTS

THE TELECASTER STORY

THE REFERENCE LISTING

"This guitar is something entirely new in the electric Spanish guitar field. The features found in this new guitar are far in advance of all the competition."

PART OF PUBLICITY RELEASE FOR FENDER'S NEW SOLIDBODY ELECTRIC MODEL

FENDER CATALOGUE, 1950

THE FENDER TELECASTER STORY

IT'S NOVEMBER 1950, and in the Riverside Rancho, the best country-music club in Los Angeles, Jimmy Bryant is puzzled. A virtuoso guitarist, renowned for his instrumental duets with pedal-steel man Speedy West and his crazy breaks on records by the likes of Tennessee Ernie Ford, he is talking to Leo Fender and George Fullerton. Leo has just handed Jimmy a prototype guitar, and Jimmy is bemused. He has never seen anything like it. Still, he plugs it in, starts to play, and begins to laugh with delight. This peculiar electric instrument is easy to work with, it's got a bright, magical tone, and Jimmy makes it sound as if a whole squad of guitarists are playing it at once. The three men exchange excited glances. They know that this is the start of something big – but just how big, they have no idea.

Fender's new solidbody electric guitar went on sale to musicians as the Telecaster in April 1951 following these guinea-pig testing sessions with musicians, as well as months of tweaking and trouble for Leo Fender and his team. The instrument had debuted a little earlier as the Esquire and then the Broadcaster. Leo's small firm was already turning out electric lap-steel guitars and amplifiers in a couple of buildings in Fullerton, Orange County, but soon the Telecaster's simple playability would lead to unimagined success and fortune.

All this was a long way from the Fender family's humble beginnings. Clarence Leonidas Fender was born in 1909 in a barn near the borders of Anaheim and Fullerton in the Los Angeles area, and the young Leo thought of Fullerton as his home town. Fullerton is in Orange County, just to the southwest of Los Angeles County, in Southern California. Leo's parents built their barn first because they couldn't yet afford to build a house, and they had a modest farm where they grew vegetables and fruit, including the county's famous oranges. Leo's father came to California from Illinois, and Leo's ancestors were American back to his great-great-great-great grandfather, who emigrated to the United States from Auerbach in Germany.

Leo's second wife, Phyllis, recalls a revealing episode from his early years. "When he was a little boy, his father told him that the only thing worthwhile in this whole world was what you accomplished at work, and that if you were not working you were lazy, which was a sin. So Leo judged himself and everyone else by that – and himself hardest of all."[1]

Leo began work as an accountant, at first at the state highway department and then a tyre distribution company, but his hobby was always electronics. In his twenties, he built amplifiers and PA systems for public events: sports gatherings, dances, and so on. He took a few piano lessons before trying the saxophone, but he was never serious, and he never learned to play the guitar.

When he lost his accounts job in the Depression, Leo took a bold step and opened his own radio and record store in Fullerton, around 1938. He called the new retail and repair shop Fender Radio Service, and it was a natural move for the ambitious and newly-married 30-year-old. He advertised his wares and services on his business card: "Electrical appliances, phonograph records, musical instruments & repairs, public address systems, sheet music." His new store on South Spadra (later renamed South Harbor Boulevard) meant that Leo met many local musicians and characters in the music and electronics businesses. During the first few years he hooked up with several people who would prove important to his future success. First among these was a professional violinist and lap-steel guitarist, Clayton Orr Kauffman, known to all simply as Doc.

The story goes that some time around 1940, Doc brought an amplifier into Leo's shop for repair and the two got chatting. Doc had amplified his own guitars and made designs for an electric guitar and a vibrato system. By this time, Leo had started looking into the potential for electric guitars and was playing around with pickup designs. They built a crude solidbody guitar around 1943 purely to test these early pickups, one design for which they patented a few years later. At the time of writing, the instrument was on display at the City Of Fullerton Museum.

Doc went to work for an aircraft company during World War II, but the two incorrigible tinkerers still found time to get together and come up with a design for a record-changer good enough to net them $5,000 in advance royalties. They used some of this money to bolster their shortlived company, K&F (for Kauffman & Fender), and they began production of electric lap-steel guitars and small amplifiers in November 1945.

Back in the 20s, many people in America had taken up the little lap-steel guitar, often called the Hawaiian guitar, and the instrument was still tremendously popular. The steel had been the first type of guitar to go electric in the 30s. Several innovative companies, with Rickenbacker in the lead, experimented with electro-magnetic pickups, fixing them to guitars and hooking them up to small amplifiers. The steel caught on as an easy-to-play instrument suitable for beginners, and the electric version also proved appealing to professional musicians, especially in Hawaiian music and among country-and-western bands.

The musician would play the steel guitar on his lap or play an instrument that was mounted on legs. The name came not from its construction – Fender's steels were all wooden – but from the metal bar the player held in his left hand to stop the raised strings, which were generally tuned to an open chord. During the 30s and later the term Spanish was used to identify the other (and then less popular) type of guitar, the one played upright against the body. Leo called this the standard guitar.

Doc Kauffman wrote later about the early days of K&F. "[Leo and I] would go down to the store, and at the rear was a metal building that housed the guitar department, and we would work till midnight." This description of a guitar department was optimistic. Most people who saw the "metal building" have described it as a tin shack hastily and cheaply put up behind Leo's radio store. Doc said: "I used to assemble all our instruments [there] and string them up and play a few steel licks, and Leo used to say he could tell how production was coming along by counting the tunes I was playing."[2]

Don Randall came next in Leo's line of important early partners. As we'll see, Randall would become a key contributor to the later success of the Fender company. For now, he was general manager of Radio & Television Equipment Co (known as Radio-Tel), based in Santa Ana, some 15 miles south of Fullerton. One of Randall's customers was the Fender Radio Service store.

Leo had not served in World War II because of a childhood illness that cost him his right eye. Randall, who spent three years in the army, recalled that Leo was able to expand his shop's trade in the war years. "During that period there weren't too many people about to do that kind of business," explained Randall. "When I got out of the service, I came back and started doing business with Leo again, selling him parts and equipment."[3] Radio-Tel, owned by Francis Hall, became the exclusive distributor of K&F products early in 1946, and salesman Charlie Hayes headed the push to persuade dealers to stock these steels and amps.

It was around this time that Leo and Doc Kauffman decided to split. "It seems Doc was afraid to carry on with the business," Randall said. Leo liked to work into the middle of the night at the tin shack making the K&F lap-steel guitars and amps, but Doc wasn't so keen to spend long hours locked away from the world. Leo said later: "It cost a lot of money to get into large-scale production, and the 30s depression was still fresh in Kauffman's mind, so he didn't want to get involved. He had a ranch or farm ... and he was afraid if we got over-extended on credit he might lose it. He thought he'd better pull out while he had a full skin, so in February of '46 he left it all with me."[4]

Doc, who remained a lifelong friend to Leo, did not resent selling out, despite the subsequent success of Fender. Doc used to joke that Leo would have killed him, anyway, if he'd stayed on, what with the long hours and tough work. "Doc liked to spend time with his family," said a colleague. "He didn't like staying down the shack till 10 or 11 at night, seven days a week. Anyone that worked with Leo had a hard time not over-working, because Leo expected you to be on call all hours."[5]

Leo and Doc parted. "His worry was right," Leo said later. "We had quite a few hard years ahead."[6] In 1946, Leo called his revised firm Fender Manufacturing, and he renamed it the Fender Electric Instrument Co in December 1947. Leo and a few employees continued to make lap-steels and amps as he had with K&F, but gradually he developed new products. He expanded into larger premises on nearby Pomona Avenue in Fullerton, at the corner of Santa Fe Avenue, separate from the radio store. The new property was described by one observer as "two plain steel buildings, not very handsome". Another Fender associate remembered that the Pomona buildings did not have their own toilets. Consequently, Fender workers had to cross the nearby railroad tracks to use the rest-rooms in the Santa Fe station. Eventually one rather elderly employee couldn't make the treacherous trans-railroad journey, and the next day Leo had no choice but to hire a portable toilet.

Dale Hyatt was another important new member of the gradually growing Fender team. He joined the company in January 1946 and would later become a crucial member of the Fender sales force. One of his early tasks, in late 1947 or early 1948, was to take over the radio store business, because Leo was busy getting started at Pomona Avenue. However, business was slow, and Fender had to rely on a loan from Radio-Tel's Francis Hall to keep going.

Leo was an introverted, hard-working man, enjoying long hours and selfless application to the task in hand. He was happiest when by himself, drawing up designs for new projects. He thought that if there was a product on the market already, he could make it better and cheaper – and make a profit in the process. Despite spectacular later successes, during these early years the new Fender company came perilously close to failing. It was Leo's sheer determination combined with his skill and luck in surrounding himself with clever, dedicated people that helped pull the business through these difficult times.

Now that the war was over, there was a general feeling that a fresh start was possible, and Americans began to consider the potential of mass production. Leo's particular application of this technique to guitar manufacturing was to be his master-stroke, but at first he still needed outside expertise in the mass-production of parts. And so another piece of the jigsaw came into place.

Karl Olmsted and his partner Lymon Race left the services in 1947 and decided to start a much-needed tool-and-die company in Fullerton, making specialist tools and dies that their customers would use to stamp out metal parts on punch presses. "We were looking for work," Olmsted says, "and Leo had reached the point where he needed dies to be made for production work. They'd been making parts by hand, cutting out the metal any way they could. But he was getting to the point where they wanted to make several of each thing." Race & Olmsted continued to make Fender's tooling and most metal parts for the next 30 years and more. "As it progressed, so we progressed to more complicated, sophisticated, high-production tooling," Olmsted says.[7]

Next to join Fender's company was George Fullerton, who became what one colleague described as Leo's faithful workhorse. The two had met at one of the outdoor events where Leo supplied a PA system, and the young George – "I was going to school," said Fullerton, "playing music, repairing radios, and delivering furniture" – started to help Leo with the PA events. Gradually, George's radio repair turned to fixing amps and lap-steels, and he began working at Pomona Avenue in February 1948. "It was only a small place then," he remembered, "only two or three people, a couple of girls."[8]

The business was not only small but still precarious. Lack of cash-flow was a regular problem. One employee reported that there were times when it was hard to cash Fender cheques locally – especially if Leo's wife, Esther, was late in receiving her wages from the phone company. An early ad for the new Fender company's wares in 1947 showed just three lap-steel models and a couple of amplifiers. Fender stressed the plus-points of the guitars: "Exclusive new patented pickup unit ... affording greater brilliance and presence. Equal volume output from all strings without compensating adjustments."

Leo and Don Randall were two highly motivated men with very different ways of working. "Leo sometimes was very resistant to change: you had to prove everything to him," Dale Hyatt says. "Nothing wrong with that; you just had to do it. Randall, of course, was much the same way: he was also rather stubborn in his realm of thinking. It's been said that they fought like cats and dogs, but I don't believe that's true at all. They couldn't fight – because they just didn't talk to each other, period. But I think one was as good as the other – and they were good for each other. I don't say that Leo Fender was the greatest thing that ever happened to Don Randall or vice versa. No, I think they were the greatest thing that happened to each other."[9]

Leo was certainly single-minded. He would have been happy if he could just continue to slave away in his workshop, sketching out pickup designs or fiddling away into the night with a new piece of machinery. As far as he was concerned, the fewer people who got in the way of all this, the better. And, generally speaking, Leo was – according to Leo – the only one able to get such things done. One of his colleagues said: "Leo might come in one morning and, buddy, he had something in his mind that he wanted to try. The place is burning down? Let it burn down. He wanted to do what he was on. And he wasn't one to give any compliments. You could tell Leo something and you'd give him an idea. He'd be looking straight at you and thinking. Wouldn't say a thing; wouldn't agree that you'd even told him anything. Then later on your idea would show up on something."[10]

Randall wanted good products at a competitive price that would rock the market, and he often had to shake things up at the factory to get results. Leo, meanwhile, would be changing a particular wiring set-up for the umpteenth time, constantly trying to perfect this guitar or that amp. "Leo was a strange man in a way," Randall said. "He had a fetish for machinery. Nothing was done economically, necessarily. If you could do it on a big machine, well, let's buy the big machine and use it – when you might have been able to buy the part the machine made a lot cheaper from a supplier."[11]

Karl Olmsted saw this, too. "Leo would say that he'd like a certain part, and we'd take it back to our workshop. Then I'd say, Leo, we'd have to hand-make every one of these, there's no way you can mass-produce it, it's going to be slow and expensive. He'd say well, what can you come up with that's cheap and that'll make me happy? Almost every job was that way."[12]

Fender's electric lap-steels began to enjoy local and increasingly wider success, on the West Coast, in the Southwest, and further eastwards. The local Fullerton paper reported in November 1949 that the Fender firm was "well known throughout the country" and yet "almost anonymous" in its home town.[13] Then Leo began to think about producing an electric 'Spanish' guitar, in other words one of standard shape and playing-style rather than his existing lap models. He had converted a few regular acoustic guitars to electric for individual customers but wanted to go further.

No one knows for sure who first thought of a Fender Spanish-style electric, although salesman Charlie Hayes may have suggested it to Leo. If he did, then it was easily the most important contribution he made to the company's prosperity, far beyond all the amps and instruments he sold and the dozens of dealers he enrolled and encouraged.

Guitar-makers and musicians really didn't understand or appreciate the potential for electric guitars, which were still in their infancy. Since the 30s, Rickenbacker, National, Gibson, and Epiphone had made regular 'Spanish' archtop hollowbody f-hole acoustic guitars with built-in electric pickups and associated controls. Aside from a handful of notable exceptions, however, guitarists in general did not see much use for these new instruments.

Rickenbacker was located in Los Angeles, not far from Fender, and had been the first with an electro-magnetic pickup – the type used since on virtually every electric guitar. Gibson set the style for the best hollowbody electrics, for example launching the accomplished ES-175 in 1949. And while demand was rising from dance-band guitarists, who found themselves increasingly unable to compete with the volume of the rest of the band, these early electric-acoustic guitars were more or less experimental, only partially successful from a technical standpoint, and still to become a commercial sensation. Nonetheless, a few guitar-makers, musicians, and amateur inventors in America were wondering about the possibility of a solidbody instrument. Leo himself had already made one: the pickup testbed that he'd built with Doc Kauffman in the early 40s. The attraction of a solidbody guitar to players was that it would cut the annoying feedback that amplified hollowbody guitars often produced. At the same time, a solid instrument would reduce the body's interference with the guitar's tone and so more accurately reproduce and sustain the sound of the strings. Rickenbacker had introduced a more or less solid Bakelite-body electric guitar in 1935 – the type that Doc Kauffman had played – but the guitar, offered in lap or Spanish forms, was small and awkward.

Around 1940, in New York City, guitarist Les Paul built what he called his log, a testbed electric that he cobbled together from a number of instruments and centred on a solid through-neck block of pine. A little later, Les concocted a couple of similar instruments for regular playing, which he called his clunkers. In Downey, California, about 15 miles west of Fender's operation in Fullerton, Paul Bigsby made a few custom solidbody electric guitars and mandolins – of which more shortly.

Fender pressed ahead on its own course, oblivious to the sneers from the guitar establishment over in the Midwest and the East. Leo would base the solid construction of the new guitar on the way he made his solid-wood steels. He wanted to maintain the advantages of these relatively easy-to-make guitars. There was absolutely no point, as far as he was concerned, to even consider the relatively complex methods used by contemporary electric guitar makers like Gibson and Epiphone. Their workers had to deal with multiple parts and spend a great deal of time and skilled effort to construct the hollowbody instruments.

It's often been said that Fender's workshop was more like a furniture factory than an instrument factory. Leo's head was ruled by expediency and straightforward practicality; so too, it followed, was the Fender shop.

We know that Doc Kauffman had a Rickenbacker semi-solidbody guitar. The inquisitive Leo must have studied the design of his friend's instrument in detail, and he couldn't have failed to notice that the Rick had a detachable neck. He would have realised this made sense for easy repair and service – returns of some early Fender products told him how important this was – and a detachable neck must have appealed to his love of simple, economic methods of working. National and Dobro, too, made their guitars with detachable necks, but along with Rickenbacker they were in the minority. Most mainstream makers employed the more time-consuming glued-on neck that, again, needed the attention of skilled workers.

Leo began to discover that he could manufacture a solidbody electric guitar practically and cheaply. He knew that such an instrument would make sense to musicians and offer them musical advantages. He explained later: "I guess you would say the objectives were durability, performance, and tone." He looked again at his existing steels when he considered the kind of tone that he had in mind for his new instrument. He said: "We wanted a standard guitar that had a little bit more of the sound of the steel guitar."[14]

Hollowbody electric guitars of the time generally delivered a warm, woody tone, in part a result of the construction of these instruments and the position of the pickup near the neck. Jazz guitarists loved that sound. Leo had something quite different in mind. Not for Fender the fat Gibson and Epiphone jazz voice. His lap-steels had a cleaner, sustained tone, and that's what he

Gearing up for a new kind of guitar

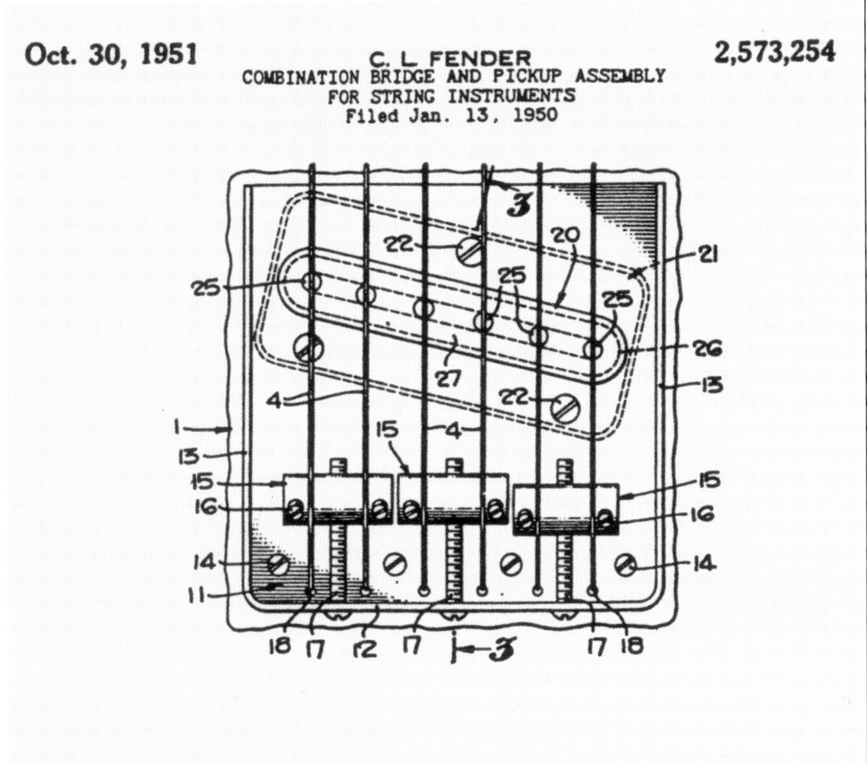

Oct. 30, 1951
C. L FENDER
COMBINATION BRIDGE AND PICKUP ASSEMBLY
FOR STRING INSTRUMENTS
Filed Jan. 13, 1950
2,573,254

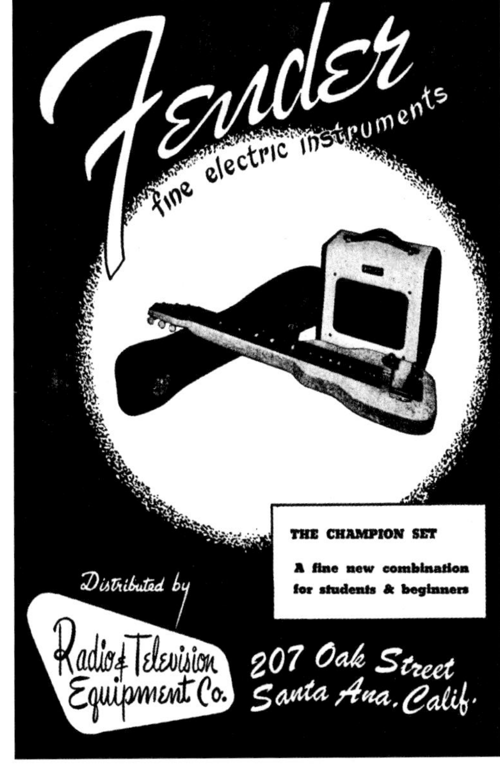

▲ 1948 Bigsby Merle Travis

The Fender company was a modest operation at the end of the 40s and into the early 50s, producing a small number of lap steel guitars and amplifiers. The ad from 1949 pictured (above) features the Champion steel, which had a slanted pickup (patent drawing, above left) that would be used for the new solidbody guitar that became the Telecaster. Another early solidbody was the instrument that Paul Bigsby made for Merle Travis (main guitar), built in 1948 about 15 miles from Fender's HQ. Leo Fender soon gathered around him an impressive team of colleagues, including the company's sales head Don Randall, pictured opposite (centre) in the early 50s showing off a new bass to a couple of trade-show visitors.

wanted for his new solidbody guitars, something like a cross between a clear acoustic guitar and a cutting electric lap-steel. Leo explained later: "I wanted to get the sound you hear when you hold the head of an acoustic guitar against your ear and pluck a string."[15]

As ever, he consulted many local musicians, trying out prototypes with them, putting testbed instruments in their hands, constantly asking their opinions on this pickup arrangement or that control set-up. One guinea pig talked about how he'd often turn around on stage at a local gig to see Leo "oblivious of musicians, audience, club management, and disruption generally," busily changing amp controls or suggesting guitar settings – and often in mid-song.[16]

George Fullerton remembered spending many long hours at Leo's side as the design for the Telecaster came together. "How do you design something that's a brand new item, a brand new thing, that will fit people and be desirable? We tried a lot of different things and finally came up with the basic design," Fullerton said. "It seemed to be the most suitable thing we had found: easy to hold, easy to play, and you could get to all the frets. Leo was very strong for building something that was very serviceable, durable, easy to repair, and, like he used to call it, built like a tank, to stand up to rough treatment. We tried to design something that would be strong and do a good job for a playing musician. We made lots of different things that we tested and tried. We didn't just decide what to do and do it; it had to be proven."[17]

Two single-pickup prototypes for the new guitar have survived. The first one dates from the summer of 1949 and has a two-piece pine body. Its headstock was based on Fender's existing lap-steel guitars – symmetrical, slightly tapered, and with three tuners each side. It had many features of the design that would go into production: an integral steel bridge-and-pickup assembly, a two-knob control plate, and a bolt-on neck. Fender based the bridge pickup – arguably the key component of the sound of the new guitar – on the one he already used for the Champion steel model, launched in 1949. The pickup was slanted to widen its tonal range – just as Gibson had done with the pickup on its ES-300 model, introduced in 1940. Fender's bridge pickup would come to be recognised as one of the firm's finest achievements. It had a tone all its own that would go on to attract successive generations of players. Not that anyone knew that yet.

Fender made a second prototype around the autumn or winter of 1949, this time from ash – which became a key timber for its early solidbody guitars – and now with an unusual six-tuners-on-one-side head, the type that we know and love today as the Telecaster headstock.

Over in Downey, 15 miles or so from Fender HQ, Paul Bigsby had a small workshop where he spent time fixing motorcycles and making pedal-steel guitars and vibrato units. He also ventured into making solidbody guitars and mandolins, hand-building a small number of distinctive instruments. Today, fewer than 25 of his guitars are known to have survived. Bigsby had started with the historic Merle Travis guitar, a solidbody that he completed in May 1948. It had through-neck construction (like the testbed guitars that Les Paul and Leo had made), through-body stringing, and a headstock that had an identical layout to Leo's, with the tuners all on one side.

Travis said that Leo borrowed his Bigsby guitar at this time. "Being a great craftsman himself, as we all knew, [Leo] wanted to build one like it. I had no use for it during the week, so I handed Leo Fender the guitar." Leo returned it the next weekend, Travis recalled in 1980, and he asked

Travis to try one "almost like it" that he'd made. "I told him I thought it was great," said Travis.[18] Don Randall wrote about Travis in a letter dated 1950: "He is playing the granddaddy of our Spanish guitar, built by Paul Bigsby – the one Leo copied."[19]

Meanwhile at Fender, the second prototype was tried and tested, and the new solidbody guitar was nearly ready to go. But Randall was frustrated. Leo did not have a finished sample good enough for the sales boss to take to the NAMM show over in New York City in summer 1949. At these important gatherings of the National Association of Music Merchants, manufacturers would show off their new models, usually before they appeared on the market. Dealers would visit from all over the country to decide which of the new wares they wanted to stock in their stores.

With time on his hands in New York, Randall took a good look around at the other makers' products. He lost no time in telling Leo his conclusion: a single pickup was simply not enough for the new guitar. He saw that Gibson was launching a new ES-5 hollowbody electric with no fewer than three pickups, and several other companies had two-pickup models at the show.

Randall battled with Leo over the need for a two-pickup guitar. Fullerton again: "Leo was a really strong-minded person with the ideas he had: you didn't change him. If he had an idea to try something, the only way you'd ever change him would be to prove that what he had would not work."[20] Reluctantly, Leo would end up with two new solidbody guitars: the single-pickup (and, briefly, two-pickup) Esquire; and, slightly later, the two-pickup Broadcaster.

But first, by April of 1950, Fender at last had the completed single-pickup instrument to promote in its catalogue. "The 'Esquire' guitar is something entirely new in the electric Spanish guitar field," wrote Randall, who named the new Esquire himself. "The features found in this new guitar are far in advance of all the competition." Today we're used to advertising hype; back then, this was more or less the truth. Randall went on to highlight the attractions of the new-fangled construction. "Because the body is solid, there is no acoustic cavity to resonate and cause feedback as in all other box type Spanish guitars. The guitar can be played at extreme volume without the danger of feedback."[21]

Richard Smith charted this early history in his book *Fender: The Sound Heard 'Round The World*, noting that Fender salesman Dave Driver got his sample of the new single-pickup Esquire on April 4th 1950, with his colleague Charlie Hayes receiving two more on the 7th and the 15th. In May, Fender had added a new concrete building alongside the two steel ones on Pomona Avenue, presumably with increased production in mind. But for now, Fender was not making the solidbody guitars in any great numbers. The Esquire, by now with two pickups, first appeared on a pricelist dated August 1st at $139.95 (plus a case for another $39.95) alongside six steel guitars and five amplifiers.

The Fender Esquire was simple and effective, with its basic, single-cutaway solid slab of ash for a body and separate screwed-on maple neck. It was geared to mass production. The slanted pickup was suspended in a steel bridge-plate carrying three brass adjustable bridge-saddles that carried two strings each. The body was finished in a yellowish semi-transparent colour known as blond (black for a few early pine-body samples) and the plastic pickguard (vulcanized fibre, to be precise) was black. The guitar was plain. It was like nothing else and it was ahead of its time. The new Esquire

Starting life as an Esquire

In its earliest guise, the new Fender solidbody electric was called the Esquire, as seen in the first advertisement to include the guitar (below) in 1950. The early pre-production sample is finished in black, like the Esquire that Spade Cooley's guitarist Jimmy Wyble plays in another 1950 ad (right). Western-swing fiddle star Cooley had a popular TV show with his band (pictured on set, left, with a Fender steel player). Guitarist Charlie 'Walkin The Guitar Strings' Aldrich was photographed by Leo in the new Fender factory in summer 1950 (opposite, inset) holding a one-pickup Esquire. Aldrich's early model was finished in the natural colour known now as blond, which became the standard look for the Esquire, Broadcaster, and Telecaster.

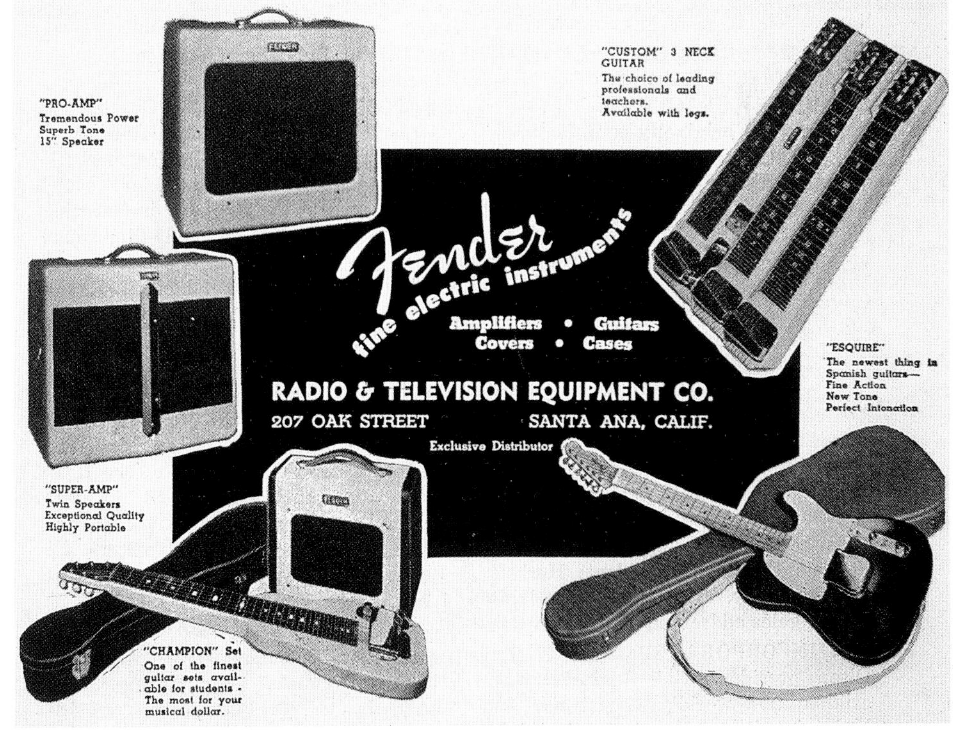

fulfilled Leo's aim to have a standard guitar that was easy to build, and as such embodied one of the reasons for Fender's coming success. It was a relatively simple, unadorned guitar that served a practical purpose: it did exactly what the player wanted as soon as he plugged it into an amp.

But it did not prove immediately easy to sell, as Randall soon found out. The next time he went to a NAMM show – in Chicago in July 1950 – he had a sample of the new guitar with him. Randall represented Fender alongside salesmen Charlie Hayes and Don Patton at Radio-Tel's display in Room 795 at the Palmer House. "I just got laughed out of the place," said Randall. "Our new guitar was called everything from a canoe paddle to the snow shovel. There was a lot of derision."

Randall did have at least one useful meeting at the Chicago trade show, however, when Al Frost from National explained that the lack of any neck strengthening in the samples would be likely to cause problems later for neck stability. "So I contacted Leo," Randall recalled, "and I says Leo, we've got to have a neck [truss] rod in there. Leo said, 'No we don't need one, it's rock maple.' I said I tell you one thing: either we put a neck rod in there or we don't sell it. Now make up your mind!

"And this was the way I had to handle Leo," Randall explained. "He was actually kind of afraid of me; I don't know why. I was the only guy who could handle him and make him do things. Rest of them it was, Oh yeah Leo, yes Mr Fender. But Leo was about two-thirds afraid of me, because I really leaned on him to get him to make changes that were necessary. So we put out just a few of them without a neck rod, and then we put a neck rod in."[22]

Salesman Dale Hyatt also had to struggle against a less than serious view of these new Fenders he was trying to sell further north. He had his Esquire samples and was out selling them in Manteca, a few miles inland from San Francisco. Hyatt's brother, who lived in the area, had tipped him off about the dozens of country musicians playing around town – and it was country players who were showing most interest in the new Fender electric guitar.

"They had these nightclubs going and guys playing honky-tonk and country-western," Hyatt says of Manteca. "I'd taken five guitars with me. So I got a guy playing one. He quite liked it – and all of a sudden it just quit, and he didn't know what was wrong with it. It was embarrassing. So I went out to the truck and got another one. It lasted about 30 minutes and it quit. Then they started saying: 'There he goes again, ladies and gentlemen – wonder how many he's got?' Anyway, the third one kept on going and worked for the rest of the evening."

Hyatt had stumbled on a weakness of the new Fender's pickup shielding in the most public way imaginable. This was the cost of trying to sell pre-production versions and working prototypes. "But anyhow, that was the start of it," Hyatt laughs. "That gentleman came down to my brother's house the next day and brought his son's electric train set, which he wanted to trade for one of the guitars. Another of the first ones sold of what we now know as the Telecaster – it might have been the second or third I sold, I'm not sure – was to a gentleman in Long Beach. He was one of the very first people to buy Leo Fender's solidbody guitar, and I know he played that thing for years and years."[23]

For now, Fender put aside the Esquire until proper production of the single-pickup model began in January 1951. But in October or November 1950, the firm started production of a two-pickup Fender, now with added truss-rod following the trade-show advice – and following some more badgering of Leo by Randall. It was Randall who came up with a new name, Broadcaster, and the retail price was set at $169.95. This put it around the same level as Gibson's fine ES-175 hollowbody electric, which sold for $175. In today's money, that would be equivalent to about $1,350, underlining the fact that these were not cheap guitars. The most basic new hollowbody electric from budget brands such as Silvertone, for example, could be had back then for around $40 ($300 in today's money).

The Broadcaster was really the first Fender solidbody electric to be made and sold in any reasonable numbers. Leo said later: "The single- and double-pickup guitars overlapped ... but the Broadcaster was the first one we built."[24] In other words, we can presume he meant this was the first model to be built in significant numbers. Richard Smith calculated that Fender sold 152 Broadcasters in the first two months of 1951. All this makes the Fender Broadcaster the historically significant solidbody electric guitar.

The Broadcaster name was shortlived, however, halted in February 1951 after Gretsch, the large New York City-based instrument manufacturer, wrote to Fender to say it already used 'Broadkaster' for drum products (and earlier for banjos). Gretsch had already stopped another drum company, Slingerland, from using the name, and evidently was sufficiently troubled by Fender's guitar to block that use, too.

Fender complied with the request to stop using the name, as Dale Hyatt explains. "There was a sense of camaraderie between the manufacturers in the early days. No one was trying to beat the other to a patent or anything like that. So Gretsch just pointed it out and we agreed to change it."[25] This was echoed in Randall's letter to Fender salesmen dated February 21 1951 where he outlined the need for a change of name. He told them that Gretsch had advised Fender of the infringement. "We have checked this and are inclined to agree that they are fair in their request," wrote Randall. "Consequently, it behooves us to find a new name. ... If any of you have a good name in mind I would welcome hearing from you immediately." At first, Fender simply used up their existing Fender Broadcaster decals on the guitar's headstock by cutting off 'Broadcaster' and leaving just the Fender logo. These rare no-model-name guitars are known today among collectors as Nocasters.

A few days later, Randall coined the new name for the Fender solidbody: Telecaster. (Randall subsequently came up with virtually all the well-known Fender guitar model names.) The Telecaster name certainly seemed appropriate, fresh from the new age of television and telecasts. Leo himself was well aware of the drawing power of TV, as George Fullerton explained. "When television was brand new, Leo's store was probably the only place in town that had televisions, and he used to have one that he'd put in the window facing out into the street, speaker outside. At night there'd be a crowd of people around watching wrestling or whatever was on. Sometimes it would be cold and foggy, but there'd still be this crowd of people."[26]

The Telecaster name was on headstocks of the two-pickup model by April 1951, and at last Fender's new solidbody electric had a permanent name. Fender's list price for the Telecaster was $189.50 (about $1,600 in today's money). The single-pickup Esquire was also available by now, priced at $149.50, and a solid case for either model added $39.95. One of the earliest players to

Broadcasting on all six strings

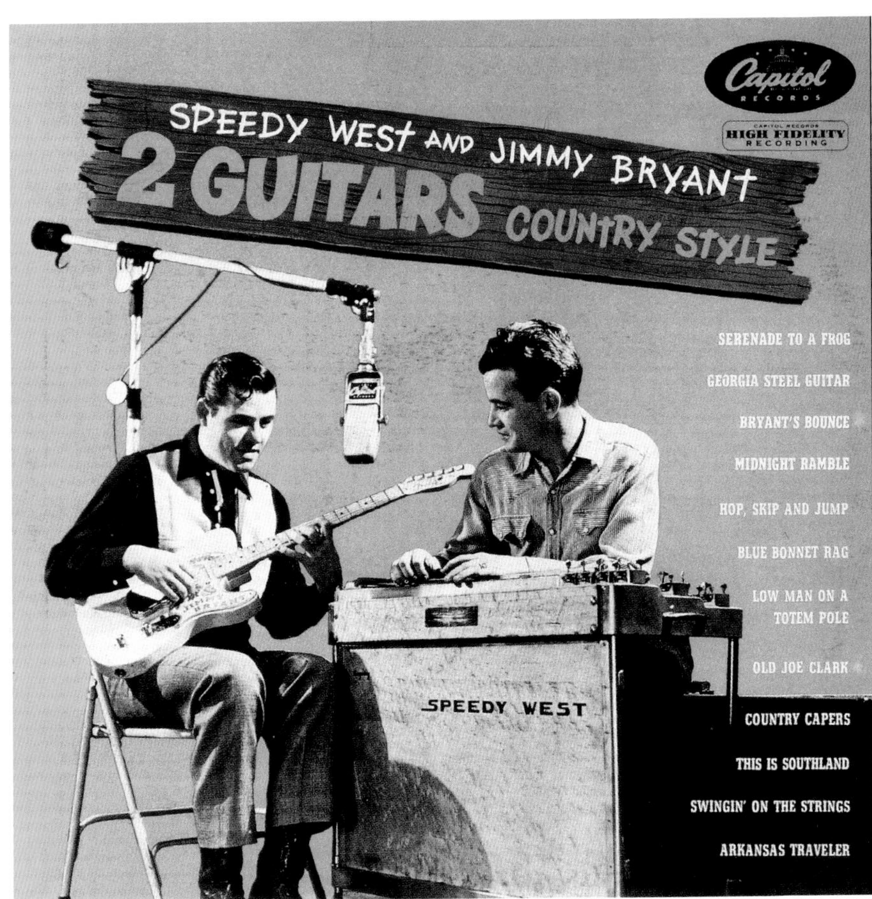

The Fender Broadcaster (main guitar) was the shortlived production model of Fender's new solidbody. Leo's old colleague Doc Kauffman is seen (opposite) at the Fender factory with a new Broadcaster in winter 1950/51. The Gretsch drum company objected to the use of 'Broadcaster' (they had Broadkaster drums) so Fender looked for a new name. In the meantime they snipped the headstock decal (below), resulting in 'Nocaster' guitars. One of the earliest notable players of Fender's new electric was Jimmy Bryant (above), often teamed with pedal-steel man Speedy West.

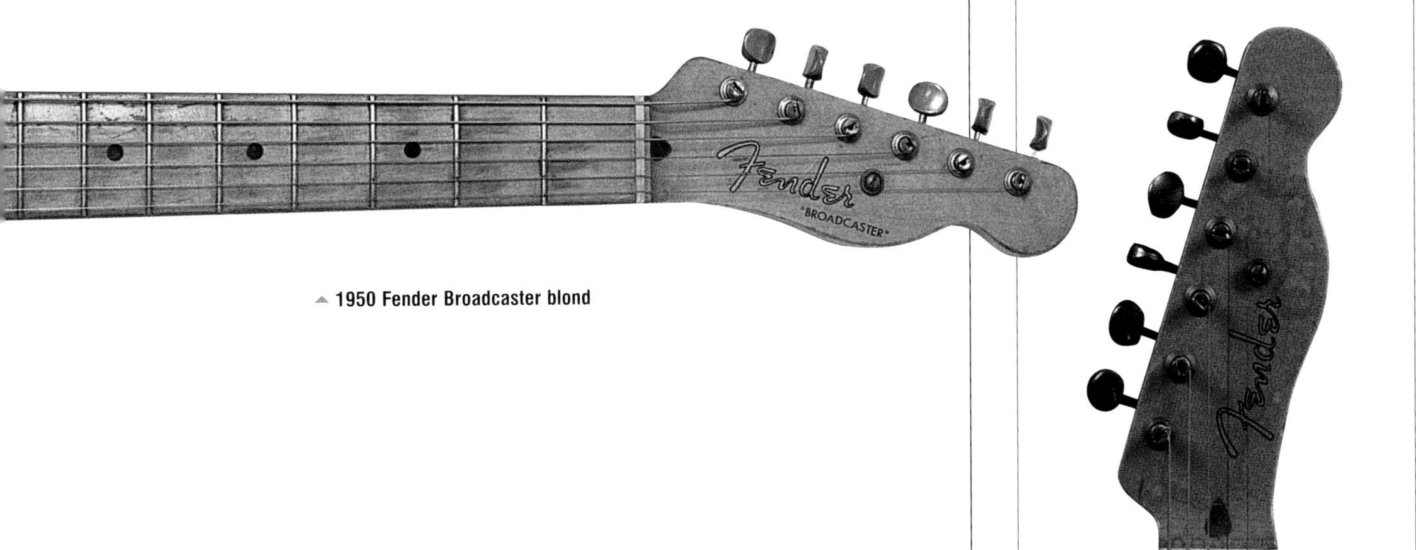

▲ 1950 Fender Broadcaster blond

appreciate the new Fender sound was Jimmy Bryant, best known for his outstanding guitar instrumental duets with Speedy West, a pedal-steel virtuoso (and Fender player). Bryant was a busy Los Angeles session player and a regular on Cliffie Stone's country TV showcase, *Hometown Jamboree*. You can hear Bryant's remarkable playing on cuts like 'Bryant's Bounce' by Speedy West & Jimmy Bryant (1952), 'Catfish Boogie' by Tennessee Ernie Ford (1953), or 'Oakie Boogie' by Ella Mae Morse (1952), each a glimpse at Bryant's clean, clever, and sometimes wild playing that ever since has had us all wondering quite how he did it.

Leo and George Fullerton took an early Broadcaster out to the Riverside Rancho, a western-music nightclub in Glendale, California, where Bryant was playing. He looked at the strange new guitar, picked it up, and started playing. Fullerton: "He got to do a lot of neat things on this guitar, and pretty soon all these people who'd been dancing were crowding around listening to what he was doing. It wasn't long before the whole band was standing around, too. He was the centre of attention. Jimmy played things on guitar that nobody could play. And of course this was an electric with low action – and with that cutaway he could go right up the neck. So naturally we put one in his hand, and this was like starting a prairie fire. Pretty soon we couldn't make enough of those guitars. That wasn't the only reason, but it was a lot of it, because Jimmy was on television shows, personal appearances, and everybody wanted a guitar like Jimmy Bryant's. That was one of the starting points of that guitar."

Fullerton said that Fender guitars were aimed at the working musician. "Think of a movie cowboy and you might remember Roy Rogers, Gene Autry: the big silver screen, and here they are in their fancy hats, shirts, and boots and shiny gold-plated guns. But did you ever see a real working cowboy? He's dirty, with rough boots on and heavy leather on his pants."

The thing was, said Fullerton, the team at Fender back then looked at guitar players as working cowboys. "If a guitar player's gonna go out on stage, say a personal appearance, and he's a top-notch entertainer, well, he might want a flashy guitar and flashy clothing. But that's not a working musician, and that's not his dress code. See, this Telecaster was so popular – still is right today – and it's part of the dress code of the musician. Take that out of their hands and put something else there, and you're taking away part of their dress, part of their appearance. It's like taking Roy Rogers but putting a cap on him instead of the hat."[27]

Meanwhile, business picked up as news of the Telecaster and Esquire spread and as Randall's five Radio-Tel salesmen – Charlie Hayes, Don Patton, Dave Driver, Mike Cole, and Art Bates – began to persuade store owners to stock the company's new solidbody instruments. Fender launched another important instrument in 1951, the Precision Bass, which was the first commercially successful solidbody electric bass guitar. (This was the exception to Randall naming the instruments; 'Precision' was Leo's idea.) The P Bass was typical of Fender's early products: it had an elegant simplicity and was designed for easy piece-together construction. Leo always opted for function over looks. "I had so many years of experience with work on radios and electronic gear," he said, "and my main interest was in the utility aspects of an item – that was the main thing. Appearance came next. That gets turned around sometimes."[28] Despite all these exciting new developments with the solidbody guitar and bass, during the early 50s Fender's main business remained in amplifiers and electric steel guitars. Those lines were of vital importance to the reorganised Fender operation, and they were rapidly expanded.

Western swing was a lively dance music that grew up in Texas dancehalls during the 30s and 40s, and its guitarists popularised the electric guitar in America, at first mostly with steel guitars. Many western swing steel players, like Noel Boggs with Spade Cooley and Leon McAuliffe with Bob Wills, played their driving electric guitar runs on Fender models such as the Stringmaster. There were also some 'Spanish' guitarists like Telecaster-wielding Bill Carson with Hank Thompson's Brazos Valley Boys, who played a commercial fusion of western swing and honky tonk and had a 1952 Number 1 country-chart hit with 'The Wild Side Of Life'.

"I didn't have the money to buy an amp and guitar outright, so Leo sold me a Telecaster and an amp for 18 bucks a month," Carson recalled, "with the understanding that I would spend a few hours each week as a musical guinea pig. He wrote our agreement on a yellow tablet sheet and stuck it in an old rickety file cabinet. That was our contract."[29] Spade Cooley's guitarist Jimmy Wyble was another early Fender player, pictured with a black-finish Esquire in a 1950 ad.

The new single-pickup Esquire and two-pickup Telecaster were on sale from the early months of 1951, and these blond-finish models would be the target of a few changes over the rest of the decade. During the following year, Fender made a fundamental change to the wiring of the two-pickup control operation. The Tele had two metal knobs and a three-way selector switch. The front knob always controlled overall volume, but beyond that it got a bit tricky.

Until the change, the two-pickup models were wired so that the selector in the rear position delivered both pickups, with the rear knob controlling the amount of neck-pickup sound blended into the bridge-pickup sound. The selector in the other two positions delivered neck-pickup only with preset tone: in the middle position with a 'natural' tone and in the front position a bassier tone; the rear knob was non-functioning in either setting.

In 1952, Fender changed that configuration: in the new two-pickup system, shoving the selector into the rear position now delivered the bridge pickup alone, with the rear knob acting as a proper tone control, while the middle position gave neck pickup alone, also with proper tone control. In the front position the effect was the same as the old system, in other words neck-pickup alone with a preset bassier tone and a non-functioning rear knob. This meant that for now (and until the late 60s) there was no both-pickups setting. As we'll see, some players soon discovered 'secret' settings between the selector switch's official stops.

The single-pickup Esquire, too, had an odd control system. Again, there were two metal knobs and a three-way selector switch, with the front knob always controlling volume. The selector in the rear position gave the pickup direct, with the rear tone knob disabled. The middle position gave what you'd expect of a simple single-pickup guitar, with regular volume and tone controls. The front position provided a preset bassier tone, again with a non-functioning rear tone knob.

On both the Telecaster and the Esquire, the original black pickguard was changed to white in 1954. The following year, both models gained staggered polepieces on the bridge pickup, giving a slightly tougher sound, and the serial number was stamped onto the neckplate rather

From henceforth thou art Telecaster

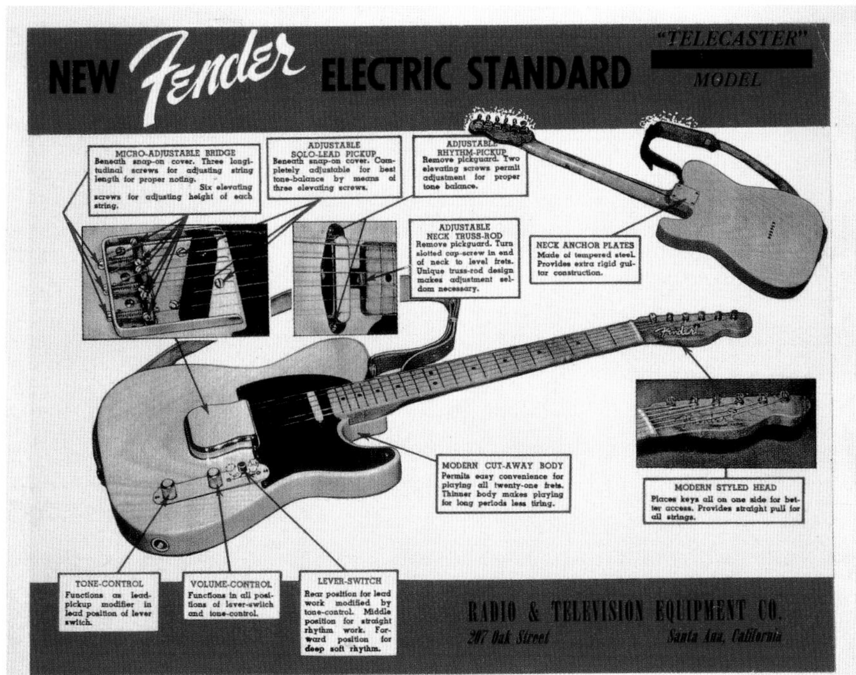

Following Gretsch's request, Fender changed the name of the Broadcaster to Telecaster – and so was born the company's longest-running electric guitar model. Fender adapted its existing promo sheet for the Broadcaster (left) to reflect the new model name. The instrument pictured (main guitar) is typical of the earliest style of Telecaster, and Fender's attorneys drew up a 1951 patent for the design (opposite, below). Bill Carson was an early player who enjoyed using a Telecaster, and he's shown (opposite) among the line-up of Hank Thompson's band at the time of their 1952 hit 'The Wild Side Of Life'. Meanwhile, a Fender ad from that same year (bottom right) underlines the availability of the new solidbody in two forms: the single-pickup Esquire and the two-pickup Telecaster.

HANK THOMPSON and his BRAZOS VALLEY BOYS

Nation's No. 1 Western Recording Artist Recording exclusively on Capitol Records

Nation's No. 1 Western Swing Band.

PERSONAL MANAGEMENT—

15½ S. WALKER, OKLAHOMA CITY, OKLA. JIM HALSEY PHONES—REGENT 6-8081, REGENT 6-0002

1953 Fender Telecaster blond

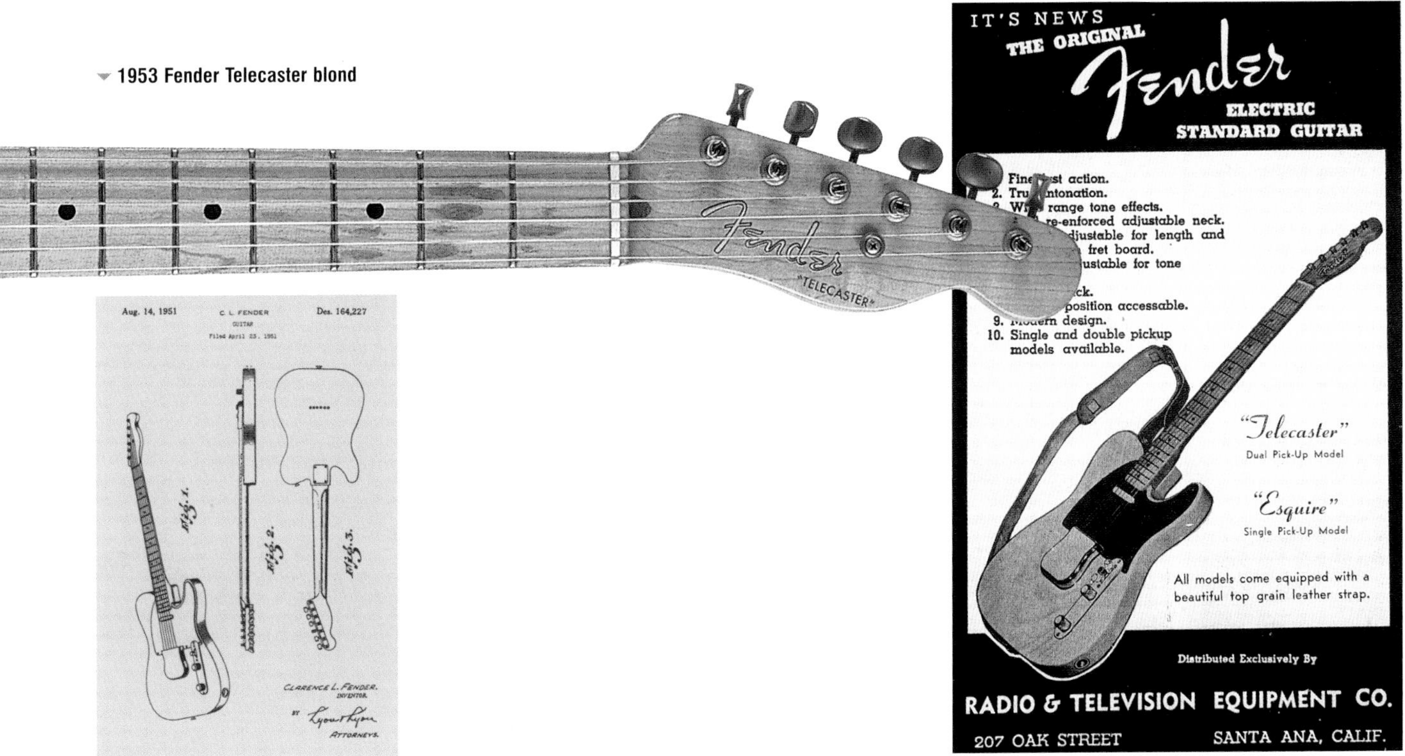

than the bridgeplate. An easy but satisfying way to empty your bank account in the 21st century is to opt for one of the all-original blackguard maple-neck Teles dating from these crucial early years of production.

Other makers at first merely continued to mock Fender's unique solidbody guitars. But soon Gibson had joined in with its Les Paul and Kay with the K-125 model (both 1952) and then Gretsch launched its Duo Jet (1953). Don Randall and his team controlled the sales side of Fender, and another important addition came in 1953 when steel guitarist Freddie Tavares joined the firm, mainly to help Leo design new products. Tavares was best known as the man who played the swooping steel intro over the titles of the *Looney Tunes* cartoons. He was a native Hawaiian, and as a young musician he bought a Rickenbacker electric steel guitar to play with a local pro dance band, Harry Owens' Royal Hawaiians.

Tavares moved to California in 1942, soon becoming a busy session player for movies, records, radio, and TV, playing on countless studio dates in Los Angeles with everyone from Doris Day to Elvis Presley. He played in local country bands and had moved to a Magnatone steel model. It was Spade Cooley's steel player, Noel Boggs, who introduced him to Leo Fender.

Freddie's son Terry recalls his father as a passionate perfectionist. Terry was just ten when Freddie went to work for Leo in 1953. "He was playing steel guitar at the time with Wade Ray & His Ozark Mountain Boys at a big club in south Los Angeles called Cowtown," Terry says. "One time, dad's friend Noel Boggs came in with Leo Fender, and after the show Noel introduced Leo to dad. Leo asked dad who made his steel guitar and amp. Dad said he did – and then proceeded to tell Leo what was wrong with his amps. Leo whipped out a screwdriver, opened dad's amp, and examined the circuits. Soon after that, he offered dad a job at his small factory shop next to the post office in Fullerton. Dad had an agreement with Leo that whenever he got a record session or movie-studio call he could leave his work at Fender and attend to it. He was very busy designing guitars and amps and with studio work."[30]

Freddie himself explained the working methods at the Fullerton workshop. "When it was just Leo and I, we did what we pleased. In other words, Leo did what he pleased, and I was just his assistant."[31] A colleague described Tavares, who died in 1990, as "one of the best musicians I have ever known, and just as good at engineering. He was a very talented man".[32]

Early in 1953, Fender's existing sales set-up with Radio-Tel was re-organised into a new distribution company, Fender Sales, and the new setup was operational by June. Based like Radio-Tel in Santa Ana, Fender Sales had four business partners: Leo, Don Randall, Francis Hall, and Charlie Hayes (the latter three coming from Radio-Tel).

Hayes, who had been Radio-Tel's first salesman, was killed in a road accident in 1955. Dale Hyatt took over his sales patch – Fender's radio store had closed in 1951. Late in '53, Francis Hall had effectively sealed his own fate by buying the Rickenbacker company and becoming a competitor. Two years later, Fender Sales would change to a partnership between just Leo and Randall, although it was Randall who actually ran this pivotal part of the Fender business. As Dale Hyatt says: "You can make the finest guitar in the world, but if you don't sell the first one you're not going to get the chance to make another."[33]

In June 1953, Fender acquired a three-and-a-half-acre plot at South Raymond Avenue and Valencia Drive in Fullerton and put up three new buildings. Fullerton's City Council was on a programme of rapid and significant industrial development. "Prior to 1950," reported the *Los Angeles Times*, "Fullerton was a citrus area with its industries primarily devoted to citrus products and food processing." The paper quoted a Fullerton official on the changes being made in the new decade. "Everyone liked the peaceful area geared to country living. But some began to realise that industry was needed to balance the economy as more and more people came in. Now there's almost 100 percent support for [the expansion]."[34]

Fender's new buildings in the heart of Fullerton's development area were a sign that the company was keen to expand its line of products. As well as the two electric guitars, the Telecaster and Esquire, Fender had a line of seven amplifiers (Bandmaster, Bassman, Champ, Deluxe, Princeton, Super, Twin Amp), five electric steel guitars (Custom, Deluxe, Dual, Stringmaster, Student), and the Precision Bass. But the firm wanted to produce more. *The Music Trades* magazine reported that, with the new property, Fender "hoped that production will be upped by almost 100 percent in the next few months".[35] First, however, the somewhat haphazard production methods had to be organised more efficiently.

This job fell into the very capable hands of another newcomer, Forrest White. He worked as an industrial engineer at an aircraft firm in Akron, Ohio, but during a business trip to Los Angeles in 1944 he fell in love with the area and resolved to move there. White had built several guitars in his spare time, including an early solidbody electric ("way before Leo did," he claimed later).

White's opportunity to move out west came in 1951 when he was hired by a Los Angeles company. He'd already met Leo a few times, and one day in spring 1954 they had lunch. Leo asked White if he'd be interested in helping him sort out some "management problems" at Fender. White remembered their conversation. "Freddie Tavares had told Leo that the company was ready to go down the drain. It was that bad," White recalled. "Leo had no credit whatsoever and had to pay cash buying any material and so on. Some of the employees' cheques were bouncing. Freddie had said that Leo didn't have anyone in the plant who could do what needed to be done. So it just so happened that my timing was right."[36]

Karl Olmsted of Race & Olmsted, Fender's tool-and-die maker, recalls how close Fender came to going broke at the time. "He tried to buy us with stock, to get out of paying our bills, and like idiots we didn't take the bait," Olmsted remembers with hindsight. "But, actually, I'm not sorry, because I'm not sure that I could have worked for Leo day in, day out. At least we had the advantage of occasionally being able to say, 'Leo, this is all we can take,' and stepping back. As good as the relationship was, once in a while you had to do that – and I couldn't if they'd taken us over. We just gave him credit and credit and credit, practically to the point where we couldn't make our payroll and bills and everything else. If this guitar craze hadn't taken off, he wouldn't have made it. So genius has to have some luck – and he had both."[37]

Meanwhile, Leo took an intrigued Forrest White to look at Fender's set-up at the new South Raymond buildings. "And it was a mess," White remembered. "There was no planning whatsoever, and that was because Leo was not an engineer; he was an accountant. Things had just been set

From B.B. to Guitar Boogie

▲ 1952 Fender Esquire blond

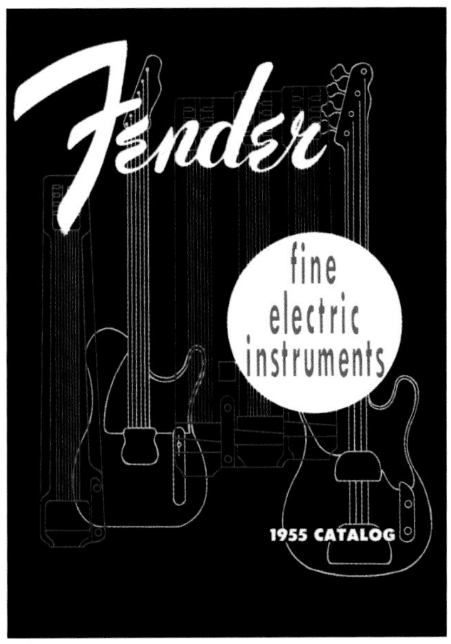

Leo Fender liked nothing better than to buy and try out new machines for his factory, such as the punch press that he stands alongside in the 50s photograph opposite. As the decade progressed, Leo's company continued to make steel guitars, amplifiers ... and the new solidbody electric models: the one-pickup Esquire and the two-pickup Telecaster. A young B.B. King is pictured here clutching an early Esquire, and the main guitar on these pages is a fine early Esquire, still with black pickguard. Fender changed this to white a few years later on both the Esquire and Telecaster. A flyer published inside *Down Beat* magazine in July 1955 (opposite, centre) included Arthur 'Guitar Boogie' Smith on the cover with a Telecaster. Meanwhile, the front of Fender's official 1955 catalogue (above) revealed a more impressive design, with the stylised outline of a Telecaster as one of the cover stars.

down any place. Man, everything was just so mixed up, you can't believe it. There was no planning whatsoever, because, in all fairness to him, he didn't have any experience in things like that."

White agreed to come in and work for Leo, beginning in May 1954. "But I said it depends on one thing. If I can have a free hand to do what I know has to be done, fine. Otherwise I'm not interested. He gave me that free hand. When I stepped in, from that point on I ran the company. He stayed in design, but I ran it."

White resolved a troubling production problem at the Fender factory by devising an incentive scheme that was tied to quality control. Assemblers on the production line were not allowed to accept a product from the previous stage unless they were happy that it was perfect – effectively making each assembler an inspector. "The reason for that," White explained, "was that if something had to be re-worked, it was on their own time. If someone loused up, then hey – once they accepted it, it's their problem. But as long as they turned out good production that passed, they made good money, darned good money."[38]

Now Leo had able men – Forrest White and Don Randall – at the head of the production and sales halves of the Fender company. He had a new factory and a small but growing reputation. And he had the start of a fresh generation of guitars – the solidbody Telecaster, Esquire, and Precision Bass – with Freddie Tavares on board and ready to help him design new ones.

Leo being Leo, he was not content to stay still. Soon, he and the team were working on a new guitar – the one that would be released in 1954 as the Stratocaster. Leo thought that the new, improved model would necessarily replace the Telecaster. Not quite. Fender's new Strat did not have an immediate impact, and only later in rock'n'roll did it find its true home. Richard Smith calculated that during 1954 and '55 Fender sold 720 Strats and 1,027 Teles. As we'll see, those proportions would fluctuate during the coming years.

Forrest White explained later that the manufacturing process for electric guitars was simple and effective at Fender in the 50s. "We bought our lumber in long lengths, 18 or 20 feet, ash or alder, depending on what we were making," he said. "We'd make the Telecasters out of ash because of their almost transparent blond finish. You'd cut the wood and glue it together so you'd have a block of wood that was the size of a guitar body."

In the Fender shop, said White, the workers then used router plates, made out of quarter-inch steel in the shape of the guitar body. "You'd attach one to the bottom with a couple of screws, and you could drill on that side, where the neck plate and everything went. On the other side went the plate where the pickups and everything ran. So you always had a minimum of two plates, sometimes three, later, depending on how sophisticated the instrument was – some might have more cut-outs and so on. You'd screw those on, trace around them, band-saw the body roughly to shape, then take off the excess on the router, and on it would go for sanding."

For shaping the necks, which Fender called ovalling, White said the factory had a couple of sanders that would swing the neck back and forth. "And then there was a mandrel that had the holes cut out for the frets. Leo designed almost all of the tooling himself. It was very simple, but it was a case of having to walk before you ran. We didn't have any computerised routers and so on like they have now, where they can cut out half a dozen necks at a time. It was one at a time back then, and everything was simple. Crude, really, but it got the job done."[39] There were more crude machines throughout Fender's factories. Some workers used ramshackle affairs with wheels and pulleys to wind pickups. There were some ad hoc finish-spray booths near a wall of racks for drying the freshly sprayed bodies. There were punch presses for making metal parts and benches at which workers did final assembly. For Telecasters, one would screw on pickguards and the neck pickup and fit the bridge/pickup unit and Kluson tuners, and then another would take over and solder the electronics together. Finally, new Teles would be strung up and tested through an amp.

Among collectors, some of Fender's shop-floor workers of the 50s have become almost as well known as Leo, Forrest, Don, Freddie, George, and the rest. This renown has developed thanks to White's approval system, where the worker would often sign parts of the guitar as it went through production. One well known signature is the pencilled TG or TAD that identifies Tadeo Gomez.

Gomez started at Fender in the late 40s and was soon working on guitar necks. Like many of the factory people that Fender employed, Gomez was born in Mexico. He moved up to the USA when he was in his teens, finally settling in La Habra, a mile or two north of Fullerton. His son Ben Gomez said: "I remember my father taking me to work at Fender's. There used to be quite a few from La Habra that worked [there]. Women worked there doing soldering and the electrical wiring. Some other [men] made the body; dad would be outside sanding and shaping the necks. Sometimes he carved a little to get it just right. He had taught himself woodworking. Nothing was too hard for him to learn."[40] Gomez left Fender in the late 50s to work at Disneyland, but he returned in the mid 60s. He died in 1986.

For now, Fender continued to sell its established lines. Steel guitars were virtually unchanged, but in 1956 the one-pickup Musicmaster and two-pickup Duo-Sonic appeared, a pair of budget solidbody guitars alongside the Tele, Esquire, and Strat. Fender's publicity described the two new models as "three-quarter size" and thus "ideal for students and adults with small hands".

There were over 50 people working at Fender, and the factory was humming with constant activity. Work would sometimes spill out into the alleyways, a distinct advantage of the California climate. But Leo was almost always inside, and often he would burn the midnight oil. Soon, his firm's problem was not how to sell the guitars, but how to make enough of them to meet the apparently ever-increasing demand. As blues, rhythm & blues, and rock'n'roll grew in popularity, Fender's place in music history was assured. "After rock'n'roll started," Fender salesman Dale Hyatt says, "of course all the dealers who had been so hesitant began teaching the electric Spanish guitar."[41]

We've already met one notable Tele player, Jimmy Bryant – but for all his untamed dexterity he could hardly be described as a rock'n'roller. Neither could B.B. King, who used a Telecaster around 1950 when he first went out on the road, nor Gatemouth Brown who played one on early-'50s instrumentals such as 'Okie Dokie Stomp'. But the most visible player of the Tele in the late 50s was James Burton, seen almost every week playing alongside pop'n'roller Ricky Nelson on the TV show *The Adventures Of Ozzie & Harriet*. Back in 1953, a 13-year-old Burton had persuaded his parents to buy him a brand new Telecaster that he'd spied in a local store. He's been a top

The Tele train keeps a-rollin'...

1956 Fender Telecaster blond

By the mid 50s, the Telecaster and Esquire had moved to a white pickguard from the original black style, shown to good effect by the fine pair of Teles pictured on these pages. As well as the new pickguard, they have the modified blond finish that Fender was using by that time. The new solidbody guitars had started to attract some action in R&B and rock'n'roll. Clarence 'Gatemouth' Brown (opposite, top left) played an attractive Texan mix of R&B and western swing on his Fender, while Paul Burlison in The Rock 'N Roll Trio (album sleeve, opposite) found a new, more angry voice with the aid of a distorted amp on the band's classic 'The Train Kept A-Rollin'', later covered by The Yardbirds. Guitarist Russell Willaford briefly played an Esquire with Gene Vincent's Blue Caps (above) in the 1956 movie *The Girl Can't Help It*.

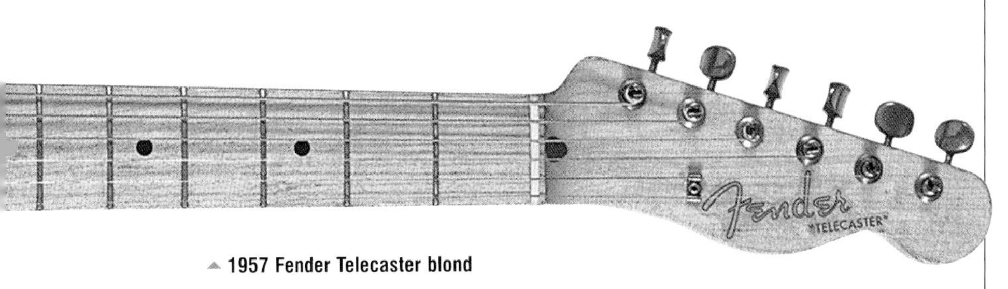

▲ **1957 Fender Telecaster blond**

Tele man ever since and became a prime influence on many other key players. Burton may well have had the first Telecaster-fuelled Top 40 hit when his guitar lick set the tone for Dale Hawkins's raw 'Suzie Q', a song that crashed into the chart in July 1957, bursting with Burton's earthy playing.

At the end of that year came the offer to join Ricky Nelson on the TV show. Burton, already a busy session player in Los Angeles, played rhythm guitar on his earliest Nelson sessions, but the first on which he played lead was 'Believe What You Say'. "Back then you played it and mixed it at the same time," Burton remembers. "I got a great sound through my Fender Deluxe amplifier. It was a slinky, spacey, energetic sound. We were into rock'n'roll, and it was rocking. It jumped right out at you!"

'Believe What You Say' was a Number 4 hit for Ricky Nelson in April 1958 and marked the start of Burton's supreme string-bending skills, aided by an experimental set of strings. "I had the first, second, third, and fourth as banjo strings," he says. "The third was unwound, which gave a much different sound to the regular wound string. I had the fifth and sixth as guitar strings, but with a D-string for where the A would be, and the E-string was an A – so I got them down to match with the light strings from the banjo. If you go back and listen to those early Ricky Nelson records you'll hear the difference."

From that point, Burton played lead guitar on all Nelson's hits. Further experimentation came later when he discovered extra sounds among the Tele's controls. "You know the three-way switch that you had back then? I was just plucking the strings, and I noticed that when you moved the switch from the middle position to your lead pickup, in between the setting I got this particular sound. The volume was much lower, but the sound was very interesting. I always call it my little Chinese tone. Very plucky, very percussive."[42] Listen to his typically concise solo on the 1961 Nelson Number 1 'Travelin' Man' for a perfect example. We'll be hearing from Burton again later.

Some of Ricky Nelson's hits were written by Johnny and Dorsey Burnette, who'd been part of The Rock'n'Roll Trio. Paul Burlison blasted out on a loose-tube-distorted Telecaster on their sweaty 1956 single 'The Train Kept A Rollin'', later covered by The Yardbirds and others.

Some American session players noted the demand for a Tele-type sound and bought the appropriate guitar. Howard Roberts, Tommy Tedesco, and Barney Kessel all acquired Teles. Kessel, described in a 1956 interview as "the busiest session guitar man in Hollywood", was a jazzer much more at home with a hollowbody Gibson. In that interview he sounded distinctly uncomfortable about the new arrival. "I had to buy a special 'ultra toppy' guitar," he complained, "to get that horrible electric guitar sound that the cowboys and the rock'n'rollers want."[43]

Luther Perkins played various Esquires on Johnny Cash's records, providing what Cash described as "one-string rhythm" and starting with the definitive 1956 hit 'I Walk The Line'. The record showed that a Tele-style guitar could highlight bright, bassy lines at the heart of simple, direct pop music. In this it would prove to be something of a blueprint.

British players got their first remarkable glimpse of a real live Telecaster in October 1958 when Muddy Waters visited. Muddy brought with him his piano player Otis Spann and his very own Fender Telecaster. The sonic bombardment of real, loud, aggressive R&B came as a shock to many in the London audiences. "There were some who could not hear [Muddy's] voice properly over the powerfully amplified guitar, and others who simply do not care for the electric instrument at all," wrote a baffled reviewer. "I liked some of the violent, explosive guitar accompaniment – although there were times when my thoughts turned with affection to the tones of the acoustic guitar heard on his first record. ... Muddy seemed able to forget where he was standing as, eyes closed, he built up patterns, sometimes walls, of electrified sound."[44]

Muddy's walls of electrified sound were transforming the blues and edging it ever closer to rock, a development that would reach fruition in the following decade. He stuck to his whiteguard maple-neck '57 Tele through the rest of his career, adding along the way a new red finish, a wider rosewood-board neck, a high nut and bridge to aid his killer slide work, and a couple of Fender amp knobs. "What would I look like with two or three guitars like these kids?" he joked with an interviewer years later. "I don't need to be bothered with that. I got my one old guitar."[45]

Most of the work on Fender's early publicity and ads fell to Don Randall, but soon he needed help to give the brand a strong push among musicians and dealers. Advertising in America was becoming a more sophisticated affair, and smart agencies were increasingly adept at convincing companies to spend more on slick ads to provide a uniform identity for a set of products.

In 1957, Fender turned to Bob Perine from the Perine-Jacoby agency of Newport Beach, California. He would continue to shape the look of Fender publicity until 1969. Perine, a keen amateur guitarist, transformed Fender's image and in the process created some of the most stylish and memorable guitar ads and catalogues ever printed. Some collectors today value prime 'Fender paper' of the 50s and 60s almost as highly as the original instruments themselves.

One of Perine's early tasks was to devise and shoot a series of press ads based on a brilliantly simple idea. He would present a Fender product in an unlikely setting, set off with the tag line "You won't part with yours either." In other words, your Fender guitar or amp is so important to you, you'll take it anywhere, just like the mad fool in this ad. The "won't part" ads began to appear in 1957, and one of the first showed a gent in a sharp suit on the top deck of a bus holding on tight to his white-finish whiteguard maple-neck Tele – as well he might. Many ads followed in the "won't part" series (along with a few variant taglines such as "Wherever you go you'll find Fender"). Guitars were seen perched on army tanks, erect at the drive-in cinema, hanging in mid-air around a skydiver's neck, strapped to a surfer ... in fact, pretty much anywhere. Perine and his team must have had a lot of fun.

The Fender catalogues, too, became beautiful objects under Perine's direction. The 1958/59 catalogue was Fender's first with a full-colour front-and-back cover, which opened out to display a luscious panorama of prime gear, including a blond Tele and Esquire, all eyed up by a couple of cool crewcut gents. The booklet was a model of clear, simple design. No matter that the pictures of the Tele and Esquire inside were of obsolete blackguard models: you couldn't help but want everything, whatever the details. And one fact in particular, tucked alongside a snap of the Esquire, might have caught your eye: "Telecaster and Esquire guitars are available in custom color finishes at an additional 5% cost," it said. That line first appeared in the previous catalogue, dated 1957/58,

Muddy won't part with his either

Muddy Waters was one of the great Telecaster players, seen here (left) with his famous red guitar. He bought it in the late 50s, later adding a rosewood-board neck and that new finish. He's pictured capo'd up and ready to go at a 60s session with label owner Leonard Chess, Little Walter, and Bo Diddley. While players such as Muddy were giving Fender high visibility on stage, the company upped its promo power when it hired a new ad agency in 1957, and specifically Bob Perine. His most famous innovation was the humorous series of ads tagged 'You Won't Part With Yours Either' that starred Fender guitars in the most unlikely situations. Two typical examples are shown here (above), while the 1959 amplification ad (right) demonstrates that almost any ad of the Perine period was full of charm and style.

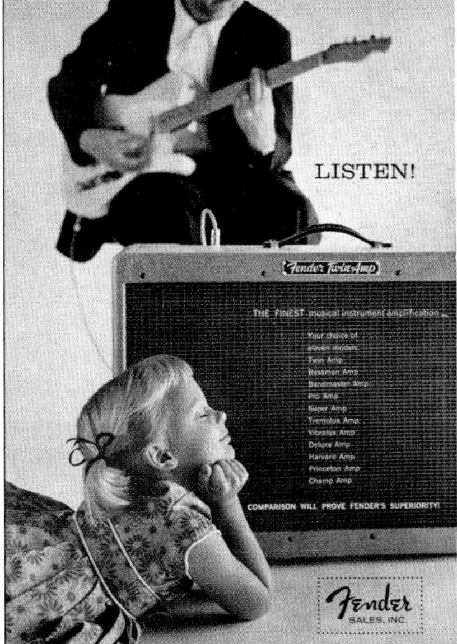

and announced that all Fenders were now officially available in Custom Colors beyond the regular finishes. Most Fenders of the 50s had come in a standard finish only: blond for Teles and Esquires; sunburst for Strats. Nonetheless a few guitars, specially made at the factory effectively as one-offs, were finished in solid colours. The rare surviving examples show this was happening by 1954, but few players back then seemed interested in slinging on a coloured guitar, and Fender's main production remained in regular-finish instruments.

Fender announced early in 1957 a Stratocaster in see-through blond finish (and gold-plated hardware), in effect Fender's first official Custom Color guitar – although the term has always been more popularly applied since to solid-colour varieties. A handful of 50s Strats were finished in solid colours, but Telecasters much less often, and some rare special-order Teles of the period were finished in sunburst.

Fender's production of special-colour guitars was certainly casual in the 50s. The informality shifted to a rather more commercial footing for the first time in the company's sales literature of 1956 when "player's choice" coloured guitars were noted as an option, at five percent extra cost. In the following year, as we've seen, these Du Pont paint finishes were described in Fender's catalogue as Custom Colors, a name that has stuck ever since, and in the pricelist as "custom Du Pont Duco finishes", still at five percent on top of regular prices.

The company eventually came up with a defined list of the officially available Custom Colors, and in the early 60s, when Fender made many more Custom Color guitars, the company even issued colour charts to publicise and help select the various shades. The original, in 1961, featured black, burgundy mist metallic, dakota red, daphne blue, fiesta red, foam green, inca silver metallic, lake placid blue metallic, olympic white, shell pink, sherwood green metallic, shoreline gold metallic, sonic blue, and surf green. The second, in 1963, had lost shell pink and gained candy apple red metallic. The third, in 1965, lost burgundy mist metallic, daphne blue, inca silver metallic, sherwood green metallic, shoreline gold metallic, and surf green, and gained the following metallics: blue ice, charcoal frost, firemist gold, firemist silver, ocean turquoise, and teal green.

The look of cars had a big effect on American guitar manufacturers in the 50s, not least in this ability to enhance the look of an already stylish object with a rich, sparkling paint job. Gretsch in New York City had been the first guitar maker to adopt car paints as standard colours for guitar models, creating new-look electric instruments such as the cadillac green Country Club and the jaguar tan Streamliner, both in 1954.

Du Pont was the biggest supplier of paint to the car factories, notably to the enormous General Motors operation. Fender used paints from Du Pont's Duco nitro-cellulose lines, such as fiesta red or foam green, as well as the more colour-retentive Lucite acrylics like lake placid blue metallic or burgundy mist metallic. Guitar historian Clay Harrell later discovered that the names Fender gave to the colours mostly came from the original car makers' terms: fiesta red, for example, was first used by Ford in 1956 for a Thunderbird colour, while lake placid blue originally appeared on a 1958 Cadillac Brougham. Candy apple red, however, was a Fender original and not a car colour. George Fullerton remembered going out to a local paint store around 1957, buying a fiesta red mix, and then returning to the factory and applying it to a guitar body. He insisted that this experiment was what started Fender's defined Custom Color line.

"That first one became fiesta red," said Fullerton. "The Du Pont company made that colour, and you could buy it right across the counter. That should have been a patent, that colour, but who knows at the time you do a thing? Meanwhile, the sales office and Don Randall laughed at it, said who in hell wants a coloured guitar, specially a red one?"[46] Don Randall had a different recollection of the genesis of Fender's Custom Color line. "Gretsch had their Country Club which was green, the White Falcon which was white, and there were others. So it was just my idea to diversify and get another product on the market. They didn't sell as well as the traditional blond and sunburst colours."[47]

Whatever the origins of Fender's Custom Colors, decades later the guitars bearing these original fiesta reds, sonic blues, burgundy mists, and the like have proved very desirable among collectors, many of whom rate a Custom Color Fender, especially an early one, as a prime catch. The colours didn't add much to the price, originally. In 1958, for example, a Custom Color would add just $9.98 extra on top of a regular $199.50 Telecaster. In today's collector market, the price differential between an original regular blond Telecaster and one finished in a genuine Custom Color is certainly greater – early coloured Teles are particularly rare – despite the prevalence of refinishes that have become so accurate that even alleged experts can be fooled into declaring some fake finishes as original. How much is a coat of paint worth?

Back at Fender in the 50s, more changes were under way. Four new factory buildings and a warehouse were added to the South Raymond site in 1958, and by the following year the number of employees topped 100 for the first time. As usual, Fender made a few small cosmetic and production adjustments to the electric models, including the addition of three screws to the Tele and Esquire's pickguards in 1959, making a total of eight. This later provided a useful visual clue to tell quickly – fakes and mods aside – between a 50s and a 60s model.

A more peculiar modification was made to the Telecaster and Esquire during 1958 when the strings were anchored at holes in the back of the bridge-plate and not passed through the body as usual. Quite what prompted this so-called top-loader bridge is unknown, but it was probably a time-saving exercise. Clearly it took the company some time to realise that many players consider through-body stringing as one of the factors that makes a Tele sound like a Tele. Within a year or so they were, thankfully, back to the original method.

During all the changes and additions to the Fender line in its first decade, visually the humble Telecaster had stayed largely the same. As we've seen, cosmetically there was a change from the original black to a white pickguard at the end of 1954. But otherwise the Telecaster looked pretty much the same blond-finished guitar it had been in 1951. In 1959, however, two new models joined the Fender line that gave a quite different look when compared to the regular blond Telecaster and Esquire. These were the Custom Telecaster and the Custom Esquire. Each had a sunburst-finish body with bound edges. Binding is the technique used to create a thin white strip on the edge of a guitar body, as on many flat-tops and other hollowbody instruments. Factory boss

Red is the colour of my true love's axe

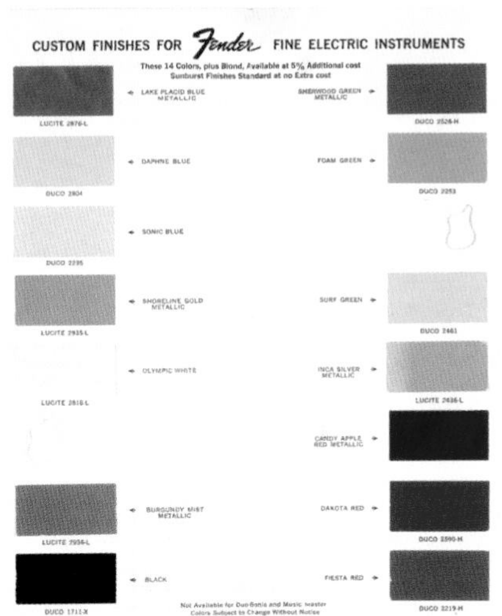

While the 1958/59 catalogue cover (left) still featured maple-neck guitars in mostly standard finishes, the big news from Fender was coloured paint and rosewood 'boards, seen in splendid confluence on our lovely Esquire (main guitar). A subtler change was the shift from five to eight pickguard screws in '59. Coloured guitars had been available from Fender for some time, but now there was an official line of Custom Colors, yours to choose from a specially devised finish chart (above). Rosewood upstaged maple during 1959, and Fender's ad from December that year (right) reflects the move to the new fingerboard wood – if not a new way to display the guitars.

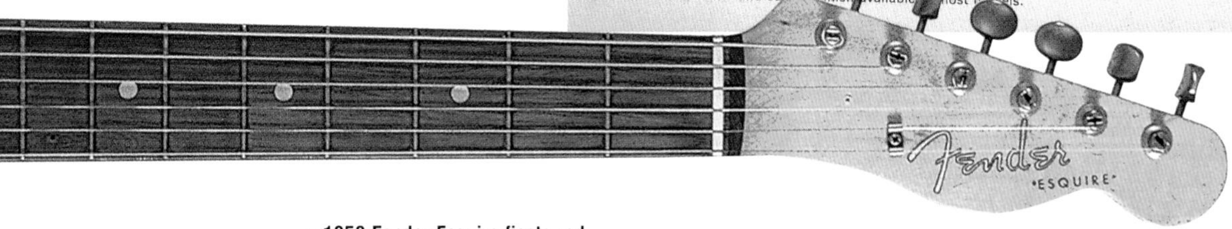

▲ **1959 Fender Esquire fiesta red**

Forrest White acquired some valuable advice on the process of binding from Fred Martin, head of the leading American flat-top acoustic guitar manufacturer, Martin. "I said Fred, I'd like to put binding around a Telecaster body, but I really don't know a darned thing about it. He showed me how they cut the binding material, which they bought in sheets and cut into strips, and he showed me what kind of adhesive to use."[48]

The bound-body Custom Esquire and Telecaster were launched at the summer 1959 NAMM show in New York City. Fender's press release described them as "improved models" and "extremely attractive instruments" with rosewood fingerboards, as on the Jazzmaster, Fender's new top-of-the-line electric introduced in 1959. During that year, the new separate rosewood fingerboard on a maple neck was adopted for all Fender models, including regular Telecasters and Esquires, replacing Fender's previous construction where the frets were set directly into the face of the solid maple neck. Some players like the smooth, almost slippery style of maple; others prefer the more textured feel of rosewood. Full maple remained as an option on the Tele (and some other models) at various times following the introduction of rosewood.

Collectors call this new style of neck and fingerboard in its first few years a slab board, with its distinctive flat joint between the base of the rosewood fingerboard and the face of the maple neck. In 1962, Fender changed the rosewood to a thinner board with a curved base, and the following year the board was made thinner still – these are known as laminate boards. Some players insist that the lam-board style helps get closer to the tone of the earlier all-maple neck because it allows the tang or base of the fret to contact the maple below the rosewood.

By the summer of '62, the pricelist included quite an array of products. A regular blond Telecaster listed at $209.50, with a colour finish at $219.98; a blond Esquire was $169.50, with a colour adding $8.48. The bound Telecaster Custom was $239.50 (plus $11.98 for a colour) and the Esquire Custom $199.50 (plus $9.98 for colour). In addition to those, there were five more electric models (Duo-Sonic, Jaguar, Jazzmaster, Musicmaster, Stratocaster) and three electric basses (Precision Bass, Jazz Bass, and VI). There were 13 amplifiers (Bandmaster, Bassman, Champ, Concert, Deluxe, Princeton, Pro Amp, Showman, Super, Tremolux, Twin Amp, Vibrasonic, and Vibrolux). Completing the line-up were five steel guitars (Champ, Deluxe, Dual, Stringmaster, and Studio Deluxe) and two pedal-steel guitars (models 400 and 1000).

The Jaguar was Fender's new top-of-the-line electric, its shorter 24-inch-scale neck a come-on to Gibson players. It shared with the Jazzmaster the novel offset-waist body shape but had a rather more complex control layout than the Jazz. The Jag was offered in four different neck widths, one a size narrower and two wider than normal (coded A, B, C or D, from narrowest to widest, with 'normal' B the most common), and these options were offered also from 1962 on the Stratocaster and the Jazzmaster, but never on the Telecaster.

The gloriously simple Telecaster and Esquire were finding a true voice in the hands of similarly uncomplicated yet accomplished musicians. In the Stax studio in Memphis, cool-hand Steve Cropper translated the good old Fender's simplicity of design into musical terms as his lean guitar lines graced the 1962 Booker T & the MGs hit 'Green Onions'. For that and other early cuts, he used a '56 Esquire, but Cropper created a fresh classic Tele look, soon opting for a new '63 Tele and its contemporary style of blond body, white 'guard, and rosewood neck. Listen for his beautifully measured opening statement and licks on Sam & Dave's 'Soul Man' hit of 1967 and his contributions to Otis Redding's 'Dock Of The Bay', added to the basic track almost immediately following Redding's premature death in '67.

A new sound emerging in the early 60s was called the Bakersfield sound (because that was the California city, 100 miles to the north of Los Angeles, where it started), although it was sometimes known as the Nashville West sound (because it was a particularly West-Coast version of country music). Whatever the description, Don Rich was the key guitarist in this danceable music based on deep, driving electric guitars. He played with Buck Owens & The Buckaroos, first on fiddle and from 1962 on guitar. Owens, a Tele player himself, was named country music artist of the 60s by Capitol Records, and with good reason: he and the band scored a remarkable 19 country-chart Number 1s during the decade.

Rich drew a cutting sound from his Telecaster and made it clear that the Tele was the perfect machine for such a noise. Cock an ear to his bassy rhythm and chicken-pickin' breaks on Owens hits like 1963's 'Act Naturally', soon covered by The Beatles, who were fans of this kind of incisive guitar twang. Two of the most famous Teles of the time were the sparkle-finish models custom-made for Rich and Owens, a pair of guitars that dazzled many an audience of the Bakersfield outfit. Rich died tragically young, at the age of just 32, in 1974, following a motorcycle accident.

Another key Bakersfield player was Roy Nichols – also a Telecaster man – who played with Merle Haggard's group The Strangers, formed in the mid 60s. James Burton played on some of these tracks, including the demure but definitive chicken-pickin' on the 1967 hit 'I'm A Lonesome Fugitive', but it was Nichols on such distinctive recordings as Haggard's live album a couple of years later, *Okie From Muskogee*. Nichols died in 2001 and is buried at Greenlawn Cemetery in Bakersfield. Pictured on his gravestone is a guitar, and it is, of course, a Telecaster.

Rich and Burton and Nichols helped to introduce chicken-pickin' to record buyers' ears, a technique based on rapid-fire picking, with a muted string click immediately followed by a clean note, and so on around and around. The stuttering result sounds something like a clucking chicken – hence the name – and is so well suited to the dry attack of a Telecaster that it has become almost entirely associated with the instrument.

In the meantime, Fender found itself in the midst of the rock'n'roll revolution of the late 50s and early 60s. Naturally enough, the company was happy to give players access to large numbers of relatively affordable guitars. In quite a short period, many musicians and guitar-makers came to think of the inventive solidbody trio of Telecaster, Precision Bass, and Stratocaster as the most desirable modern guitars. What is remarkable is that in these circumstances Fender got so much right, and nearly always the first time. In short, the company had become remarkably successful.

Exporting became an important part of that success. Don Randall began the process in 1960 when he visited the leading European trade show at Frankfurt, Germany. "Our products were known over there because of the GIs playing our guitars," he recalled, "and they were very much prized. So we started doing business in Europe."[49] Britain became an especially important market

Green onions, Bakersfield twang

◀ 1963 Fender Custom Telecaster sunburst

The Custom Telecaster and Esquire models, launched by Fender in 1959, had a quite different look, finished in the sunburst style of the Stratocaster and with bound white edges to the body. The Custom Telecaster pictured has the three-tone sunburst of the period, while the binding is clearly visible in the period ad (far left). The original Custom Esquire would last in the company's lines until 1969, the Tele for three years longer. Meanwhile, a host of players were discovering the tone and playability of the classic Telecaster, few to more impressive effect than Steve Cropper (opposite) whose economically graceful lines were heard on Stax sessions, not least Booker T's memorable 'Green Onions'. A driving, twangier sound came from Bakersfield, California, in the 60s, led by Buck Owens and Don Rich, guitarist in Buck's band The Buckaroos, pictured on stage (above) with their custom-made sparkle-finish Teles.

because of the worldwide success of its pop groups. Musicians in the UK had found it almost impossible to buy Fenders until the early 60s, because from 1951 to 1959 the British government banned imports of some American merchandise, including guitars.

In 1960, Jennings became the first official British distributor of Fender gear, joined by Selmer two years later. A Jennings pricelist from 1961 pitched the Telecaster at £107/9s/7d (£107.48; about $300 at the time); three years later the Tele had crept up to £122/17/0 (£122.85; nearer $340). By summer 1965, both Selmer and Jennings had been replaced as the British Fender distributor by Arbiter, who would continue for many years as the brand's UK agent. "Fender was the biggest musical instrument exporter in the United States," said Randall. "In fact I think we exported more US-made musical products than all the other companies combined. We had it to ourselves for maybe three or four years."[50] Western Europe was the biggest export market, but Fender also did well in Scandinavia, South Africa, Rhodesia (now Zimbabwe), Japan, Australia, and Canada.

Many buildings had been added to cope with increased manufacturing demands, and by 1964 Fender employed some 600 people (500 in manufacturing) spread over 29 buildings. Forrest White said his production staff were making 1,500 guitars a week at the end of 1964, compared to the 40 a week when he joined the company ten years earlier. As well as electric guitars and amplifiers, Fender's early-60s pricelists offered acoustic guitars, effects units, a host of related accessories, and Fender-Rhodes electric pianos, which were added to the line in 1963.

Don Randall remembered writing a million dollars' worth of wholesale business during his first year in the 50s, but in the mid 60s that had risen to some ten million dollars' worth, translating to about forty million dollars' worth of retail sales. The beat boom, triggered by The Beatles and the so-called British Invasion of pop groups, swept the United States. Electric guitars were at a peak of popularity, and Fender was among the biggest and most successful producers.

Suddenly, however, in January 1965, the Fender companies were sold to the mighty Columbia Broadcasting System Inc, better known as CBS. *The Music Trades* magazine reported in somewhat shocked tones: "The purchase price of $13 million is by far the highest ever offered in the history of the [musical instrument] industry for any single manufacturer. ... The acquisition, a sterling proof of the music industry's growth potential, marks the first time that one of the nation's largest corporations has entered our field. With sales volume in excess of half a billion dollars annually, CBS currently does more business than the entire [US musical instrument] industry does at retail. Actual purchase of Fender was made by the Columbia Records Distribution Division of CBS, whose outstanding recent feats have included the production of *My Fair Lady*."[51]

Economic analysts were advising big corporations to diversify and acquire companies from a variety of different businesses. Presumably they also advised the corporations that all they had to do was finance and expand the new acquisitions, and rich pickings would follow. Columbia Records boss Goddard Lieberson said of Fender: "This is a fast growing business tied into the expanding leisure time market. We expect this industry to grow by 23 per cent in the next two years."[52]

Leo Fender was by all accounts a hypochondriac, and he decided to sell Fender because he was worried about his health, principally the staph infection in his sinuses that had troubled him for many years. Also, he was nervous about financing expansion. He recalled later: "I thought I was going to have to retire. I had been suffering for years with a virus infection of the sinuses and it made my life a misery. I felt that I wasn't going to be in the health to carry on."[53]

Don Randall said: "Leo was a faddist, and he'd get on these health kicks. One time, he heard that carrot juice was the thing, the panacea, so he and his friend Ronnie Beers got these big commercial juicers, and they went and bought carrots by the sackload. And all of a sudden they started turning red. That cured him of that. Then his next kick, he'd come and say hey, try this, this is the best thing for you – you can't believe how good it makes you feel. You had to have a tablespoonful of cider vinegar in a glass of hot water. I said, Leo … ."[54]

Randall handled the sale of Fender to CBS. He said that Leo had earlier offered him the company for a million-and-a-half dollars, but he didn't feel he was ready for that kind of career move and so suggested to Leo that they might see what he could get from an outside buyer. Leo agreed, and Randall's first tentative discussions took place in early 1964 with the Baldwin Piano & Organ Co of Ohio. Randall also contacted an investment banker, who at first suggested that Fender go public, an idea with no appeal for Leo or Randall. The bankers then came up with CBS as a potential purchaser. "Now we had two companies up there," Randall remembered, "but Baldwin's attitude to purchasing turned out to be totally unsatisfactory for our purposes. So finally we got down to the nitty gritty with CBS, and I made about half a dozen trips back and forth to New York: jam sessions with attorneys and financial people."

CBS came in with a low offer at first, Randall recalled. "But eventually, we came to a fairly agreeable price. So I called Leo and said how does that suit you? He said oh Don, I can't believe it, are you trying to pull my leg? And I said no – does that sound like a satisfactory deal we can close on? 'Well anything you say Don, that's fine, you just go ahead and do it,' he said. And so the rest is history: we went on and sold it to CBS after a lot of investigation. They did a big study on us – people came in to justify the sale and the price paid – and we consummated the deal. Leo wouldn't even go back to New York for the signing, for the pay-off or anything. 'You get the money and you bring it out to me,' he said."[55]

In the year following the Fender acquisition, CBS published a survey that estimated the number of guitar players in the USA at nine million and placed total American retail sales of guitars during 1965 at $185 million, up from $24 million in 1958. CBS was clearly enthusiastic about the potential for music and went on to buy more instrument companies, including Rogers (drums), Steinway (pianos), and Leslie (organ loudspeakers).

Over the years, the sale of Fender to CBS provoked much retrospective dismay among guitar players and collectors, some of whom consider so-called pre-CBS instruments – in other words those made prior to the beginning of 1965 – as superior to those made after that date. This is a meaningless generalisation. But there is little doubt that, over a period of time after the sale, CBS did introduce changes to the production methods of Fender guitars, and a number of those changes were detrimental to the quality of some instruments. According to insiders, the problem with CBS at this time was that it seemed to believe that all it had to do was simply pour a great

Shake your money maker

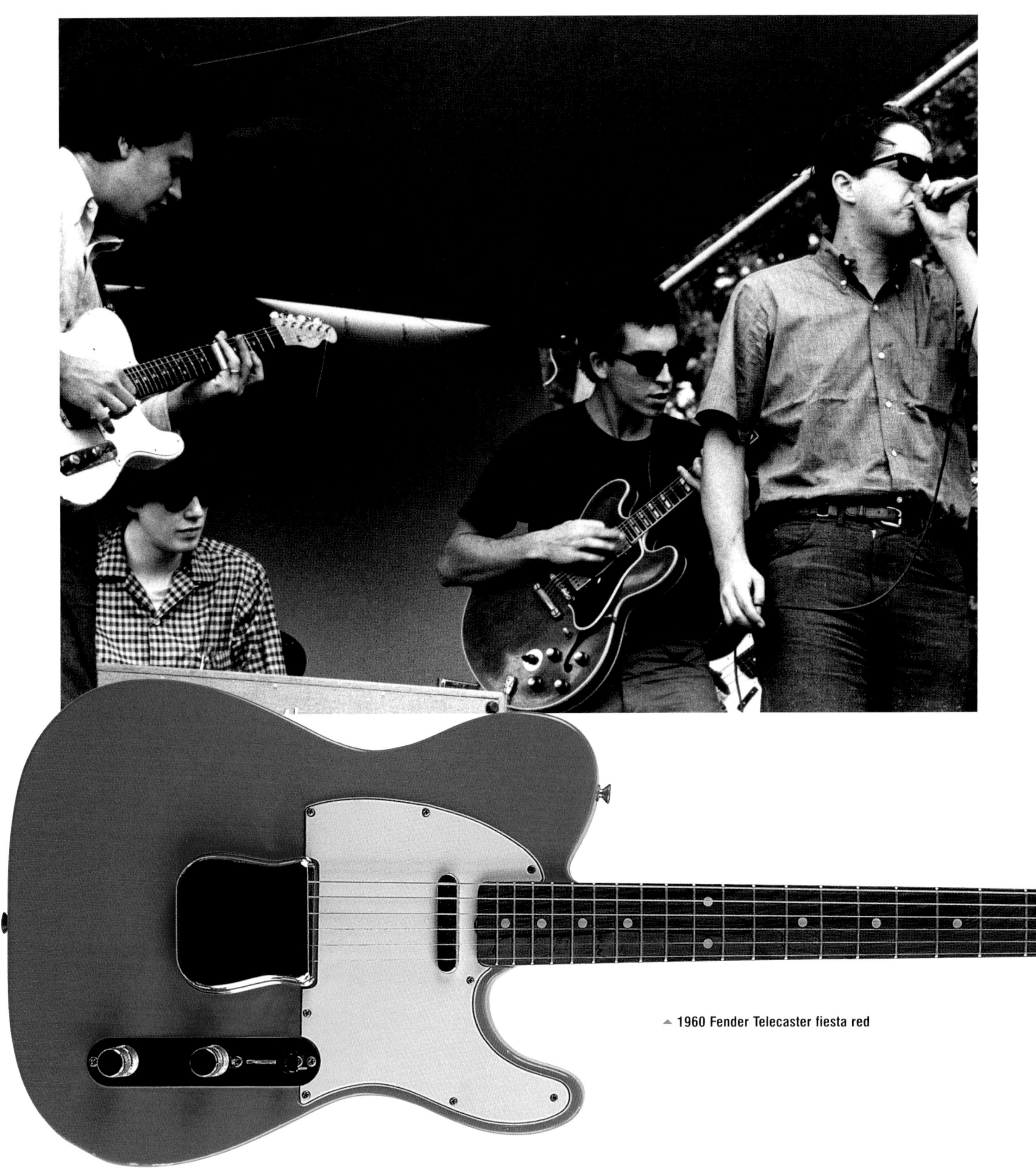

▲ 1960 Fender Telecaster fiesta red

FROM **arbiter** THE MOST WANTED GUITAR IN BRITAIN TODAY

TELECASTER by Fender

See your Arbiter dealer today, see the whole fabulous range of Fender Guitars from the sensational solid electric guitars right through the range to the finest country & western round holes. You want the worlds best in amplification? Turn again to Fender for the last word in Style, Selection, Power and Performance!

PRECISION BASS
NEWPORTER
SHENANDOAH 12 STRING
MALIBU

SHOWMAN
TWIN REVERB
BASSMAN

arbiter ltd
41 GERRARD STREET
LONDON W.1 · REG 1561

Mike Bloomfield is captured on film with his cutting Tele onstage with the Butterfield Blues Band (left) at the 1965 Newport festival. At the same event Bloomfield played with Bob Dylan, famously bringing Fender electricity to acoustic folk. Fender's 1963/64 catalogue illustrated a rare 'red-mahogany' option (above, far left), with a see-through red finish on a mahogany body, while the 1965/66 catalogue (below) featured a regular blond ash-body Esquire, the red-mahogany Tele again, and a sunburst bound-body Custom Telecaster. Meanwhile, Fender guitars had been unavailable in Britain throughout the 50s because of a trade ban, but in 1960 Jennings and then two years later Selmer were appointed as distributors. In 1965, Arbiter became the new UK agent, and the firm promoted the Telecaster in its ad (pictured, above right) as "the most wanted guitar in Britain today".

deal of money into Fender. And certainly Fender's sales did increase and profits did go up. Randall recalled income almost doubling in the first year that CBS owned Fender. Profit became paramount, said Forrest White, who remained as manager of electric guitar and amplifier production. "CBS had a vice president for everything. I think they had a vice president for cleaning the toilets. You name it: whatever it was, it had a vice president."[56]

Here was a significant clash of cultures. The new CBS men, often trained engineers with college degrees, believed in high-volume production. Fender's old guard were long-serving craft workers without formal qualifications. A job ad in the *Los Angeles Times* in March 1966 summed up the changes. It was for a Systems Analyst to oversee a computer feasibility study at Fender, for a "management information system" covering "sales order processing, material control, manufacturing systems, and accounting systems". It's not hard to imagine the rumours that probably rattled around the old team. They want to run the place with computers! Whatever next?

When the old-guard men talked later about the effect of the CBS takeover on Fender's guitars, they had different opinions. George Fullerton said management was first alerted to criticisms when complaints started to filter back from the dealers through the sales reps. "They'd say the guitars don't play like they used to, they aren't adjusted like they used to be," Fullerton remembered.[57]

Salesman Dale Hyatt reckons that the quality stayed relatively stable until around 1968, and then quality-control deteriorated. "It got to the point where I did not enjoy going to any store anywhere, because every time I walked in, I found myself defending some poor piece of workmanship. They got very sloppy with the finish, with far too many bad spots. They created their own competition, letting the door wide open for everybody else, including the Japanese."[58]

Under the new owner, Randall became vice president and general manager of Fender Musical Instruments and Fender Sales (both now part of the new CBS Musical Instruments Division). To him, the supposition that quality deteriorated when CBS took over was a fallacy. "I will say this for CBS: they were just as interested in quality as we were. They spared no amount of time or effort to ensure the quality was there. There's always this suspicion when a big company takes over that they're going to make a lousy product and sell it for a higher price, and that's not true here. But the other problems that existed were multiple."[59]

CBS retained Leo Fender's services as "special consultant in research and development". The corporation's confidential pre-sale report into the Fender operation had concluded that Randall was a necessity to running the business – but that Leo was not. It said "a competent chief engineer" could easily keep products moving forward in the contemporary marketplace, but it would be "highly desirable, at least for a period of four or five years, to maintain the active interest and creativity of Mr Fender".[60]

In other words, CBS didn't want Leo taking his ideas elsewhere, but didn't particularly want him getting in the way of the newly efficient Fender business machine. So he was set up away from the Fender buildings and allowed to tinker as much as he liked – with very little effect on the product. A 1965 CBS brochure showed the key personnel at Fender, and Leo was listed way down in 18th place among the 28 management posts. A couple of years after the sale to CBS, Leo changed doctors, who prescribed antibiotics and cured his sinus complaint. He completed a few projects for CBS but left when his five-year contract expired in 1970. He went on to make instruments for the Music Man company (originally set up in 1972 although not named Music Man until 1974) and his later G&L operation – where the ASAT model was more or less a Telecaster with a different name.

Leo was not the first of the old guard to leave CBS. Forrest White departed in 1967, because, he said, "I wouldn't build some products – the solid state amps – that I thought were unworthy of Leo's name."[61] He went on to work with Leo at Music Man, as well as for CMI, which owned Gibson, and Rickenbacker. White died in 1994. Don Randall resigned from CBS in 1969, disenchanted with corporate life, and formed Randall Electric Instruments, which he sold in 1987. He died in 2008. George Fullerton left CBS in 1970, worked at Ernie Ball for a while, and with Leo formed the G&L company in 1979, although Fullerton sold his interest in 1986. (G&L at first stood for "George & Leo", later "Guitars by Leo".) Fullerton died in 2009. Dale Hyatt resigned from CBS in 1972. Hyatt, too, became part of the G&L set-up, which was sold to BBE Sound Inc after Leo Fender's death in 1991 at the age of 82.

One of Fender's first CBS-era pricelists, dated April 1965, revealed a burgeoning line of products. Tele and Esquire prices hadn't shifted since the '62 list mentoned earlier, and there were now seven accompanying electric guitar models: Duo-Sonic, Electric XII, Jaguar, Jazzmaster, Musicmaster, Mustang, and Stratocaster. The other lines included bass guitars, flat-top acoustics, amplifiers, various Fender-Rhodes keyboards, steel and pedal-steel guitars, a solidbody electric mandolin, and reverb and echo units.

Back around 1960, Fender had started to use a modernised chunky Fender logo in company literature. The first electric model to brandish the new design on its headstock was the new-for-'62 Jaguar. During the following years, Fender had gradually applied it to all guitars, although it didn't arrive on the Telecaster until about 1966. This new logo, drawn up by adman Bob Perine, is known today among collectors as the transition logo, because it leads from the original thin 'spaghetti' logo to a bolder black version, sometimes known as the CBS logo, introduced around 1968. In 1965, Fender began to stamp the modernised 'F' of the new logo on to guitar neckplates and, shortly after, on to new-design tuners.

Aside from the comings and goings of personnel and all the other day-to-day details of running a guitar business, CBS had little cause to worry about demand. Pop music was, of course, flourishing in the 60s, and Telecasters were everywhere. Michael Bloomfield turned up with one for an apparently casual Bob Dylan performance at the Newport folk festival in July 1965, introducing an audience used to acoustic guitars to the capabilities of a turned-up Tele. A month earlier, Bloomfield had played his Tele on the recording of 'Like A Rolling Stone'. The following year, Robbie Robertson toted a Tele when The Hawks backed Dylan for a series of now legendary live shows that staked out the ground for amplified folk-rock, and Dylan himself later played a Tele.

In Britain, despite strong competition during this heady decade from the Gibson Les Paul and the Stratocaster among pro players, the Telecaster held its own. An early boost came from Mick Green with Johnny Kidd & The Pirates, notably on hits such as 'I'll Never Get Over You' (1963)

Talking 'bout the CBS generation

Pete Townshend was probably more associated with Rickenbacker guitars in the 60s, but in the middle of the decade he took up a Telecaster. Our picture of The Who (opposite) clearly shows that he added an extra pickup to give something like a Stratocaster layout. A number of players modified the Tele's electrics, most often the 'weaker' front pickup, and the idea became popular in the 70s. But the 60s were a time of great upheaval for the Fender operation, which in 1965 was sold to the vast and powerful CBS corporation for $13 million, an unprecedented figure in the musical instrument industry. There has been a great deal of debate ever since about how the new owner's actions affected the quality of Fender guitars. Whatever the changes, Telecasters continued to pour from the California factory, and as ever the coloured-finish instruments remained in the minority. Two CBS-era Custom Color examples are pictured here – and one of them has the newly reinstated maple-fingerboard option.

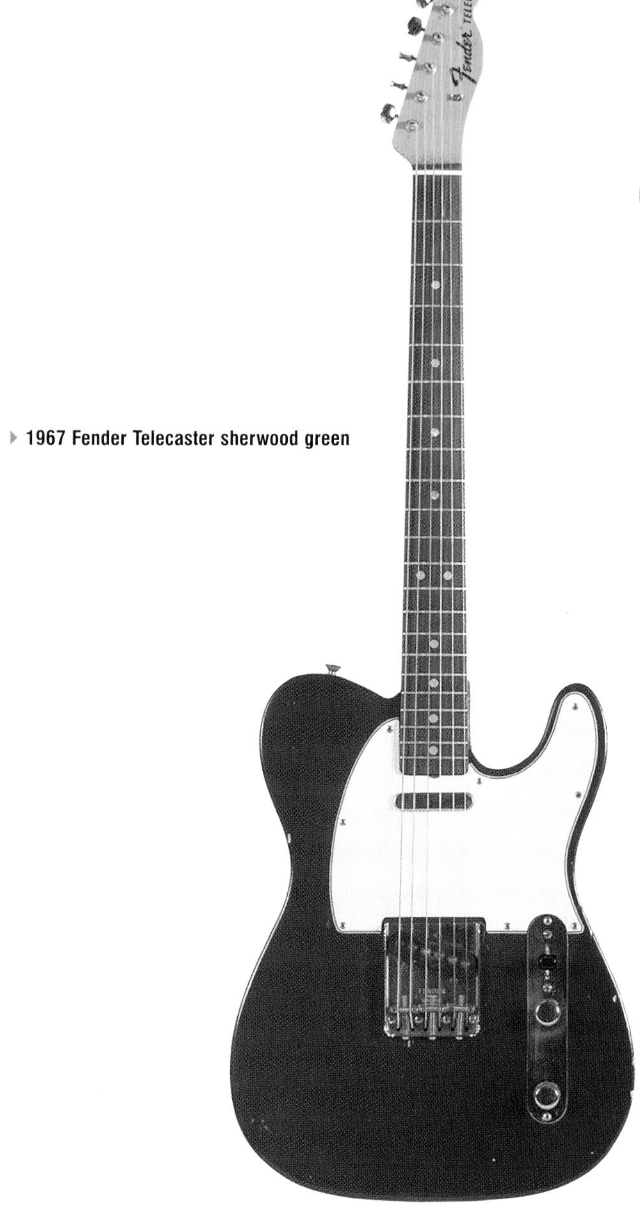

1967 Fender Telecaster sherwood green

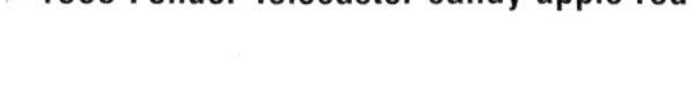

1969 Fender Telecaster candy apple red

where Green's mix of chords and single-line work benefited from his Tele's cutting sound. In 1965, The Who's Pete Townshend, renowned for on-stage guitar destruction, briefly favoured a Tele, telling an interviewer that it was the "toughest guitar". The journalist agreed, revealing a less well-known attribute of the instrument. "The final proof came when [Townshend] whacked it against an 18-inch-thick pillar, chipping the concrete but only bruising the guitar."[62]

As psychedelia loomed, Syd Barrett of Pink Floyd was setting the controls of his Esquire for a series of long experimental work-outs. Barrett exploited the guitar's potential for noise and sound effects as well as its more customary sonic values. He used a typical blond rosewood-board Esquire of the time, probably bought new around 1964. "It's been painted several times, and once I even covered it in plastic sheeting and silver discs," Barrett said in 1967. "Those discs are still on the guitar, but they tend to look a bit worn."[63]

Jimi Hendrix was the quintessential Strat player, although his sound wizard Roger Mayer recalls how a couple of classic solos were recorded on a Telecaster. Mayer built Hendrix a new effects unit, a frequency-doubler known as the Octavia. Early in February 1967, there was a plan to try the new unit at a London recording session following a gig. At the evening's show, Mayer says, "Jimi had a Strat with him and put it through the ceiling, bashing up the tuners. So when we went to Olympic studio later that night to do some overdubs using the Octavia, Jimi had to send [bassist] Noel Redding out to get a Telecaster. He used it for the overdubs to 'Fire' and 'Purple Haze', including the Octavia solo on 'Purple Haze'."[64]

More Brits valued the Tele's worth, and 1968 proved a good year: Justin Hayward of The Moody Blues played some great Tele licks on the group's single 'Ride My See-Saw', and Davy O'List wrestled howling, squealing solos from his Tele's neck pickup on The Nice's Top 10 hit 'America'.

Just before Eric Clapton left The Yardbirds he played a red Telecaster, owned by the group's management. Jeff Beck inherited the guitar briefly when he replaced Clapton in February 1965. "I had to use that because I didn't have a guitar when I joined," Beck recalls. "I'd already sold my first Fender, a Strat, but I got rid of the red Tele soon after. It was a terrible guitar. John Owen, a friend of mine, had a Telecaster. I would ogle this thing, and I spent more time playing it than he did. Then I borrowed it – and I never gave it back."

Beyond the brief red Tele, it was Owen's blond '59 or '60 rosewood-neck Tele that Beck used at first in The Yardbirds. But why did he want a Telecaster? "Because of the sound that Ricky Nelson's records had. We all thought that was a Telecaster. We weren't sure, because there was no information on the records at all. I don't know who told us, but we all assumed it was a Tele because it sounded so close when we plugged in our one: on the back pickup it sounded a lot like James Burton.

"And then I saw that film *The Girl Can't Help It* at the Sutton Granada, after school, in May or June of '56. It was the most pivotal film in my career, and my life, really." Beck watched slack-jawed as Little Richard's band performed. There in the background was a chap – probably Nathaniel Douglas – with a lovely battered maple-neck blackguard Tele. "It was just mouth-watering for us!" Then on came Gene Vincent & His Blue Caps. Beck knew that Cliff Gallup played guitar with this lot – and there on film was a 15-year-old blond kid playing an Esquire. Must be Gallup, he concluded. Turned out it was a stand-in, one Russell Willaford. "He remains a massive mystery," Beck explains. "No one ever found out anything about the guy. He just came and did the film and some publicity shots, with an Esquire, and then disappeared."

Fast forward to April 1965, and Beck got a '54 Esquire to use alongside his borrowed-but-it's-mine Tele in The Yardbirds. His *Girl Can't Help It* guitars were complete. "I bought my first Esquire from John Walker," he says. The Yardbirds were on a Kinks package tour, but The Kinks pulled out after an on-stage brawl, replaced by The Walker Brothers. "First thing I saw at rehearsals was this really good-looking pair of brothers, and one had an Esquire with a white pickguard and blond neck – and I wanted that blond neck. You couldn't get the blond neck after a certain run, they changed it to rosewood. I said I want that guitar! He said oh, 75 quid then. Give over! They're only about 85 quid new! And his had been shaved into a contoured body. I bought it anyway."

Beck made his great series of Yardbirds recordings, each an object lesson in how to present inventive, experimental electric guitar in a bluesy-pop framework. 'Heart Full Of Soul' was the Tele; 'Shapes Of Things' the Esquire. But surely it couldn't have been easy to persuade the Esquire to feed back for 'Shapes'? "That was done in Chess Records," Beck remembers, "where we were all completely blown away with the way they did things. The drum sound was great, and everything was like a dream come true – because we were playing in Chess, albeit the last throes of it. Marshall Chess was there and the guys that used to record Muddy. Really great! I was standing right next to an AC-30 on a chair, which I used so that I could easily reach the controls. I just moved around to get the right noise, you know? It was madness: pure experimentation.

"I wanted a Les Paul, but when I got it, it was so refined, and not really the tool you need on stage, for some reason. The controls were in the wrong place: I kept hitting the pickup selector into the wrong position. But the Esquire was no problem at all. I used to spin it around on top of the amp and change the speed of the echo while it was feeding back. Total lunacy! I used to try and break it – and I never could."

When he left The Yardbirds at the end of 1966, Beck passed on the Telecaster to Jimmy Page, by now the group's other guitar player. "I left The Yardbirds in a huff," Beck says. "I just decided in a minute I was going to leave. So I didn't take the guitar, and Jimmy carried on playing. Because he was now the only lead guitarist, he had to mimic what I did, and that's how come he got the guitar. Jimmy plastered it with psychedelic paint, and all the early Zeppelin stuff was done on that, on John Owen's Telecaster."[65] We'll discover the fate of Beck's Yardbirds Esquire a little later.

Meanwhile, Eric Clapton hadn't given up entirely on the Telecaster. He botched together an odd hybrid while in Cream and Blind Faith, at first adding a contemporary rosewood Strat neck to a bound Custom Tele body, and later – as seen at Blind Faith's famous Hyde Park concert in June 1969 – he tried it with the maple neck from his 'Brownie' Strat. Clapton was simply exploiting the modular bolt-together nature of Fender guitars. But his experiment was shortlived, and soon he moved almost exclusively to Stratocasters.

Over in California, CBS completed the construction of a new Fender factory in 1966 (although it was planned before its purchase of the company). The new plant cost $1.3 million and was next to

Set the controls for some groovy naturals

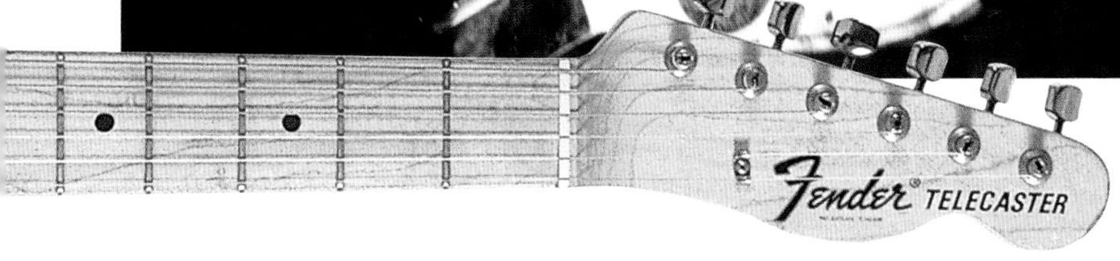

▲ **1968 Fender Thinline Telecaster sunburst**

The 60s proved a good time for British guitarists with Teles in tow, and fans looked no further than The Yardbirds for a run of great Fender men. Eric Clapton (opposite, left) often played a red Telecaster in the group, which upon leaving he passed to Jeff Beck (opposite, right). The new boy disliked the hand-me-down and quickly acquired his own weapons: an enviable and effective pair of Esquire and Telecaster. Syd Barrett (left) had a much more impressionistic role in mind for his Esquire amid the psychedelic ramblings of Pink Floyd. Fender, meanwhile, decided to bring some acoustic tone to the Tele and launched the Thinline model in 1968 (main guitar), complete with hollowed-out body chambers and a token f-hole. As well as the sunburst finish pictured, the Thinline came in what Fender's 1968 ad (above) called the 'groovy naturals': ash or mahogany.

Fender's existing buildings on the South Raymond site. Clearly the new owners were getting ready for a push on production. But in the late 60s at Fender there were unusual signs of weakness. The firm tried and failed with some solid-state amplifiers, quietly dropped most of its relatively new hollowbody electric models, and knocked together some ugly 'new' solidbody models designed to soak up unused parts.

Around 1967, Fender changed the control wiring of the Tele, altering the circuit that had been used since 1952. Now, the Tele operated pretty much as you'd expect with a two-pickup guitar: with the selector in the rear position, you got bridge pickup only; in the middle position, both pickups; and in the front position, neck pickup only. The tone control worked with all combinations. Also starting in '67, a Fender/Bigsby vibrato was offered as an optional extra on Teles and Esquires, lasting for about seven years.

Fender pressed forward with a new plan intended to gain some ground from its rivals – primarily Gibson, which dominated hollowbody electrics. This time, Fender took the Telecaster and produced a lighter version, the Thinline, beginning in 1968. It was designed by Roger Rossmeisl and Virgilio 'Babe' Simoni, Fender's product manager of stringed instruments. Leo brought Rossmeisl to Fender in 1962 to design those earlier and unsuccessful hollowbody guitars. He was the son of a German guitar-maker, and he went to the States in the 50s, at first working for Gibson in Michigan but then moving to Rickenbacker in California. There he made a number of one-off custom guitars, but he also designed some stylish production models, too, notably Rick's classic 330/360 series.

Rossmeisl's Thinline Telecaster had three hollowed-out cavities, or chambers, inside the body, made in his Rickenbacker style by taking a slice off the back, routing out the cavities, and then gluing the back in place. The guitar had a modified pickguard shaped to accommodate the single, token f-hole. At first the Thinline retained the regular Telecaster pickup layout, although later, as we'll see, it gained humbuckers.

Fender's press release said: "[The] famous Telecaster guitar is now available in a semi-acoustic model with a choice of two natural wood finishes, mahogany or ash. The lightweight hollowbody guitar incorporates Fender's distinctive f-hole design and new styled pickguard. The polyester-finished maple neck comes equipped with special lightweight strings for fast playing action."

Rossmeisl did not last much longer at Fender. George Fullerton echoed a general feeling when he said: "Roger was a marvellous designer and didn't become the person he should have been. I think he was his own worst enemy. Such a waste."[66] He died in Germany in 1979 at the age of 52.

It was around this time that two members of The Byrds, guitarist Clarence White and drummer Gene Parsons, came up with a new B-string-pull device, ingeniously controlled by a sprung lever fitted inside a hacked Tele body and attached to the strap button on the top. White's first electric band was Nashville West in 1967, where he moved from a Martin D-28 to a '56 Tele, but it was at a Byrds session that he told Parsons he needed a 'third hand' to help play some complicated string-bends. Parsons obliged with the necessary engineering. If the player pulled down on the neck, the strap button moved up, shifting a lever and some springs and rods inside, and raising the pitch of the B-string by a whole step. Presto! String-bends within chords to emulate pedal steel-type sounds. Following a hiccup with Leo and the CBS management, in October 1968 Parsons and White applied for a patent themselves for their B-Bender (also known as the StringBender), granted 17 months later. Parsons began custom-building and retro-fitting the devices into Teles around 1973. (After a long wait, the Fender connection did come good, with a Clarence White Custom Shop model that ran from 1993 to 2001, an American Standard version for a few years from 1995, and a three-pickup Nashville model from 1998.)

B-benders are rarely heard in action because few guitarists find the awkward shoulder-and-arm co-ordination worth the effort. However, the co-inventor, Clarence White, injects some carefully-positioned licks into 'Chestnut Mare' by The Byrds in 1970, Bernie Leadon gracefully bends the notes on 'Peaceful Easy Feeling' by The Eagles in 1972, and Jimmy Page shoulders a Tele to good effect on 'All My Love' from Led Zeppelin's final group album, 1979's *In Through The Out Door*.

In 1968, psychedelia hit Fender. The company's designers had fun applying self-adhesive wallpaper with a paisley or floral pattern to some Telecasters, presumably to give them fresh flower-power appeal. Certainly the Paisley Red and Blue Flower Teles could not be described as examples of CBS's boring approach to guitar design. But the Tele seemed the least likely target for the creation of such far-out psychedelic art objects.

The Paisley Red quickly became identified with James Burton who, since we left him back in the late 50s with Ricky Nelson, had played with scores if not hundreds of artists. But in 1969 he landed a plum gig with Elvis Presley, and Burton would remain as Presley's guitarist until the singer's death in 1977.

"When I first went to work with Elvis I was playing my early-'50s Tele that my dad got me, the one I used on 'Suzie Q' and all the Ricky Nelson songs," Burton says. "In '69, the vice president of Fender, Chuck Weiner, called me and said I have a guitar here that has your name on it. I said really? Send it to me. He said no, I want you to come down and check it out. Come and have lunch. So I drove to Fullerton, went in his office – and he said it's over there, in the corner."

Burton opened up the case and was shocked by what he saw inside. "Oh! Pink paisley! I said no, no, no, no. I said maybe a heavy rock'n'roll guitar player, but not me. He said oh yeah, it's yours, take it. He was sure, his mind was made up, and he was not going to let me get out of there without the guitar. So I said OK, I'll take it."

He decided to take his new acquisition to Las Vegas and check it out in working conditions. "About two weeks into the Elvis Vegas show, I decided to bring it out. I didn't know what Elvis was going to say on stage. I was nervous, but I thought I'd take my chance. So I took the guitar out, we're doing the first show, and he comes over to me, we're doing 'Johnny B Goode', and he's making like he's playing the guitar next to me. But he didn't say a word on stage."

After the show, Red West, one of Elvis's Memphis Mafia, told Burton that Elvis wanted to see him in his dressing room. "I go down and talk to Elvis," Burton recalls. "He says, 'I notice you've got a different guitar tonight.' I said yeah. I told him the story about it, said I was a little nervous because maybe it was a little too flashy or something, didn't know how you'd accept that on stage. 'Oh,' he said, 'I love it! Looks great, sounds great.' Incredible! I had been so nervous. I thought he might say where'd you get that horrible guitar? But he loved it. He said, 'Man, it looks great.' And

From Presley's Paisley to a Byrds B-Bender

FENDER'S
Blue Flower
Blue Flower bursts forth in a dazzling array of subtle purple and green patterns. Never before has such an exciting profusion of color been offered.
Telecaster $279.50, Telecaster Bass $289.50
(These finishes are available on the Telecaster and Telecaster Bass only.)
Fender
FENDER
TELECASTER

▸ 1968 Fender Paisley Red Telecaster

James Burton (opposite, centre) plays his famous Paisley Red Tele with Elvis, almost in danger of upstaging the King. Burton has been one of the most influential Tele men of all time. Two new gaudily decorated Fender finishes were launched for Esquires and Telecasters in 1968: Burton's vibrant Paisley Red, or the marginally more restful Blue Flower, promoted in a Fender flyer (opposite, below) as "bursting forth in a dazzling array". Unfortunately, most players other than Burton were not impressed, and the models did not last long on the Fender pricelist. Another strange idea was the B-Bender, devised by Byrds guitarist Clarence White and drummer Gene Parsons. White wanted a 'third hand' to help with complex string bends; Parsons came up with a system of levers and a spring inside a hacked Tele body (the back cover hides the work, right). Pulling down on the neck raises the pitch of the B-string, giving the athletic guitarist pedal-steel-like bends within chords. Officially from 1968, the Tele was offered with the option of a factory-fitted Fender/Bigsby vibrato, as seen (below, far left) in the catalogue from that year.

▸ **1964 Fender Telecaster sonic blue**

this guitar had a sound, you know? It was different to my original Tele, a little fatter," says Burton. "I had my back pickup custom wound by a friend of mine, Red Rhodes. Hit that switch, and the notes sound that big and round."[67]

Much as it suited Burton – and he used the guitar not only with Presley but also for work with Emmylou Harris, Gram Parsons, and many others – Fender's dazzling wallpaper experiment with the Paisley Red and Blue Flower Telecasters did not last long.

Alongside the amps, speakers, effects, pianos, organs, steel guitars, banjos, acoustics, and all the rest on Fender's bursting 1968 pricelist were eight solidbody electric models in addition to the Tele and Esquire: the Bronco, Duo-Sonic, Electric XII, Jaguar, Jazzmaster, Musicmaster, Mustang, and Stratocaster. The Thinline Telecaster listed for $319.50, $90 more than the regular $229.50 Tele, and the Paisley Red and Blue Flower Teles were $279.50 apiece. The regular Esquire listed at $194.50, the Custom Tele $259.50, and the Custom Esquire $224.50, with colour finishes as usual adding five percent.

The Beatles had nothing to do with Fender, or at least not as far as most casual onlookers were concerned. In fact, George Harrison and John Lennon each acquired a Stratocaster in 1965 for studio use, and Paul McCartney, increasingly confident with six rather than four strings, got himself an Esquire two years later, using it for his soaring, concise solo on *Sgt Pepper*'s 'Good Morning, Good Morning'. However, the public face of The Beatles remained distinctly Fender-less – leading Fender's Don Randall to try to persuade manager Brian Epstein to get his boys more visibly into the brand. "It was the only time we ever tried to buy somebody off," Randall recalled. "I sent a member of my staff to try and buy Brian Epstein off. But no, it was a pittance."

In summer 1968, Randall managed to secure a meeting with Lennon and McCartney at the band's Apple headquarters in London. "I was still kind of interested in getting them to use our products. So we went up there and had quite a long conversation with Paul. He had some great ideas, a real animated guy. Finally John and Yoko came in, and we all sat down at this big conference table."[68]

The meeting resulted in the band receiving some Fender-Rhodes pianos, a VI six-string bass, a Jazz Bass, a number of amplifiers, including a PA system, and George Harrison's Rosewood Telecaster. From this point, Fender's UK agent, Arbiter, supplied the group with more or less whatever they wanted.

The Beatles famously played their last ever 'concert' on the rooftop of their Apple HQ in London in January 1969, and it featured in the subsequent movie *Let It Be* that effectively charted their break-up. On the roof and at a few other points during the making of the film and the accompanying album, Harrison played his Rosewood Telecaster, an unusual and shortlived model. Fender had sent a prototype to Harrison in December 1968. Fender had made two prototypes of the Telecaster and two of a Rosewood Stratocaster, one of the Strats apparently intended for but never reaching Jimi Hendrix.

The Rosewood Telecaster went into production later in 1969 and lasted a couple of years in the line. It had a body constructed from a thin layer of maple sandwiched between a solid rosewood top and back. It made for a striking yet heavy instrument. Fender attempted to lighten the load by moving to a two-piece construction with hollowed chambers inside, but the weight and unusual tonality meant it was never a popular instrument. It has been revived a number of times in more recent years.

Some players and collectors believe that the 70s are the poorest years of Fender's production history, while others who got their first instruments then are likely to have fonder memories. There's little doubt, however, that quality control slipped and more low-standard Fenders were made during this decade than any other. But Fender made some decent guitars in the 70s as well. It's just that the company made more average guitars then than good ones, and it seems like it produced the good ones in spite rather than because of its policies.

During the 70s, CBS management cut back on the existing Fender product lines and offered hardly any new models. The last Esquires and Duo-Sonics of the period were made in 1969. George Fullerton recalled: "The powers that be also came up with the idea to drop the whole Telecaster line. And I just blew up! I went to Leo and I said no way: we will never, never, never drop this. I said, 'That's our beginning, that's our roots.' We'd have to be absolutely ashamed if we dropped that."[69] The Jaguar disappeared in 1975, and by 1980 the Thinline Telecaster, the Jazzmaster, the budget Bronco and Musicmaster – all these had been phased out of production. Most were later reissued, but back in the day it made for a bare catalogue. Elsewhere in Fender's guitar lines, the original acoustic flat-tops had all gone by 1971, and ten years later, the steels and pedal steels had all disappeared from the pricelists. Only amplifiers (some 14 models) offered anything like the previous market coverage.

As far as the Telecaster was concerned, the 70s might well be described as the decade of the humbucker. Part of Fender's distinction had come from using bright-sounding single-coil pickups; the warmer, fatter-sounding humbucking types were always seen then as a Gibson mainstay. Humbucking pickups had two coils wired so that they cancelled the noise that often plagued single-coil pickups. The bridge pickup on a Telecaster (or an Esquire) is widely praised as the heart of its sound, but the neck pickup ... well, that has been seen by some as the guitar's weak link. Some players simply didn't use it; some found it had a useful jazz-like tone; others took the matter into their own hands, or at least passed the problem on to their repairman.

A popular choice for some was to replace the mellow neck pickup with a ballsier humbucker, often lifted from a Gibson. Steve Marriott of The Small Faces had given this a try back at the time of the group's enjoyable *Ogden's Nut Gone Flake* album of 1968. But the most visible user of a humbucker'd Tele in the 70s was Keith Richards. He was playing Teles regularly on stage with the Stones from around 1972, even though he'd flirted with them live as early as 1966 (and Brian Jones used Keith's first Tele to record the slide part on 'Little Red Rooster' back in '64).

Keef's most famous Fender is his blackguard '52 (or perhaps '53) Tele, nicknamed Micawber, complete with 'backwards' Gibson humbucker added in 1972. It's also one of the guitars he uses with five-string open tuning, effectively open G with the low D removed (G-D-G-B-D low to high), heard live on classics like 'Brown Sugar'. "I use a whole load of different guitars, that's true," he

Shine until tomorrow

Fender sent George Harrison a prototype of an unusual rosewood-body Telecaster, and the Beatle used it during the making of the group's *Let It Be* movie and album. Harrison is pictured with the Tele (left), which he played most famously during The Beatles' last concert, filmed on the roof of their Apple HQ in London. Fender put the model into production in 1969 (main guitar), but the instrument's relatively heavy weight and unusual tonality meant it was a shortlived item. An ad from 1971 (opposite, bottom) revealed that Fender, like most people at the time, was unaware that its first solidbody had debuted in 1950. Changes to the 70s line continued: the earlier f-hole Thinline model, with its single-coil pickups (late example, right, bottom), was altered in 1971 to incorporate two of Fender's new humbucking pickups (example shown right, top).

▲ **1969 Fender Rosewood Telecaster rosewood**

▲ 1972 Fender Thinline Telecaster sunburst

▼ 1971 Fender Thinline Telecaster shell pink

said in the early 80s, "but they're not all that dissimilar in type. I mean, 90 percent are probably Telecasters, old ones."[70] He has a couple of regular backup Teles, too: Malcolm (a blond-finished '54) and Sonny (a sunburst '66).

Denny Dias in Steely Dan went further and replaced both pickups of his Telecaster with humbuckers. Perhaps that means it's not really a Tele at all any more. No matter: Steely Dan made remarkable records in the 70s, and on the first two albums Dias and Jeff Baxter provide some of the most exhilarating guitar playing of the decade. Dias solo'd less, but his highly modified Tele – a beast remodelled by Baxter with twin 'buckers, multiple coil switching, big frets, and a Strat bridge – can be heard on his breathtaking, tumbling solo on 'Bodhisattva' from 1973's *Countdown To Ecstasy*. Baxter, too, often played a modified Tele, and you can hear him alongside Dias on, for example, 'Reelin' In The Years' from the band's first album, *Can't Buy A Thrill*.

In 1973, Jeff Beck exchanged his Yardbirds Esquire with pickup maestro Seymour Duncan for a Tele with humbuckers. Duncan had put together this 'Tele-Gib' from a '59 Telecaster body, a '63/'64 neck, and a Gibson Flying V's pair of humbuckers. "It had the feel of a Tele and just this big fat sound of the humbuckers," is Beck's summation. "It's a really good combination. Just doesn't look that great."

One of the finest moments for Beck's Tele-Gib came when he used it to record 'Cause We've Ended As Lovers' for the 1975 album *Blow By Blow*. "The Les Paul – well, I thought everybody's got those," Beck says. "I wanted to speak quite clearly as me. My Les Paul sounded good, but it just sounded like … well, I won't mention who it sounded like. But as soon as I picked up this Tele, there was something there."[71]

Beck dedicated 'Cause We've Ended As Lovers' to Roy Buchanan – of whom more shortly. What the Tele master made of Beck's gesture is unknown, but in an interview the year after *Blow By Blow* came out, Buchanan had a warning for all those busily bolting 'buckers on to old Teles. "They're antiques, really," said Buchanan, "and putting a humbucker on them would be like putting a moustache on the Mona Lisa."[72]

Buchanan's note of caution was largely ignored, and for some players the Tele-plus-humbucker trend continued through the 70s. Steve Howe, a keen guitar collector, bought a mid-'50s Tele while on tour with Yes in the States in 1974. He quickly added a neck humbucker and used it for quite a lot of that year's *Relayer* album. "The Tele was great for me then," Howe says, "and although I could make it sound like a Gibson thanks to the humbucker, the back pickup is what makes it a Telecaster."[73]

Andy Summers came to prominence with The Police later in the 70s, although he'd had a long apprenticeship, notably with Hammond-organist Zoot Money's bands. On stage with The Police, Summers played almost exclusively a bound Custom Telecaster, which he'd bought for $200 in Los Angeles while teaching there in 1972. It had been heavily modified, with a 50s maple neck, an added humbucker, and various electronic changes.

His fragmented, small-chord approach worked well on that Tele. "I've never found another guitar that sounded better," Summers says. "It's a '61 sunburst Custom with a Gibson humbucker in front. The back pickup has been packed underneath so it doesn't feed back at all. There's a little pre-amp built into the back of the guitar so that it will overload for a great, strong lead sound, plus an out-of-phase switch. I like simple guitars."[74]

The guys at Fender were gripped by the humbucker trend. They modified the existing Thinline Telecaster model in 1971 with two new Fender humbuckers, presumably with the intention of sending out a signal that Fender was invading Gibson territory. Fender's official word, in a press release, went like this: "The humbucking pickups not only help eliminate feedback, they also add a gutty mid-range and bass sound." It was about as close as Fender would come officially to say: "This Fender is like a Gibson."

Seth Lover came to California in 1967, enticed by Fender away from the Gibson company in Michigan where, famously, he had invented Gibson's humbucking pickup in the 50s. Warm, clear, powerful humbuckers gave a distinctive edge to dozens of Gibson models, not least the Les Paul electrics that came back into vogue toward the end of the 60s.

Lover later explained what his new employers were after. "The Fender sales force wanted a copy of a Gibson humbucking pickup, they wanted it to sound exactly like that," he said. "The patent had not quite run out, so I designed them a pickup that looked a little different." He used magnets of cunife, an alloy of copper, nickel, and iron, rather than Gibson's alnico, which mixes aluminium, nickel, and cobalt. "I hesitated in making it sound exactly like the Gibson – I figured Fender was known for a brilliant type sound, so I kept a little more brilliance in the Fender pickup than there was in the Gibson."[75] Lover divided the polepieces into two lines, too, with the three bass ones to the front of the cover and the three treble ones to the rear.

Fender had blatantly replaced both pickups with humbuckers on that revised Thinline model, but the designers' next move was to a more restrained arrangement for the Telecaster Custom, in 1972. This time the classic Tele lead pickup stayed put. Just the neck pickup was changed to a humbucker, and the control layout was opened out to a Gibson-like two volumes and two tones. Fender's marketing director Dave Gupton combined hype with prescience in his press statement about the new instrument. "Musicians looking for sound versatility will be able to do just about anything with the new Telecaster Custom," he boasted in typical ad-speak. But then he got real. "By incorporating the latest humbucking-design Fender pickup along with the unique world-renowned Telecaster lead pickup, a whole new spectrum of sounds is created."

Next came the Telecaster Deluxe, in 1973, and Fender was back to twin humbuckers. The Deluxes seemed like a cross between the big-headstock neck of the contemporary Stratocaster (some even had Strat-style vibratos), the body of a Telecaster, but with a Strat-like rear contour, and the pickups and controls of a Gibson. As with the Custom, there were four controls on the Deluxe: two volumes and two tones.

None of these humbucker'd Teles were overly successful at the time. Potential customers were often confused and, at the time, they stayed away. The humbucker-equipped Telecaster Deluxe and Custom models both disappeared from the pricelist during 1981, the Thinline two years earlier. As we shall see, they have become enormously popular in recent years, with many players now discovering for themselves the potent combination of the playability of a Tele and the

Two more ways to buck that hum

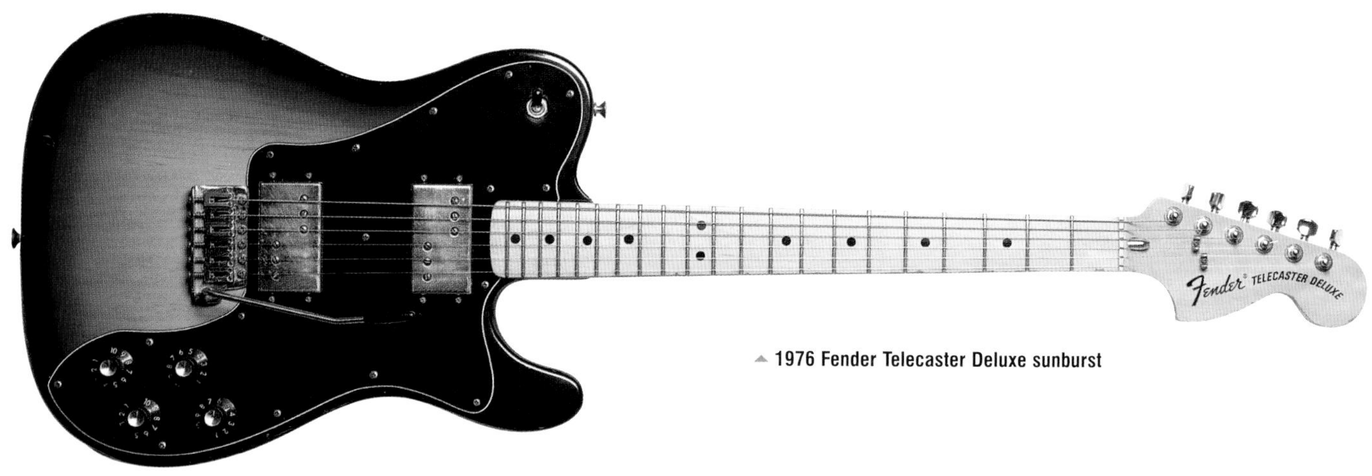

▲ 1976 Fender Telecaster Deluxe sunburst

▼ 1977 Fender Telecaster Custom sunburst

Two new Telecasters with Fender's humbucking pickups appeared in the early 70s. The Telecaster Custom (main guitar) acknowledged one of the most popular modifications that guitarists made to the instrument: to replace the 'weak' neck pickup with a ballsier humbucker. Fender also threw in a new-shape pickguard and a Gibson-like four-control layout. Keith Richards often used an old Telecaster with added neck 'bucker on-stage at the time, but he was also seen with one of the new Customs (above). Another player keen on the humbucker'd Tele approach was Steely Dan's Denny Dias, pictured (above right) in the early 70s with his highly modified Tele. The new Telecaster Deluxe (opposite, top) was similar to the Custom, but it had two humbuckers and a Stratocaster-style neck and headstock.

usefulness of that humbucker – more of which later. Like many Fenders of the period, the humbucker'd Teles were fitted with a bullet truss-rod adjuster and a neck-tilt system. The 'bullet' term described the appearance of the truss-rod adjustment nut at the headstock, while the neck-tilt system was a Fender device at the neck-to-body joint that allowed easier adjustment of neck pitch, or angle. They also came with the company's new high-gloss 'thick skin' finish, achieved by spraying more than a dozen coats of polyester on to the unfortunate instrument, and today its plastic appearance is a giveaway sign of a 70s Fender.

The December 1974 pricelist revealed just a few options for new Telecasters. Most of Fender's original Custom Colors had been discontinued in the late 60s and early 70s, and the Tele was available in just six finishes in '74: standard blond ($315), or natural (ash), sunburst, black, white, or walnut ($330 each). The regular model had the rosewood fingerboard of the period, but a maple board was an option. Left-handers and Bigsby-vibrato versions were also available (although this was the last year for now of the Bigsby option). The basic two-humbucker Telecaster Deluxe, in walnut, was pitched on that list at $440, the single-humbucker Custom, in sunburst, at $345, and the two-humbucker Thinline, in sunburst, at $410.

In spite of all this twin-coil excess, many players continued to favour the original, unadulterated single-coil Tele, and few with more effect on their fellow guitarists than the great Roy Buchanan. He had it all: a keen melodic sense coupled to economic note choice, an astounding flair for solo dexterity, and an ability to shine with singers (including himself) as well as in instrumental territory. Buchanan's main guitar was a '53 Tele, which he got around 1968 and soon christened Nancy. "I like the old Teles because of the wood," he said, "the way the pickups are wound, the capacitors – the whole works."[76]

He set the bar in 1972 with an early single, 'Sweet Dreams', a languid, bluesy romp full of clean, instinctive Tele lines. Many good records followed. Robbie Robertson of The Band said Buchanan had a command over the Telecaster that he couldn't quite comprehend. "He bent the neck; he bent the strings behind the bridge," said Robertson. "He played with both hands on the fingerboard. He used every ornament on the thing to get a noise out of it. It was like the guitar came to life. It started speaking. [And because] Roy was such a complicated person, he never played with anybody where he could be shown in his proper light. I remember hearing [that] The Rolling Stones were talking to him, wanting to try him out – and he didn't even show up."[77]

For his comeback in 1986, Buchanan evidently had a change of heart and decided to give up his beloved old Teles. "A lot of people won't want to hear this, but the new guitars are actually better than the old ones," he said, explaining that he was now using a new '86 Tele. "I mean, I would rather be driving a brand new Rolls Royce than a '55 Chevy."[78] Buchanan had a continuing battle with drink and other drugs, and he committed suicide in 1988 at the age of 48.

Robbie Robertson himself did some fine stuff with a Telecaster at the end of the 60s and into the 70s with The Band and Bob Dylan. One of Robertson's best recorded achievements came in 'King Harvest' on The Band's second album, from 1969, where his thoughtful Tele support culminates in a wonderfully dry, spiky, hesitant solo at the close of the track. But he shines almost everywhere he plays, and it's impossible not to smile and enjoy such a masterful minimalist as he deploys harmonics, drones, volume effects, and more to create a distinctive guitar voice. Much of the great work is on a Tele, but Robertson shifted to Strats in 1975.

We learned earlier about Jeff Beck's generous gift of a Telecaster to Jimmy Page. Page used that guitar in The Yardbirds and on a good deal of early Led Zeppelin material, on stage and in the studio. He pulled out the Tele again for one of his most revered solos, on 'Stairway To Heaven'. Page was better known by the time of its release on the untitled fourth album in 1971 for big, thick Les Paul sounds, but the 'Stairway' lead is pure Telecaster. About six minutes into the marathon, Page builds a logical, satisfying statement on his Tele that perfectly suits the lofty surroundings.

The decade was chock full of other great Tele moments. Catfish Collins defined funk rhythm playing on James Brown's 'Sex Machine' in 1970, and Bill Harkleroad, aka Zoot Horn Rollo, hit long, meaning notes and let them float all over Captain Beefheart's 1972 LP *Clear Spot*. Status Quo boogied endlessly on a pair of road-weary Teles, Rick Parfitt's a battered home-painted white '65 and Francis Rossi's an equally careworn '57 that went from sunburst to black to green. "I really love the shape," Rossi said of the Telecaster. "And it's workmanlike, solid, basic-looking. No-nonsense. There's no fragility about it. It's like a tool."[79]

Sly Stone and his brother, guitarist Freddie, deployed Teles throughout the Family Stone's funky stuff, Bruce Springsteen drove a hard-working Esquire (possibly a '56 or '57, with added black 'guard and Telefied with a second pickup), and Marc Bolan posed on television with a sunburst Custom Tele as he mimed to 'Hot Love', T.Rex's British Number 1 smash of 1971.

Fender's Dave Gupton announced that 1972 had been a record year for the company, with unit production and dollar sales figures both higher than ever before. He was in little doubt that 1973 would yield still higher figures and that the trend would continue upward. A major expansion program was on at the Fullerton plant to boost output still further, completed in summer 1974 and providing the Fender operation with about 290,000 square feet of space for production, warehousing, and shipping.

This is precisely why CBS had purchased Fender back in 1965. But the increase in the number of instruments leaving the factory inevitably affected quality. A feeling was beginning to set in that Fenders were not made like they used to be. A number of top musicians were regularly to be seen playing old guitars, now described as 'vintage' instruments, and it added to the growing impression that numbers might be more important to Fender than quality. Some guitarists were becoming convinced that older instruments were somehow more playable and sounded better than new guitars.

An early sign of this new old-is-best vibe came in the *Washington Post* at the end of 1972. Reporter Tom Zito had spotted a trend among local musicians who hunted for original Telecasters. "Available for a mere $150 in 1952," wrote Zito, more or less accurately, "this humble electric guitar has already increased in value some 500 percent. ... Proof, in the buy-it-on-time, wear-it-out, and throw-it-away world of rock, that enduring value does indeed exist."

Zito met Leo Fender and told him how some musicians were now considering a vintage Telecaster in much the same light as the hallowed and immensely valuable Stradivarius violins of

Sounds of the Seventies

Time now to stop for a moment and enjoy a 70s interlude as we consider more musicians from that decade who helped to keep the Fender Telecaster on the guitarist's map. But keep in mind what the Fender factory was up to: check out this '72 Tele (main guitar), another example of blue faded to green. The chap with the flowing locks (above) is Bill Harkleroad, better known to Captain Beefheart fans as Zoot Horn Rollo, his glassy Tele tone an appropriate foil for the Captain's vocalising. Note the humbucker in the neck position.

1972 Fender Telecaster lake placid blue

Bruce Springsteen hit it big in the middle of the decade with *Born To Run*, and on the jacket (left) you can see him, alongside saxophonist Clarence Clemons, brandishing his Fender, thought to have started life as an Esquire but now with Tele-fying pickup modifications.

Tele-toting Robbie Robertson is seen (right) at work on material for The Band, here in rehearsal with Levon Helm. Above that is the great Roy Buchanan, the fabled melodic stylist who knew exactly how to get the most from his Telecaster (here with a Strat pickup added at the neck).

17th century Italy. Apparently the 65-year-old Leo paused, as well he might. Then he said: "Well, I'm sure a lot of musicians feel just like that about 'em. Now I'll give you an example. In 1929, I bought a Model 12 Remington. I mean, I could really hit a target with that old rifle. One time I got a jack rabbit at better than 300 yards. You see, some pieces of machinery just suit people."

The reporter next turned to Freddie Tavares at Fender, who told him that the continuing demand for Teles, old and new, was down to the sound. "Now how do you describe that? I'll tell you. It's the kind of sound that says, 'Listen, you bugger, I'm talkin', so shut up!' It's a piercing, whining sound that forces you to pay attention, and it's filled with clear high-range harmonics. What makes it so appealing is that it makes the average ear say, 'My god, what brilliance!'"

Zito at the *Post* had the good luck to come upon guitarist Danny Gatton. Of course, we know now that he was one of the great Tele players, but back then he was just another struggling Washington guitarist, and one who sold and repaired instruments as a sideline. Gatton told the *Post* the reason players were looking for these early-50s Telecasters was because they had what he called the old funky Fender sound. "I've been getting calls for them like hotcakes," he said. "People have been paying five beans [$500] for them. ... Not that I really blame them. It's all I'll play. You can do everything – squeeze all that country funk out of them. If there's a sound you can't get, don't blame it on the axe. It means you can't pick."

Tavares and Leo naturally thought that new Teles sounded as good as the old ones. Gatton was equally sure that pre-1956 Teles were best. "There's all the difference in the world," he said, and continued with a list of significant changes: thicker-gauge wire now in the pickup coils, reducing fidelity; raised rather than flat pickup polepieces, producing muddier tones; less wax potting, or filling, for the newer pickups, fuelling feedback problems; and different value capacitors, altering the Tele's classic tone.[80]

Gatton would become a Tele player's Tele player in years to come, making influential records like *Redneck Jazz* (1978) and *88 Elmira Street* (1991) before his untimely death by his own hand in 1994. He was a constant fiddler, modifying and adapting his guitars and working closely with Joe Barden in search of the perfect pickup. A couple of Teles, a '52 and a '53, were his workhorses.

"[Guitarist] Bob Berman, a good friend of Roy [Buchanan's], would come to hear me play," Gatton told an interviewer in 1983. "He'd say, 'I like what you're doing, but you've got to play an old Tele like Roy's – that's the sound!' I said that they were cheap, and pointed to the pearl on my Les Paul. Then Bob hired me on a demo session he was recording. I was about to record a solo when he handed me his '52 Tele and said, 'Play something that'll knock my socks off, and it's yours.' So I pulled out all the stops, and he gave me my first Telecaster," said Gatton. "Most important, the Tele gives me that dirty blues sound that I can't get from my Les Pauls."[81]

The search for old guitars and the notion that they were mysteriously and inherently better grew steadily during the 70s. Stephen Stills summed up the attitude to vintage axes in a 1975 interview, when he said: "Nothing new has been built since the 60s that's worth a damn."[82] Norman's Rare Guitars, established in California during the middle of the decade, was one of the newer dealers specialising in the vintage requirements of rock players. Proprietor Norman Harris was in no doubt why so many guitarists were taking up older instruments – like those he offered for sale. "You simply cannot compare what I have to offer with what the big companies are mass producing today," he boasted.[83] The first published attempt to sort out the various old Telecasters and their dates of manufacture came in Tom Wheeler's *The Guitar Book* in 1974, and later more definitively in André Duchossoir's *The Fender Telecaster* (1991).

Freddie Tavares's son Terry recalls how one person's junk can become another's collectable. "I can remember dad bringing home trunk-loads of rejected necks and bodies which the saws and routers had nicked, and we burned them in the fireplace. Little did we know that if we had just saved them for 45 years they'd be worth millions today as ding'd-up mid-50s Strats and Teles."[84]

In Britain, punk – depending on your viewpoint – gave a welcome opportunity to fresh young hopefuls or wiped out the idea of good musicianship. There was some good Tele action among it all, most visibly by Clash mainman Joe Strummer grinding out rhythm on his bashed-up black Tele covered in stickers, while Mick Jones's Gibsons provided most of the band's leads. Strummer bought his '66 sunburst Tele secondhand for £120 in 1975, when he was in a pub-rock band called The 101ers. He joined The Clash the following year and took his guitar to a car body shop, where he had it painted black over a grey undercoat. He decorated it with stickers and stencils, most famously an Ignore Alien Orders sticker and a NOISE stencil. He played that Tele until The Clash split in the mid 80s, and Fender issued a signature version in 2007.

Strummer was inspired to play a Telecaster by Wilko Johnson, guitarist in Dr Feelgood. Johnson's band straddled the stylistic gap between pub-rock and punk, mixing old-style R&B with a thoroughly modern brutality, thoughtfully supplied by the manic Telecaster-wielding guitarist. Punks in almost everything but name and sartorial style, the Feelgoods achieved their peak of success in October 1976 when their third album, the live *Stupidity*, topped the British album charts. Johnson generally turned to one of a pair of '63 Teles to deliver his brittle, fragile, collapsing-any-second sound, which harked back to the lead-and-rhythm-all-at-once style of his chief influence, Mick Green of The Pirates.

Meanwhile at Fender, the catalogue was settling down to a revised pattern. After the so-so reception for the recent spate of new humbucker-equipped Teles, Fender's taste for fresh designs slackened off considerably. A glance at the chronology at the rear of this book reveals the lack of new models in the 70s. It's clear that Fender was concentrating in general on its strengths – and as a result was enjoying its most commercially successful period yet, producing a greater quantity of instruments than ever before.

Fender began a shortlived revival in 1977 of the antigua finish, a light-to-dark shaded colour at first offered as an option during the late 60s on some Coronado models. Back then, it was an emergency measure to disguise manufacturing flaws. This time around, for just a couple of years, Fender used it purely for the look. Several Teles had antigua options, including the regular model, the Deluxe, and the Custom. This new antigua style, now with more of a graduated tone, was matched to similarly finished pickguards. It was briefly revived on a Japanese-made Tele in 2004.

Also featured on the antigua guitars was the new black hardware introduced in 1975. All the plasticware – knobs, pickup covers, switch caps – was black, and this certainly enhanced the overall

Punkcaster rockers

In the late 70s came punk, and the British version at least had a fair showing of the Fender Telecaster. The most visible Tele player was Joe Strummer of The Clash (right), whose stickered and stencilled instrument became a punk icon right through the band's rise from London pubs to worldwide stadiums. The punk guitarist's punk guitarist was Wilko Johnson of Dr Feelgood (opposite), a manic onstage presence whose fluid rhythm-and-lead style drove the band with a distinctive brittle edge. Over in California, at the Fender factory, the weather was still sunny and punks rarely seen. Just take a glance at these ads from the period: there's the Telecaster as a walking vinyl record machine (opposite), as lead guitar in a Three Bears jam session, or as a kind of techno-bird (above). And all the while, the 70s Tele itself (main guitar) continued to reflect the current state of Fender guitar-making.

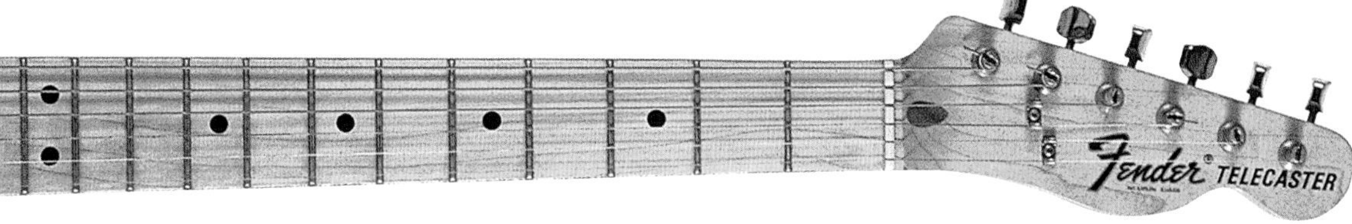

▲ **1974 Fender Telecaster blond**

look of the antigua-finish instruments. It was also around this time that Fender replaced its tuners with closed-cover units bought in from the German Schaller company, a supplier used until 1983.

CBS was selling 40,000 Fender instruments a year by the end of the 70s. A further sign of such an enormously increased production rate was the end of the tradition for putting a date on an instrument's neck. Since the earliest days of Esquires and Broadcasters, workers had almost always pencilled and later rubber-stamped dates on the body-end of necks. It remains about the most reliable way to date a Fender of the period (leaving aside the question of fakes). But from 1973 to the early 80s, Fender stopped doing it. Presumably they were simply too busy.

By 1976, Fender had a five-acre facility under one roof in Fullerton and employed over 750 workers. John Page, who would run Fender's Custom Shop from the late 80s until the early 2000s, started working for Fender in 1978, spending some months on the production line before moving to R&D. There was rampant departmentalism at Fender in the late 70s, he recalls. "You couldn't even tell Purchasing what part you wanted or where you wanted it from; all you could tell them was the spec of the part you wanted," Page explains. "It was so compartmentalised, and virtually no one got to know anyone else in any of the other departments. There was no communication."

Page remembers his horror when he discovered a CBS executive cheerfully disposing of Fender's history. "This guy came through our office putting green dots on all our guitars. I asked what he was doing. 'Oh well, I got this great programme: I'm gonna give these away to dealers, yes sir.' What! And before we were able to stop it, he had given away about 80 percent of our original prototypes and samples."[85]

By 1979, the Fender pricelist showed ten electric models in the line, with a basic Tele at $535 (rosewood neck) or $580 (maple), a single-humbucker Custom listing at $580 (rosewood) or $615 (maple), and a two-humbucker Deluxe at $685 (maple only). The Teles sat among seven other electrics (Bronco, Jazzmaster, Lead, Musicmaster, Mustang, Starcaster, and Stratocaster).

Colour schemes brightened during the 80s: the shortlived International Colors came along in 1981, and then the Custom Colors and Stratobursts in '82. Some of the new hues were distinctly lurid, such as capri orange, aztec gold, or bronze stratoburst, and players didn't much care for them at the time. In 1983, there was a short run of marble 'bowling ball' finishes, in red, blue, or yellow. At least the notion that a decent selection of Custom Colors was a good idea seemed to be back in place.

With generally trimmed model lines and a massive output from the factories, it was hard to resist the feeling as the 80s dawned that the newly-important calculations of the balance sheet were now firmly established at Fender and had taken precedence over the company's former creativity. At the start of the decade, CBS management decided they needed fresh blood to encourage some new enthusiasm at the firm. Income had been climbing spectacularly to 1980 – it had tripled in that year from 1971's $20 million – but re-investment in the company was wavering.

Beginning in 1981, CBS hired key men from the American musical-instruments division of Yamaha, the big Japanese company famous for pianos, electronics, and, increasingly, guitars. John McLaren was recruited as the new head of CBS Musical Instruments overall. Bill Schultz was the new president of the Fender/Rogers/Rhodes division (guitars/drums/keyboards), Dan Smith became director of marketing electric guitars, and Roger Balmer, who came from Music Man but had been at Yamaha before, was installed as head of marketing and sales. From within CBS, Bill Mendello, chief financial officer of the instruments division, relocated to California and based himself at Fender. These key managers would guide the firm through the tricky years ahead.

Dan Smith, the new man in charge of guitars at Fender, says CBS brought in the team to turn around Fender's flagging reputation and to regain the market share the brand had lost since the late 70s. "At that point in time everybody hated what Fender had become," he recalls. "We thought we knew how bad it was, but we took it for granted that they could make Telecasters and Stratocasters the way they used to make them. We were wrong. So many things had been changed in the Fender factory at Fullerton."

Smith already knew that Fender quality was not good, and that everybody – players, dealers, the company itself – knew the quality was not good. Before Yamaha, he'd worked as a guitar repairer in Rochester, New York, and there Smith saw for himself some of the poor instruments his customers brought in. He worked at Yamaha from 1977, and when he visited dealers, often they wanted to talk more about how awful Fender and Gibson guitars were than about Yamaha.

When Smith arrived at Fender in 1981, he had an early shock as he toured the factory. "I remember looking at the body contours," he says. "People were complaining about contours, and here I am looking at racks of hundreds of guitars. Every one of those guitars had a different edge contour! We went and pulled instruments out of the warehouse and did general re-inspections on 800-plus guitars. Out of those, I think only about 15 passed the existing criteria."[86]

Among the first improvements Smith made was to revise the look of the Telecaster. "One of the things that had happened in the 70s was that CBS had brought in a CNC [computer controlled] machine and modified the shape of the Telecaster so it would work with that machine," Smith explains. "If you look at Teles from the 70s to about 1982 or so, when we got it back to where it should be, the shoulder on the left-hand side is weird. It was too low, and that little cut-out that happens right at the neck had a larger radius. They had lost the curve that goes from the left side shoulder down into the cutaway on the right side." To many, the subtle change to the shape of the Tele was symptomatic of CBS's wider disregard for how things ought to be. "We said hey, you can't change that shape! We fixed it so your eye picks up a nice smooth transition, a nice French curve from one side to the next."[8]

Another new idea was, quite simply, for Fender to copy itself, by recreating the guitars that, as we've seen, many players and collectors were spending increasingly large sums of money to acquire: the vintage Fender guitars made back in the company's glory years in the 50s and 60s.

Freddie Tavares, one of the original Fender men from the 50s, still worked in Fender R&D, and in 1980 he began work on a Vintage Telecaster. The idea was to re-create a 1952-style original, prompted by an idea from marketing manager Paul Bugelski. It was planned to be the first modern reissue of a vintage-style Fender guitar. At the July NAMM music-trade show in 1981, organised by the National Association of Music Merchants, Fender showed a prototype.

Dan Smith arrived at the company a month later. "This supposed '52 Telecaster had polyester finish, the wrong body shape, a whole bunch of stuff wrong with it," Smith says. "I told them we

Redneck jazz and bowling balls

▸ 1984 Fender Telecaster Standard bowling ball blue

▴ 1984 Fender Telecaster Standard bowling ball gold

Into the 80s, and our two representatives of Tele-playing supremacy are from each end of the spectrum. Danny Gatton (above) is a Tele player's Tele player, with the title of his 1978 album *Redneck Jazz* hinting at two of the constituents of his remarkable playing. Gatton would benefit from a lofty reputation among his peers, as well as a Fender signature Telecaster in 1990, but four years later the troubled musician committed suicide. Andy Summers (opposite) was an experienced player when he joined The Police in the 70s, enjoying huge success at the end of that decade and into the 80s. Summers used a Custom Telecaster with added neck humbucker, aiding his small-chord effects-assisted sound. In the early 80s, Fender decided to draw attention to the shortlived Telecaster Standard (the one with no through-body stringing) and produced a trial run of 50 guitars in three marble or bowling ball finishes, examples of which are shown on these pages. Fender did not pursue the idea further.

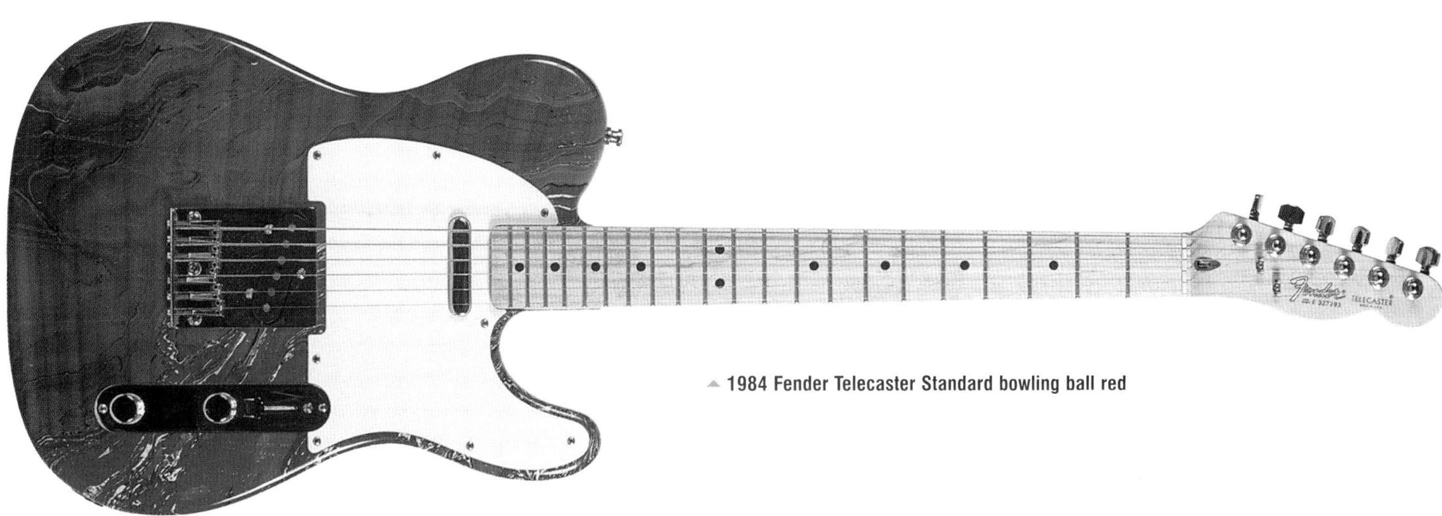

▲ 1984 Fender Telecaster Standard bowling ball red

can't ship that. So we shut down the vintage reissue series. We brought in Ted Greene, a great guitar player here in Southern California, who had I think 13 or 14 old Broadcasters and Nocasters and Telecasters. We spent a lot of time with him and his Teles, making sure we had all the details right."[88]

The team searched further to assist in their proposed re-creations of vintage instruments. R&D man John Page travelled with Smith to a vintage guitar dealer, Ax In Hand in Illinois, where they took more measurements and photographs and paint-tests from a few old guitars. They also bought some vintage Fender instruments. "That's right," laughs Smith, "we went out and bought back our own product!"[89] Such industry resulted in Fender's first Vintage reissues. The models consisted of the revised '52 Telecaster, plus a maple-neck '57 and rosewood-board '62 Strat. Production of the Vintage reissues was planned to start in 1982 at Fender's US factory at Fullerton – and also at the newly formed Fender Japan operation.

Fender/Rogers/Rhodes president Bill Schultz had recommended a large investment package, primarily aimed at modernising the Fullerton factory. This had the immediate effect of virtually stopping production while new machinery was brought in and staff re-trained. But he also wanted to start production of Fender guitars in Japan. The reason was relatively straightforward: Fender's sales were being hammered by the onslaught of copies produced in the region. The Japanese copyists made the biggest profits in their own domestic market, so the best place to hit back at them was in Japan – by making and selling guitars there.

In the early 70s, when the Japanese began manufacturing electric guitars in the style of classic American models, most Western makers didn't see much to worry about. Later, the quality of the Japanese instruments improved, but some American makers had their heads stuck firmly in the sand. Dave Gupton, vice president of Fender by 1978, said: "Fender is not adversely affected by the Japanese copies as perhaps some of the other major manufacturers, because we have been able to keep our costs pretty much in line."[90]

That casual attitude changed dramatically in a few short years. By the start of the 80s, the US dollar had increased in value relative to the Japanese yen. It shifted from a low in 1978, when a dollar was worth around 200 yen, to a high in 1982, when it rose to nearly 250 yen. Coupled with the high quality of many Japanese guitars, this meant that instruments built there were making a notable impact on the international guitar market. Many copied Fender and Gibson models. "We had to stop this plethora of copies," Smith recalls. "A lot of these companies basically told Bill Schultz and me that they were going to bury us. They were ripping us off, and what we really needed to do was to get these guys where it hurt – back in their own marketplace."[91]

With the blessing of CBS, negotiations began with two Japanese distributors, Kanda Shokai and Yamano Music, to establish the Fender Japan company. The joint venture was officially established in March 1982 combining the forces of Fender, Kanda, and Yamano. Fender USA licensed Fender Japan the right to have Fender guitars built within Japan for sale on the Japanese market.

After discussions with Tokai, Kawai, and others, Fender Japan chose Fujigen to build its guitars. Based in Matsumoto, some 130 miles north-west of Tokyo, the Fujigen factory was best known in the West for the excellence of its Ibanez-brand instruments. Fujigen made good Greco-brand copies of Fender, and Kanda Shokai had been selling them, so the Japanese were well prepared to make and sell Fender guitars.

The changes under way at the US factory meant that American versions of the new reissue series did not come properly on-stream until early 1983, and the factory there was not up to full speed until the start of '84. No such problems detained Fujigen and Fender Japan. Smith and his colleagues at Fender USA received samples of the Japanese-made Vintage reissues before American production started, and he remembers their reaction to the high quality of these Fender re-creations. "Everybody came up to inspect them and the guys almost cried, because the Japanese product was so good. It was what we were having a hell of a time trying to do."[92]

The July 1983 US pricelist pitched the '52 Telecaster reissue at $785, which was $335 more than the regular Tele. That same month, Guitar Trader, a dealer based in New Jersey and specialising in vintage instruments, offered a 1954 Tele for sale at $3,000. It was the most expensive guitar in their inventory except for a handful of 50s Les Paul Standards and a Flying V. Their Telecaster was blond with maple neck, black pickguard, and level-polepiece lead pickup. Guitar Trader said it was "fully intact and supplied with original formfit hardcase" and described it as "the most sought-after style of Telecaster produced".[93]

Fender's Vintage Tele reproduction was not exact enough for some die-hard collectors, but the idea seemed sound enough. If there was a market for old guitars, then why not for guitars that looked like the old ones? Guitarists knew that the instruments had to feel and play right, too, of course – the very attributes that made the older Teles so appealing. Fender had more work to do. But they were definitely on to something.

As we've learned, Fender Japan's guitars at this stage were being made only for the internal Japanese market. But Fender's European agents were putting pressure on the Fullerton management for a budget-price Fender to compete with the multitude of exported models being sold in Europe and elsewhere by other Japanese manufacturers.

This led in 1982 to Fender Japan making some less costly versions of the Vintage Tele and Strat reissues for European distribution, distinguished at first by the addition of a small 'Squier Series' logo on the tip of the headstock. This was soon changed, with a large 'Squier' replacing the Fender logo, and the Squier brand was born.

The name was much older, however. It came from a string-making company, V.C. Squier, and the V.C. in question was Victor Carroll Squier, a 19th-century Michigan-born violin maker who, in the 1890s, added a successful string-making operation to his business. The firm operated at the same Battle Creek building from 1927 to 1972, with Fender acquiring Squier in the 60s. The new owners at Fender pounced on the name when they needed a brandname in a hurry for these cheaper Japanese guitars.

Toward the end of 1983, with the US Fender factory still not up to the scale of production the team wanted, Schultz and Smith decided to have Fender Japan build some instruments for the US market, too. They approved Japanese production of a Squier-brand 70s-style Telecaster and Stratocaster. These, together with the earlier Squier Vintage-style Teles and Strats, marked the start of the sale of Fender Japan products around the world and the move by Fender to become an

Yesterday once more

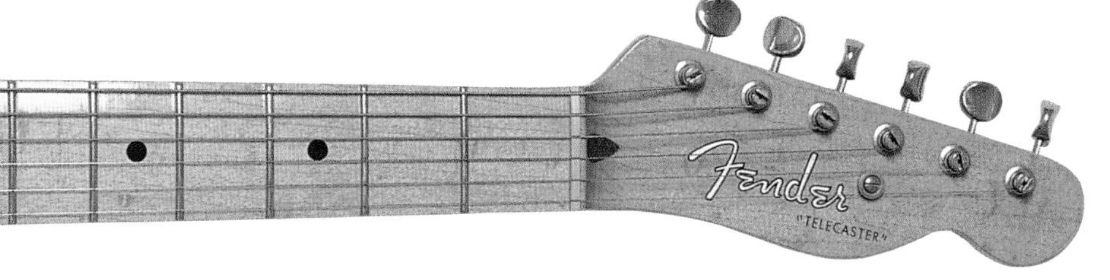

▲ **1984 Fender '52 Telecaster blond**

Old Fender hand Freddie Tavares, seen with the company's new guitar boss Dan Smith (opposite), began work on Fender's first modern reissue in 1980. Vintage instruments had grown in stature during the 70s, and prices rose for good original guitars, especially early Fenders and Gibsons. The result of Tavares's industry was the '52 Telecaster (main guitar). It was publicised in Fender's 1982 catalogue (opposite), even though US-made examples did not appear until the following year. Fender began Japanese production at this time, with some of the earliest models branded Squier (ad, above), a name that came from a string company that Fender owned. Meanwhile, one of the few jazz guitarists attracted to the Tele was Mike Stern (above, left) who played with Miles Davis in the early 80s and released his first solo album, *Neesh*, in 1983.

international manufacturer of guitars. "It taught us, contrary to what the guys believed at Fender six or seven years before, that people would buy Fender guitars with 'made in Japan' on them," Smith says. "In fact, I really believe that our introduction of those instruments, worldwide and in the USA, was what legitimised buying Japanese guitars."[94] Certainly many musicians had resisted the cheap image at first associated with Japan-made guitars, but the rise in quality of instruments from brands such as Ibanez, Yamaha, Greco, Aria, and Tokai – as well as Fender and Squier – wiped away a good deal of this prejudice and gave Japanese guitars a new popularity and respectability.

At the US factory in 1983, Fender made some cost-cutting changes to the Fender-brand Telecaster Standard (and to the equivalent Strat). These were the result of the dollar's continuing strength and the consequent difficulty in selling US-made products overseas, where they were becoming increasingly high-priced. Savings had to be made, so the Tele was deprived of its tone-enhancing through-body stringing – just as Fender had done briefly back in the late 50s. The revisions were ill-conceived, and many who applauded the improvements made since 1981 groaned inwardly at the familiar signs of economics again taking precedence over playability and sound. Fortunately, this mutant variety of Fender's key Telecaster model lasted only until the end of 1984.

Another shortlived guitar from the same period was the Elite Telecaster, which together with an accompanying Stratocaster was intended as a radical new high-end version of the old faithful. The Elite Tele sold for $895 and had two new pickups designed to deliver humbucking noise-cancellation and single-coil brilliance, all linked to active circuitry, a popular system at the time but a first for Fender. The guitar incorporated a battery-powered pre-amp to boost the signal and widen the tonal range – and only a few of its new sounds would have been familiar to traditional Tele players. The bridge/tailpiece was also restyled to incorporate six individual saddles. There were good points – the new pickups, the effective active circuitry, an improved truss-rod design – but they were mostly overlooked. The Elite Tele was dropped by the end of '84 (as was the Elite Strat, which was lumbered with a poor vibrato system called the Freeflyte).

The look of the Elite Tele may have been a reaction to Schecter and in particular to Pete Townshend's use of a Tele-style guitar made from Schecter parts. Schecter was a US firm among the leaders of a fad for replacement parts intended to help players revamp existing guitars. Larry DiMarzio had spearheaded the new business, introducing his Super Distortion replacement pickup in 1975, with Mighty Mite, Seymour Duncan, Schecter, and others soon following. Now it was brass hardware and fancy pickguards and knobs, too – in fact anything to give a new look or fresh tone to a dusty guitar. Fender had already reacted to the craze with its own lines of brass hardware, Standard Brass and Brassmaster, launched in 1980, claiming like the rest that brass aided sustain and improved overall tone. Fender ought to have been well aware of the theory, given that the Telecaster's original three-saddle bridge had brass saddles.

Fender's business and production headaches didn't help them in the 80s, and it now faced new competing styles of solidbody electric guitars, notably in the superstrat style. This was primarily devised by Grover Jackson, who headed the US Charvel/Jackson firm, which manufactured in America and then Japan. The Jackson Soloist model, which appeared around 1983, was one of the first superstrats. Subsequently, many brands such as Ibanez, Washburn, Kramer, and others adopted elements of the design in various forms, often with notable success.

The Telecaster could still be seen and heard in engaging company. Fender's image did not suffer much when Freddie Mercury picked up a white Tele to strum as Queen began 'Crazy Little Thing Called Love' at 1985's Live Aid, the famine-relief benefit that grabbed a global audience of millions. Chrissie Hynde was seen with a striking blue Tele at Pretenders gigs, and guitarist James Honeyman-Scott grabbed it in the studio for his gorgeously crafted solo for 'Kid' on the band's 1980 debut album. Prince prominently played a Telecaster-style guitar – a 70s Japanese-made H.S. Anderson Madcat, which was later reissued by Hohner – to fuel almost all his 80s funk. Supreme country Tele picker Ray Flacke could be heard on the Ricky Scaggs LPs *Waiting For The Sun To Shine* (1982) and *Highways And Heartaches* (1983), while Mike Stern contributed to 1982's live Miles Davis album *We Want Miles,* marking a relatively rare example of a Telecaster in jazz.

Albert Lee was a confirmed Tele fan who'd played with Sonny Curtis's Crickets and Emmylou Harris – and at one point had the unlikely job of guitarist with Eric Clapton. His solo albums, too, pricked the ears of other guitarists – the 1986 instrumental album *Speechless* was a particularly good example – but it was the 1979 track 'Country Boy' that for many fellow players defined his deft picking, full of tumbling arpeggios from a steely Tele alongside some fierce flat-top work.

In a later interview, Lee said he'd played a Tele since 1963. The first one had been a rosewood-board model, probably a '59 or a '60. "It was pretty beaten up," he recalled. "The guy at the store said, 'Look, a James Burton guitar.' It seemed really Mickey Mouse compared to [my previous guitar, a] Les Paul Custom, but as soon as I played it I thought: this is great. It sounded so alive, so electric – more so than anything I'd ever played. From then on it was always number one. My style evolved around that guitar. … You develop a style on a Tele that you don't develop on another guitar. I suppose my favourite now is my '53 Tele."[95]

Jerry Donahue was another Tele man who'd played widely with others – as a member of Fotheringay and Fairport Convention, and with Joan Armatrading, Gerry Rafferty, Chris Rea, and many others in the studio and on the road. In 1986, he released a firm solo statement of his guitar preference, the *Telecasting* album. When someone like Danny Gatton called him "the string-bending king of the planet" any players who hadn't already twigged Donahue's importance were sure to take notice. Later, in the early 90s, he became a founder member of an astonishing Tele trio, the Hellecasters, along with Will Ray and John Jorgenson.

"First thing I did with my Tele back in the late 60s, when I moved to one after using Strats, was to get rid of the neck pickup," Donahue says. "I never thought it was balanced with the bridge pickup. It's great if you want to play country and then you want to play jazz. That was probably Leo's goal, for people who wanted to play what he would have considered 'both styles'.

"I put a Strat pickup in the neck position because that was the sound I probably liked most from the Strat," Donahue continues, "besides the in-between sound that I'd found by accident along with a host of others on the three-way switch. I never fell out of love with the Strat, but the Tele just gradually became my main instrument over the years. With Fairport and Joan Armatrading I'd be swapping back and forth, but when I put out that album called *Telecasting*, the

Getting close to that elite country boy

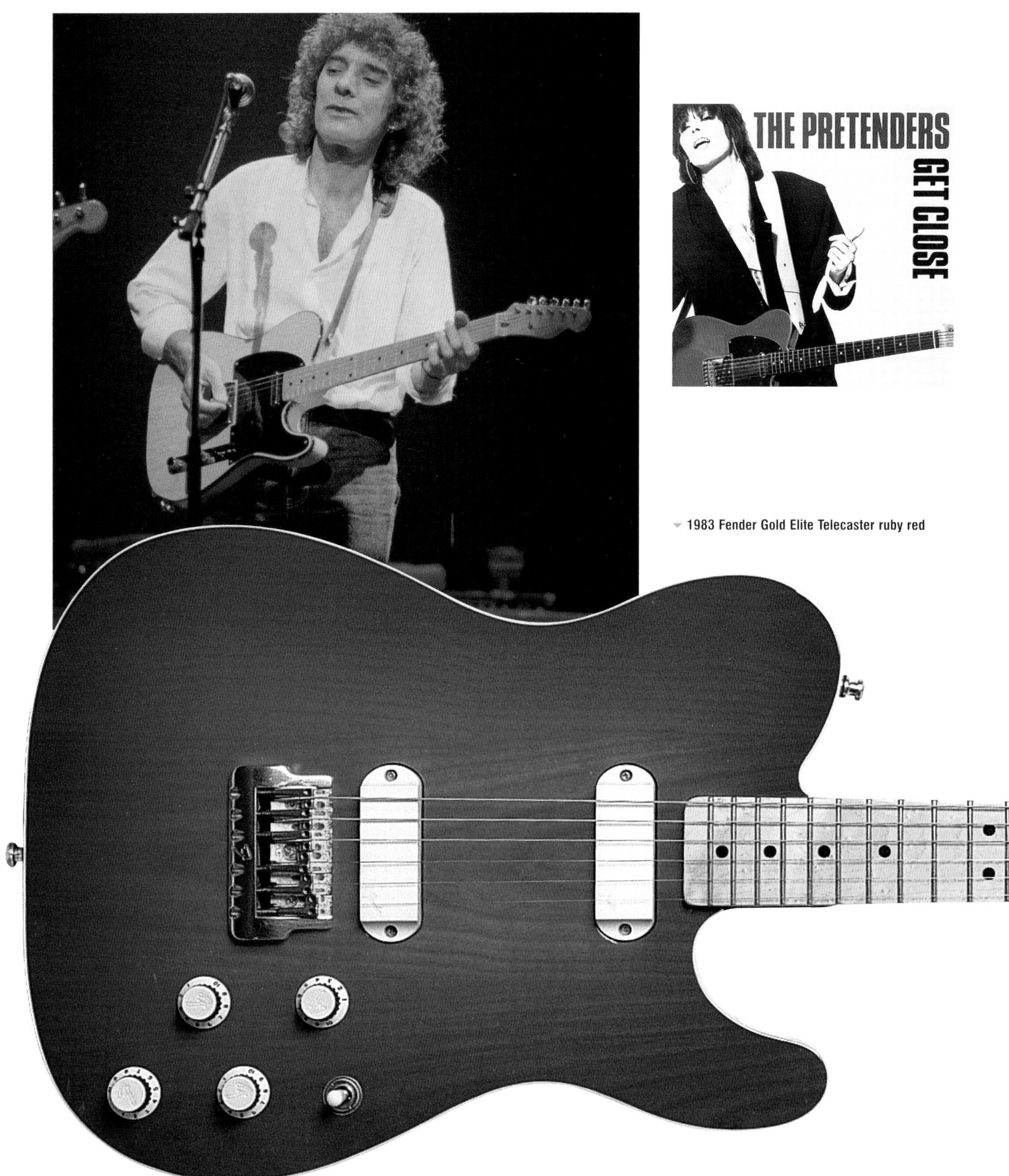

▼ 1983 Fender Gold Elite Telecaster ruby red

▲ 1983 Fender Gold Elite Telecaster emerald green

The Elite Telecaster (two examples pictured) was a radical departure away from traditional design, intended to stake out new ground for the modern instrument in contrast to the successful vintage-style reissues. But the Elite, launched in 1983, did not last for much more than a year on the Fender pricelist, even in the upscale gold-hardware variant shown here (the Gold Elite above has the optional stick-on pickguard). Telecasters continued to attract high-profile pop players: Chrissie Hynde of The Pretenders (above) featured her favourite blue Tele on the jacket of the band's 1986 album *Get Close*. Albert Lee (opposite) was a confirmed Tele fan for much of his career and played one on many of his recordings, solo and for others, including his influential electric-and-acoustic cut 'Country Boy'.

Tele became the guitar for me."[96] At the time of writing, Donahue played his Tele-style signature Fret-King JD with The Acoustic Gathering, and also used it at an enjoyable Hellecasters reunion during the 2012 Winter NAMM show.

For a variety of reasons, CBS decided during 1984 to sell Fender Musical Instruments. In January 1985 the *San Francisco Chronicle* detailed the reasons, with CBS blaming Japanese competition for Fender's recent losses. "The Fullerton-based firm's last domestic guitar manufacturing unit, which employs 60 senior craftsmen who build top-of-the-line instruments for professional musicians, is scheduled to be shut down February 1st," added the reporter. "Company officials say tentative plans call for the continued manufacture of electric pianos until the end of February at the plant in this Orange County community 25 miles south-east of Los Angeles. The future of the company's famed product lines – the guitars pioneered by Leo Fender, pianos by Harold Rhodes, Rogers drums, and Squier guitar strings – will depend on Fender's new owner, who must decide which ones to continue and which, if any, will be made in the United States."

The report went on to explain that CBS was offering the Fender name and business for sale separately from the vast manufacturing plant. John McLaren, the former president of the CBS musical instruments division, was quoted as saying that there were a lot of "broken hearts" around Fullerton. The newspaper pointed out that McLaren and Bill Schultz and their team tried to turn the company around in the early 80s (McLaren had left Fender in '84). One estimate put sales of Fender guitars down 50 percent in the last three years. "CBS does not report financial statistics for its division separately," said the *Chronicle*, "but attributed an $8.3 million Columbia Group operating loss for the third quarter of 1984 in part to 'continued losses in the musical instruments business'."

The newspaper report speculated that the US guitar industry's problems were not due solely to the Japanese. It suggested that the baby-boom generation was past the prime instrument-buying age and, in a phrase still familiar to us today, that "today's young people seem to be more interested in video games and computers than guitars". The *Chronicle* reckoned that some fault lay also with the corporate giants who began snapping up the best instrument manufacturers during the 60s but were "ill-suited to running businesses in which success depended so much on craftsmanship and personal service".[97]

CBS invited offers for Fender, and various groups made bids, including some existing employees. "I was in the process of developing with Fujigen in Japan a complete line of Fender products for sale worldwide," Dan Smith says. "When we put in our bid with CBS, I was going back and forth to try and put this line together – even though we didn't know if we were going to get the company. Fujigen stood by us. They really respected Bill Schultz and the rest of us, so they let us put a product line together. And they made these guitars, not knowing at all what was going to happen."[98]

Bill Mendello, the company's chief financial officer and part of the Schultz-Smith bidding team, recalls another way in which the new Japanese partners helped. The team knew they had to raise a large amount of money but, Mendello says, none of them had any experience of doing so.

"Then Bill came up with a great idea: he said let's go talk to Mike Yamano." Masamitsu Yamano was president of Fender's longstanding Japanese distributor, Yamano Music, and a partner in Fender Japan. Like many Japanese businessmen who deal with American firms, Masamitsu adopted a Western forename. Schultz and Mendello flew to Japan, sat down with Mike, and explained the problem.

"Mike looked at us and said: here's a blank cheque; you fill it in," Mendello remembers. "See how much money you can raise – and what you can't raise, I'll make up the difference. Well … when we'd got on the plane to come out to Japan, we felt we probably couldn't buy the company. On the way back, we knew we'd got the financing. We knew we could do it." It's something Mendello will never forget. "Without that, we would not have succeeded. It was that confidence which really made a big difference."[99]

By the end of January 1985, almost exactly 20 years since the corporation had acquired it, CBS confirmed it would sell Fender to "an investor group led by William Schultz, president of Fender Musical Instruments". The contract was formalised in February and the sale completed in March for $12.5 million. This figure compared conspicuously with the $13 million CBS paid for the company back in 1965.

With the hectic months of negotiations and financing behind them, Schultz and his team faced many problems. Probably most pressing was the fact that the Fullerton factory was not included in the deal. US production of Fenders, such as it was, stopped in February 1985. The US company employed over 800 people in early 1984; that went down to about 100 by early '85.

George Blanda was a new arrival at Fender that year, and he recalls the scene. "I don't think people realise what a little mom-and-pop business it was then. I'd seen the gigantic CBS building, 800 or so people. I was employee number 76. They envisioned they were going to be a distribution company of import instruments – which they were doing well with. They were going to have US production of just the vintage models, at a very small rate, like the Custom Shop does now."[100]

"Scary but exciting" is how Dan Smith described it at the time. "We're not going to be in the position to be able to make any mistakes," he said. "There'll be nobody behind us with a big cheque-book if we have a bad month."[101] The new firm established administration headquarters in Brea, California, not far from Fullerton. Six years later, Fender would move admin from Brea to Scottsdale, Arizona, where it remains today, relocating within the city in 2012.

The Japanese operation became Fender's lifeline, providing much-needed product to a company with no US factory. Every guitar in Fender's 1985 catalogue was made in Japan, including the new Contemporary Telecasters and Strats, the first Fenders with the increasingly fashionable heavy-duty vibrato units and string-clamps, although these seemed particularly unlikely on a Telecaster. Production in Japan was based on Smith's handshake agreement with Fujigen that it would continue to supply Fender and Squier-brand guitars after CBS left the picture. One estimate put as much as 80 percent of the guitars that Fender USA sold from around the end of 1984 to the middle of 1986 as made in Japan.

Back in the United States, Fender finally established its new factory. The new team had machinery from the purchase plus some stockpiled parts. They found a 14,000-square-foot

Casting around for a new standard

Fender's new American Standard guitars redefined the modern look of the regular model, following the management buy-out of the company in 1985. The revised Tele (main guitar) appeared in 1988 with 22 big frets, a fatter-sounding bridge pickup, and a six-saddle bridge, all designed to appeal to modern players. It worked: with tweaks along the way, it's still in production today. Tele supremo Jerry Donahue (pictured opposite) made a statement of intent on his 1986 *Telecasting* album (right), and Fender offered two Donahue signature models (prototype, opposite) from 1992 to 2001. A Japanese-made attempt to embrace fashionable superstrat-style features resulted in the shortlived Contemporary Telecaster (opposite, below).

Jerry Donahue
Telecasting

▼ 1991 Fender American Standard Telecaster sunburst

▲ 1990 Fender Jerry Donahue Telecaster prototype

▲ 1987 Fender Contemporary Telecaster black

building in Corona, about 20 miles east of the defunct Fullerton site, and started production on a limited scale toward the end of 1985. "Initially we only produced vintage reissue guitars – fewer than ten a day," Smith says. "We thought we would gradually build up to 150 or so a day over a five-year period. We still had Fujigen, who at one point were producing over 10,000 guitars a month for us, and we naively thought that would go on forever. The weakening of the dollar and the strengthening of the yen would change all that."[102] At the end of 1984, the yen stood at around 250 to the US dollar; by the end of 1986, it was half that. It meant that, from a Western perspective, Japanese guitars were becoming too expensive.

Fender shifted production of its cheaper Squier brand to Korea in 1988 and used factories there for Squier as well as a few Fender-brand models until 2010. At the time of writing, Fender manufactured Squier-brand electrics in China, India, and Indonesia, and occasionally made some Fender-brand electrics offshore, in Indonesia and, more recently, China – of which more later.

In the mid 80s, Fender officially established a Custom Shop at the Corona plant. It began so that the company could build one-offs and special orders for players who had the money and the inclination. As Dan Smith says, they were only planning to make ten Vintage guitars a day. "So we were going to start a Custom Shop to build special projects for artists, to make certain that the prestige was still there for the company."[103] That role remains today – customers over the years have included everyone from Bob Dylan and Pops Staples to David Bowie and John Mayer – but as time went on, the Shop came to play a wider role in Fender's expanding business.

When guitar builder George Blanda joined Fender in 1985, he was recruited to make artist guitars, but a year later, as those shifting exchange rates began to favour exports, demand for US-made product increased dramatically. Fender needed an R&D specialist to come up with new models, and the job fell to Blanda. He had the perfect combination of an engineering capability and a love of guitars. Blanda's move left vacant the Custom Shop position, which earlier had been offered to John Carruthers.

Fender then discussed the idea with guitar maker Michael Stevens and with former Fender R&D man John Page, who had left the company a year earlier to concentrate on his music. The result was that Stevens and Page joined Fender to start the Custom Shop in January 1987. Their first official order was to make two guitars for Elliot Easton of The Cars, one of which was a left-handed Thinline Telecaster in Foam Green. The order was placed at the end of February 1987, and John Page completed Easton's luscious Tele on August 10th.

A year or so later, the Shop turned out its first numbered limited edition, the 1988 40th Anniversary Telecaster. At that time, most people – including Fender itself – believed that the first Broadcaster/Telecaster had been produced in 1948, which explains why the anniversary date was, we know now, two years adrift.

The expansion of the Custom Shop's business prompted a move in 1993 to new buildings – still close to the Corona factory – providing extra space and improved efficiency. When Fender's new plant was unveiled five years later, the Custom Shop was shifted into the factory, where it remains today. By that time, the Shop was building about 7,000 instruments a year. Fender will not discuss recent numbers, but it's safe to assume they have not gone down. We'll catch up with the Shop's current activities later in the book.

Smith and his colleagues wanted to re-establish the regular US side of Fender's production, too, with a good, basic Telecaster – and, of course, a Stratocaster, P Bass, and Jazz Bass. The attraction was that these models would involve very little new costs, and they would, the company hoped, be accepted by players as a continuation of the very best of Fender's long-standing American traditions. The plan translated into the first American Standard models.

The team had learned from recent work that the focus of the new American Standard had to be on the Telecaster's great strength: its simplicity. The result of their efforts appeared in 1988, the $599.99 American Standard Telecaster. Smith says they'd started the idea rolling with the first Standard models in the early 80s. "We wanted to make a good-quality standard instrument that better addressed modern playing styles, and at a reasonable price. As George Blanda and I worked on the American Standard Strat and its bridge design, we knew the bridge saddles would work nicely for the Telecaster. So George designed a bridge plate. We gave the guitar a bigger fingerboard radius that we figured could help get an action that appealed more to Gibson guys but didn't feel much different to Fender guys, and we made the neck a little wider to accommodate modern styles, with bigger frets."

All that was pretty obvious, Smith says. A bolder change came with the redesigned bridge pickup. "We found that by eliminating the plate on the bottom of the pickup and moving to a brass bridge plate, in combination with the saddles, it made for a fatter sounding bridge pickup, which is what a lot of guys were looking for. It still had a nice twank, or whatever you want to call it, a nice spiky, bitey sound, but it was fatter sounding, and it sounded better through distortion."[104]

In this way, the American Standard drew from the original, but was updated with, for example, that 22-fret neck and six-saddle bridge. At first the new model was offered in four finish options, black, sunburst, vintage white, and gun metal blue, with crimson metallic soon added and various changes and additions following. Once the Corona plant's production lines reached full speed, the American Standard proved a successful model for the revitalised Fender company. It was renamed as plain "American" in 2001, and then back to American Standard from 2008 – and it gained a 'belly' body contour in 2012 – but it has always been a dependable beacon in the Fender line.

Fender's first signature guitar was the Eric Clapton Stratocaster, which went on sale to the public in 1988. However, Fender had talked informally to Telecaster king James Burton some time before that about the possibility of a signature model. "I figured that Leo Fender had already made two of the finest guitars," recalls Burton. "What do you do to improve those or make them different? And I thought well, factory-wise, Fender hasn't put together a three-pickup Tele. So my idea was to make a three-pickup Tele and to experiment with the pickups I liked. My first intention was to do the pink paisley Tele as my signature model, but Fender made an agreement with the Japanese to take over the copy of the pink paisley. My guitar would be made in the States."[105] Burton had to wait until 1990 for his signature Telecaster to appear. It had three single-coil pickups in a Strat

Strange customs and signed headstocks

1994 Fender Egyptian Telecaster

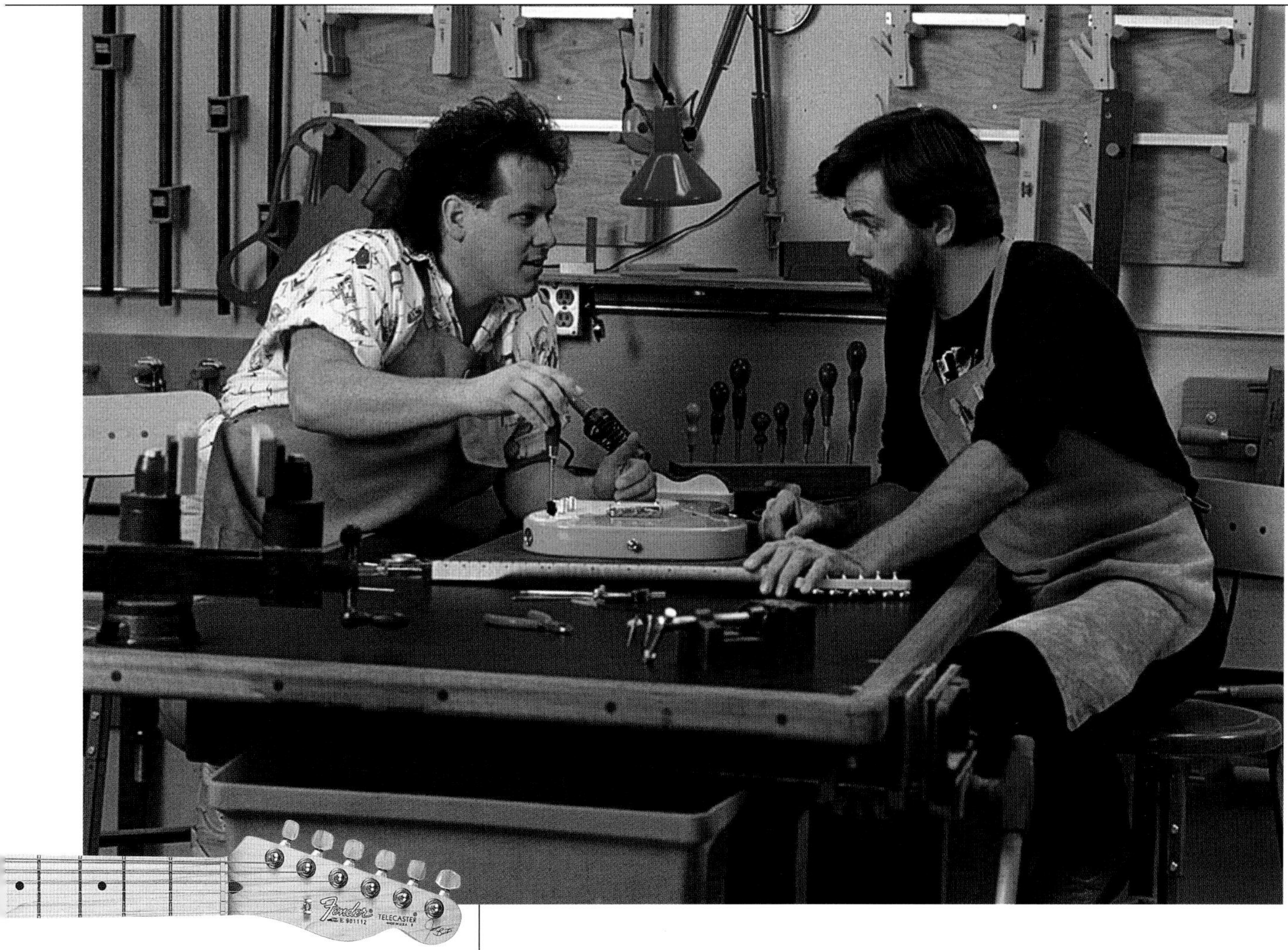

▲ **1990 Fender James Burton Telecaster black w/gold paisley**

▼ **1989 Fender Telecaster 40th Anniversary**

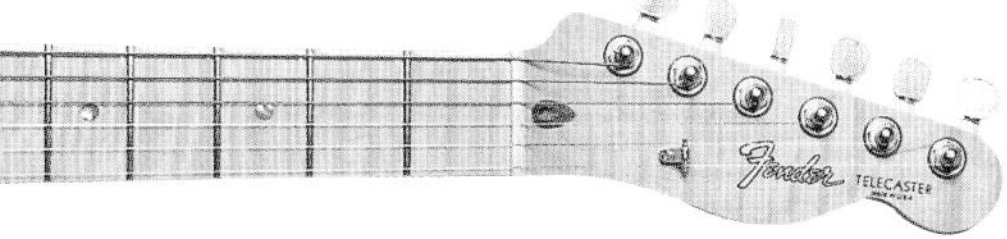

Fender's Custom Shop was officially started at the Corona factory in California at the start of 1987. The intention at first was to make one-off guitars for individual customers. Shop founders John Page (above, left) and Michael Stevens (right) are pictured early in 1987 working on their first commission, a foam green left-handed Thinline Telecaster for Elliot Easton of The Cars. Since then, the Shop has developed to its present three-way role. First are the continuing one-offs, such as this Egyptian Tele (opposite) by Master Builder Fred Stuart. Second are limited editions, like the 40th Anniversary Telecaster (left, below), produced in an edition of 300 instruments. The third type of Custom Shop guitar comes as a line of catalogued models, including the period-detailed Time Machine instruments (see pages 106–107) and various Artist guitars. Fender's first signature guitar was the Eric Clapton Stratocaster, of 1988, but the firm had started discussions earlier with Tele king James Burton, who had to wait until 1990 for his first Fender signature Tele to appear (pictured left).

layout, and some examples were finished in a paisley pattern much more lurid than his original Red Paisley model. A new version in 2006 offered a blue or red paisley "flames" finish, as well as a two-pickup option in plain candy apple red.

There have been other three-pickup Telecasters since. At the time of writing, in addition to the Burton models, they included the various American and Mexican Nashville Teles, first seen in 1999, the J5 Triple Tele Deluxe (2007), the Blackout Tele (2008), and the Modern Player Telecaster Plus (2011). A shortlived version of the Tele Plus from 1995 opted for the Burton-type layout with three single-coils arranged Strat-style, and the original Tele Plus, launched in 1990, also had three of Fender's Lace Sensor single-coils – a pickup offering low noise and no string-pull – but with two grouped at the bridge that could be switched together as a humbucker.

Many Fender signature Teles followed the original Burton model – some made in the Custom Shop, others from Corona or further afield – and each one is endowed with features favoured by the named artist. At various times, there have been signature Telecasters named for Jim Adkins, Jimmy Bryant, James Burton, Albert Collins, Graham Coxon, Jerry Donahue, Nokie Edwards, Danny Gatton, Merle Haggard, Waylon Jennings, John 5, John Jorgenson, Richie Kotzen, Buck Owens, Rick Parfitt, Will Ray, Jim Root, Francis Rossi, G.E. Smith, Joe Strummer, Muddy Waters, and Clarence White.

In 2003, a Seymour Duncan Esquire appeared, modelled on the guitar that Jeff Beck swapped with pickup-man Duncan back in the 70s. Naturally, Beck was sent one of the new models. "I opened the box and I thought they were having a laugh, that they'd sent my guitar back," he recalls. "It had every dig, every scratch, every little bit of ink stain. I'd written something on it and it sank into the wood: they'd done that. Quite amusing. So I've got the repro and someone else has got the real thing. They'd even got it accurate to the point where the treble control didn't work, because it didn't work on mine. Either that," laughs Beck, "or they didn't hook it up."[106]

CBS had used a few firms based in Mexico for packing and making strings, but in 1987 a Fender engineer, Bashar Darcazallie, went to Mexico and established low-key manufacturing there for the new Fender operation. Darcazallie set up in a converted church in Ensenada, a city about 180 miles south of Los Angeles, just across the California–Mexico border and about a three-hour drive from the Corona factory. With that facility running successfully and making some electronics, it seemed logical to make guitars there, too.

Fender enlisted the help of Fujigen, the factory building its Japanese guitars, and the two firms set up a joint venture, F&F, to develop a guitar manufacturing facility at Ensenada. Key people came over from Fujigen's plant in Japan and trained the workers at the new Mexican guitar factory, modelling the processes and layout on the factory back in Matsumoto. With this level of training, the Mexican workers soon became adept and skilled, and by 1991 the first guitars appeared from the plant, including the Standard Telecaster plus a Standard Strat, P Bass, and Jazz Bass. Fender bought out Fujigen's interest and successfully continued alone to develop the Mexico plant. In the years that followed, the factory has become an important part of Fender's manufacturing capability, including the production of many Telecaster models.

Aside from two shortlived models launched back in 1984 – the Esprit and the Flame – Fender had not strayed much from its customary bolt-on-neck construction. However, three new Set Neck Teles in 1991 offered a glued joint, enabling a smooth heel-less junction where neck meets body, in the style traditionally used by Gibson and other makers. Some players find this more comfortable and usefully playable. "We always try to have something in our line to interest someone who likes Gibson," is how a Fender exec puts it.[107] Other Teles of recent years with set necks have included the Special Edition Custom FMT HH and two signature models, the Merle Haggard and the Jim Adkins JA-90.

Following the success of the Vintage reissue series introduced in the early 80s, Fender Japan began to issue more models that re-created guitars from Fender's past, including Paisley, Blue Flower, Rosewood, and Thinline Teles. In 1992, Fender USA came up with the series name Collectables to cover a selection of these Japanese instruments sold in the US, including various vintage-style Teles and Strats. In more recent years, the series names have changed again, and at the time of writing reissues from a variety of sources were organised into the Classic and Road Worn series from Mexico, the American Vintage and Vintage Hot Rod guitars from the US Corona factory, and the Time Machine models from the Custom Shop.

Fender's 1992 pricelist showed the following Teles: Standard $389.99; 50s, $669.99; Custom '62, $749.99; Thinline '69, $799.99; American Standard, $839.99; HMT acoustic-electric, $849.99–$1,199.99; Tele Plus, $999.99; Deluxe Tele Plus, $1,099.99; US Vintage '52, $1,199.99; James Burton, $1,399.99; Set Neck, $1,999.99; Jerry Donahue, $2,099.99; Albert Collins, $2,499.99; Danny Gatton, $2,499.99. These sat alongside a slew of Strats, a pair of passing Prodigys, and a bevy of basses.

There was no shortage of good Tele players during the 90s. Blur's *Parklife* album appeared in 1994, and the band's guitarist, Graham Coxon, preferred a US reissue '52 Telecaster, which he described as his shiny butterscotch job. "I used that throughout the whole of Blur's career," said Coxon. "It ended up with a Mr Smiley sticker and an Air India sticker on it, and a really bad drawing that I did on the back. That was my workhorse, and I've still got it."[108] After he left Blur in 2002, he continued to use '52s and also discovered the older humbucker'd models. Fender issued a Coxon signature Tele in 2011, with 70s head, rosewood board, shell pickguard, and a Duncan humbucker at the neck.

Frank Black of The Pixies and Chuck Prophet (ex-Green On Red) often selected a Tele, and Beck was regularly seen live with a stock new Tele, sometimes with a friendly unicorn decoration on the body (that's Beck Hansen; Jeff was well into Strats by now). Jeff Buckley, meanwhile, appeared with little more in support than his '83 American Standard Tele on *Live At Sin-E*, his pre-fame EP that came out in 1993.

Bill Kirchen had been in Commander Cody & His Lost Planet Airmen in the 70s and used his Telecaster to play the fine lead on the group's only hit single, 'Hot Rod Lincoln', in 1972. By the 90s he was out on his own and in 1997 included a remarkable remake of that song on *Hot Rod Lincoln Live!*, where Kirchen impersonates everyone from Buck Owens to The Sex Pistols in a

Scruggs, set necks, and classics

The 90s saw Fender attempting to diversify the Telecaster line while still recognising that a regular trad-style model held sway with many guitarists. Frank Black (right), of The Pixies, was one of those enthusiastic Tele players. Signature models continued to bolster the Fender catalogue, including a tribute to Byrds man Clarence White (main guitar), who died at the age of just 29 back in 1973. It duplicated White's favoured neck pickup, Scruggs tuners, and on-board B-bender string-pull device. The Custom Shop's American Classic (opposite, centre) was a three-pickup upscale take on the American Standard, while the Set Neck models (Country Artist, opposite, left) allowed Fender a rare move away from its customary bolt-on neck joint, into Gibson territory. The vintage look did survive: on the Japanese 50s model (opposite, right) and the continuing US '52 Telecaster (catalogue, opposite, bottom).

▲ **1993 Fender Clarence White Telecaster sunburst**

◀ 1992 Fender Set Neck Telecaster Country Artist sunset orange

▶ 1995 Fender American Classic Telecaster sunburst

▶ 1997 Fender 50s Telecaster blond

brilliantly conceived guitar interlude. "You can hear the same Telecaster recorded in 1971 with its original pickups on the Commander Cody version, and then again on the same song more than a quarter of a century later," Kirchen reports, marvelling at the longevity of his enduring axe. He made another great Tele-centric track in 2007, 'Hammer Of The Honky Tonk Gods', which is all about our favourite guitar, "born at the junction of form and function".

Kirchen got his Tele upon moving to San Francisco in the late 60s. "Pete Townshend had just come through and busted his SG, and this guy sitting next to me at the gig wanted an SG and I wanted a Telecaster. I wanted to be like Don Rich and he wanted to be like Pete Townshend – so we traded. Bingo! And I still use that Tele today."

Kirchen's nickname for his Tele is the coal-burner. "I tell people I've had it for so long that we had to convert it from coal power to electricity. Young kids are not exactly sure of their timelines and scratch their heads and think about that. If you tell them that when you first got this guitar, pterodactyls filled the sky, some of them will actually stop and wonder if that's true."

As far as Kirchen can tell, his Tele is a late-50s model with a factory three-colour sunburst. "It's like the story of the woodsman who's had the same axe in his family for six generations – but it's had five new heads and four new handles. Every single piece of metal on that guitar has been changed, save the six ferrules that the strings run through. They're original. But every peg, screw, wire, strap button ... everything has been changed numerous times. Right now I have Don Mare pickups in it, JT saddles, and a friend of mine carved me a new bridge out of a piece of steel. No matter what you do, though, to me it still sounds like a Telecaster. The thing that gets me is that, no matter what I change on that guitar, the sound inherent to that body is always there."[109]

In 1992, Fender had a special Telecaster signed by a host of country stars and then presented it to President Bush (senior). But the real president of the Tele was honoured at a Rock & Roll Hall Of Fame ceremony the same year. Leo Fender was one of 12 music legends inducted into the Hall that January, alongside Jimi Hendrix and others. Leo's second wife, Phyllis, was there for Leo, who had died the previous year. "When I accepted his award, I said that Leo truly believed that musicians were special angels, special envoys from the Lord," Mrs Fender says. "He believed he was put here to make the very best instruments in the world, because these special angels would help us get through this life, would ease our pain and ease our sadness, and help us celebrate."[110]

Keith Richards also spoke on behalf of Leo, rather more prosaically. "He gave us the weapons," Richards told the Hall Of Fame gathering, leaving them with what he called the guitar players' prayer: "Caress it. Don't squeeze it."[111]

Keef was well aware how useful Fender's historical achievements could be to a musician. A common request at the time from some artists was for the Custom Shop to make a replica of a favourite old guitar, usually because the original was too valuable – financially and emotionally – to risk taking out on the road. The story goes, according to a Fender insider, that Richards thought that some replicas the Shop had made him for a Stones tour looked too new. Bash 'em up a bit and I'll play 'em, he said. So the Shop began to include wear-and-tear distress marks to replicate the overall look of a battered old original. It was not a new idea, but it was certainly an effective one.

J.W. Black, a builder at the Custom Shop who had been working with the Stones, showed John Page an aged Fender that a friend, Vince Cunetto, had made. Black came up with the idea of offering aged replicas as regular Custom Shop catalogued items, called Relics. "It started almost as a tongue-in-cheek thing," admits John Page, "like worn-in Levis or something. It would look cool – and in the first three rows it would look like you're playing a valuable Nocaster. But only you know that it's not really. That was how it started."

Black and Cunetto made two aged 50s-era samples: a Nocaster (nickname for the transitional Broadcaster/Telecaster) and a 'Mary Kaye' Stratocaster (blond body, gold-plated parts). "We took them to the January 1995 NAMM trade show," recalls Page, "and we put them under glass cases like they were pieces of art. Everyone came along and would say oh, that's really cool, you brought original ones as a tribute. And we were saying, er, yeah ... how many do you want? People went nuts! It was amazing."[112]

Soon the Custom Shop was reacting to the demand, offering a set line of a Relic Nocaster and three Relic Strats. At first, Cunetto worked off-site, at his workshop in Missouri, ageing the bodies, necks, and parts that Fender sent him, starting in summer 1995. Four years later, the work was all handled within the Custom Shop. The line was expanded in 1998, when Fender established three strands of these 're-creations' in what is now known as the Time Machine series.

The Relic finish has 'aged' knocks and the look of heavy wear, as if the guitar had been out on the road for a generation or so.

The Closet Classic finish (seen less often in recent years) is made to look as if the guitar was bought new way back when, played a few times, and then stuck in a closet.

The N.O.S. (New Old Stock) finish looks as if an instrument was bought brand new in the 50s or 60s and then put straight into a time machine that transported it to the present day. The kind of thing, in other words, that vintage-guitar collectors and dealers regularly fantasise about, but which rarely happens in real life.

By 2012, the Custom Shop's Time Machine series featured a '51 Nocaster (N.O.S. or Relic) and a '61 Custom (Relic), listing between about $4,000 and $5,000. These may seem high prices, but when you consider what you might have to pay now for genuine originals – tens of thousands of dollars for a Nocaster, for example – then the attraction becomes clearer. And even if you could find originals, there's always the worry among collectors with a vintage piece about the veracity of this paint finish or that pickguard screw or those solder joints. The Time Machines at least take away any niggling doubts about originality.

These Custom Shop specials appeal to guitar fans keen to acquire a new Fender with the feel and sound of an oldie – and, in the case of the Relics, they're made to look as if decades of wear-and-tear have stained the fingerboard, scuffed the body, and tarnished the hardware. The Time Machine series was a clever move, the nearest Fender came with new instruments to the almost indefinable cool of vintage guitars. It was something that many thought was firmly and safely locked away in the past.

Fender marked its 50th anniversary in 1996. As you may recall from many pages back, Leo Fender split with his original partner, Doc Kauffman, in 1946. Leo dissolved their K&F company,

Bashed-up relics from the time machine

◀ 1997 Fender HMT Acoustic-Electric sunburst

In 1995, Fender decided to market 'aged' new oldies, and among the first releases was a '51 Nocaster (flyer, opposite, top). Today, the Time Machine line includes models in three levels of ageing, including the 'knocked about' Relic style (main guitar). A further step into the past came in '96, upon Fender's 50th anniversary, with a limited edition of 50 Pine Telecaster & Amp sets (catalogue cover, opposite, below), with the guitar re-creating the original Tele prototype. Another 90s trend was the hybrid guitar, mixing regular magnetic and 'acoustic'-sounding piezo pickups. The HMT model (later version, far left) was Fender's take on the idea. Influences on new musicians came not only from retro-styled catalogue shots (left) but also from players such as Thom Yorke of Radiohead (pictured right) who regularly used a 70s humbucker'd Telecaster Deluxe.

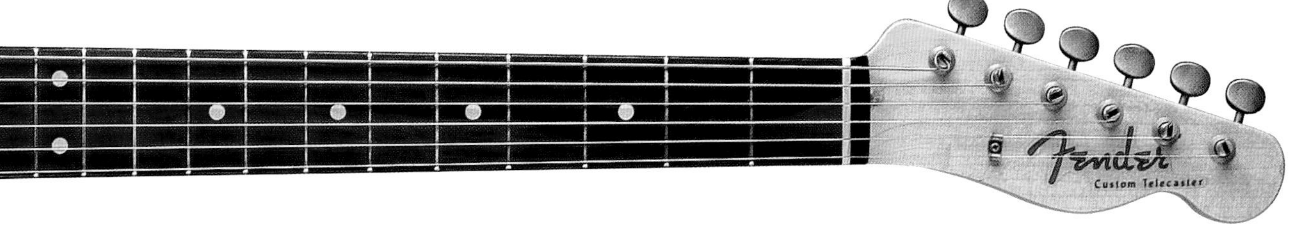

▲ 2003 Fender Time Machine '60 Custom Telecaster Relic sonic blue

called his revised operation Fender Manufacturing, and then renamed it the Fender Electric Instrument Co in December 1947. The modern company celebrated what it tagged "50 Years of Excellence" in 1996 with some factory-made limited-edition anniversary models – the apparently timeless quartet of Telecaster, Precision Bass, Stratocaster, and Jazz Bass – each with a special commemorative neckplate. Also, Fender attached a 50th Anniversary decal to many regular products sold that year. The Custom Shop made some anniversary models, too, notably 50 examples only of the Pine Telecaster & Amp set. The guitar recreated the original solidbody prototype with its steel-like headstock shape and angled control plate (and the amp was a replica of an early Model 26).

Fender opened a new factory late in 1998, still in Corona, California. The company proudly described the impressive state-of-the-art plant as the world's most expensive and automated guitar factory. Since starting production at the original Corona factory back in 1985, Fender had grown to occupy 115,000 square feet in ten buildings across the city. Such a rambling spread proved increasingly inefficient, and during the early 90s Fender began to plan a centralised factory. The new $20-million facility provided a potentially growing production capacity for the future. Some models were reorganised into new series in 1998, with new high-end US models grouped as American Deluxes and reissues brought together as American Vintages.

The 1998 pricelist had the following Teles: Standard $409.99; Deluxe Nashville, $549.99; 50s, $599.99; James Burton Standard, $599.99; '72 Custom, $659.99; '62 Custom, $669.99; J.D., $709.99; '69 Thinline, $749.99; '72 Thinline, $799.99; California Tele, $799.99; American Standard, $979.99; Tele Plus, $1,299.99; American Vintage '52, $1,499.99; James Burton, $1,599.99; 90s Thinline, $1,799.99.

We saw how Fender started to offer humbuckers on various new Telecaster models back at the start of the 70s. There were three key models: the second version of the Thinline (1971–79), which had two humbuckers, regular Tele controls, and an f-hole in the body; the Deluxe (1972–81), with two humbuckers, a Strat-like head, and four knobs; and the Custom (1972–81), which was fitted with a neck humbucker, a regular bridge pickup, and four knobs. None of these models were particularly successful at the time, but they showed that Fender was at least aware that quite a few players were replacing pickups on their Teles, very often putting a humbucker in place of the neck unit.

In the late 90s, fashion began to turn again to these models, probably originating with Radiohead, whose 1997 album *OK Computer* was a big hit. Thom Yorke was seen regularly with a 70s two-humbucker Tele Deluxe (with modified controls and various stickers), and on some live dates there was the compelling sight of Yorke on Deluxe, Jonny Greenwood on a Tele Plus with bridge humbucker, and Ed O'Brien on a regular American Standard Tele. Radiohead's popularity certainly helped along the new hipness of the humbucker'd Tele, and soon members of The Hives (Custom), Snow Patrol (Deluxe and Custom), Gomez (Thinline), Maroon 5 (Deluxe), and many others lined up to play them.

Alex Kapranos of Franz Ferdinand opted for a Deluxe. "It's the one with a Stratocaster-type headstock and double humbuckers," he explained, "a totally amazing guitar. It's still got that Tele sound but it drives a little more. I play a lot of rhythmic stuff with my left hand and it picks up all the harmonic sounds from that, which other guitars really don't seem to. You can get some really strange sounds that you wouldn't expect to come from a guitar, I think probably because of those humbuckers."[113]

Jonny Buckland of Coldplay had a humbucker'd Thinline. "My favourite guitar is the first sunburst Thinline that I bought in 2001," he said later. "I'd seen them around but I'd never seen one for sale anywhere. I just fell in love with it and played it on everything on *A Rush Of Blood To The Head*," he explained, namechecking his band's second album, released in 2002.[114]

Fender reacted to the new popularity and reissued the 70s humbucker'd Teles as part of the Mexican-made Classic series: the '72 Telecaster Thinline (two humbuckers) and the '72 Telecaster Custom (neck humbucker), both starting in 1999, and the '72 Telecaster Deluxe (two humbuckers) in 2004. US-made versions appeared in 2011 in the shape of the American Vintage '72 Telecaster Thinline and '72 Telecaster Custom.

"Everybody likes the aesthetic of those instruments," says Justin Norvell – Fender's vice president, marketing – and then he adds with a smile: "It's just that some of the originals weren't that great – so we wanted to make good ones."[115]

With Fender's greater confidence in playing around with the feature set of Telecasters, there is now an abundance of humbucker-equipped models to choose from beyond the 70s reissues. The first Fenders with the company's new US-made humbuckers had been the California 'Fat' models of 1997, including a Fat Tele with neck humbucker. Then, in 2004, a new wave of stack-coil pickups appeared, the Somarium Cobalt Noiseless (SCN) units designed by veteran pickup designer Bill Lawrence, as seen on American Deluxe and some American Series Telecasters. A new switching system, known as S-1, enhanced the new pickup capabilities.

Fender's Pawn Shop series, launched in 2011, took another of the ideas that first appeared on that first wave of non-traditional Teles, transferring the Thinline's chambered f-hole body to a Strat-style guitar and simply calling it the '72. Back in the late 60s and early 70s, however, Fender obviously felt more able to mess with the layout of the Tele rather than the Straocaster, which was seen then as the superior relation. But that's turned into a real benefit for the Telecaster, because it's the historical fallout from the experimentation of that era – in part, at least – that has led to the Telecaster's rebirth and remarkable new popularity today.

All of this is not to say that the classic two-single-coil Telecaster has lost fans. Players such as Vince Gill, Brad Paisley, Keith Urban, Dierks Bentley, and others highlight the longevity of the Tele twang, and the instrument's long and distinguished career in country's mainstream – as well as in its many backwaters and alts and tributaries – looks set to run for a long time yet.

John 5 is the guitarist with Rob Zombie and a continually surprising artist in his own right. Have a listen to something like 'Bella Kiss' on John's *Devil Knows My Name* solo album or 'J.W.' on *The Art Of Malice* if you have him categorised as a particular kind of player. He's a keen student of Fender history, too, with an extensive collection of Telecasters, and he's become part of that history himself, with several signature models to his name – and, naturally, the electrics are all Tele-based. He's had

Bring on the humbucker revival

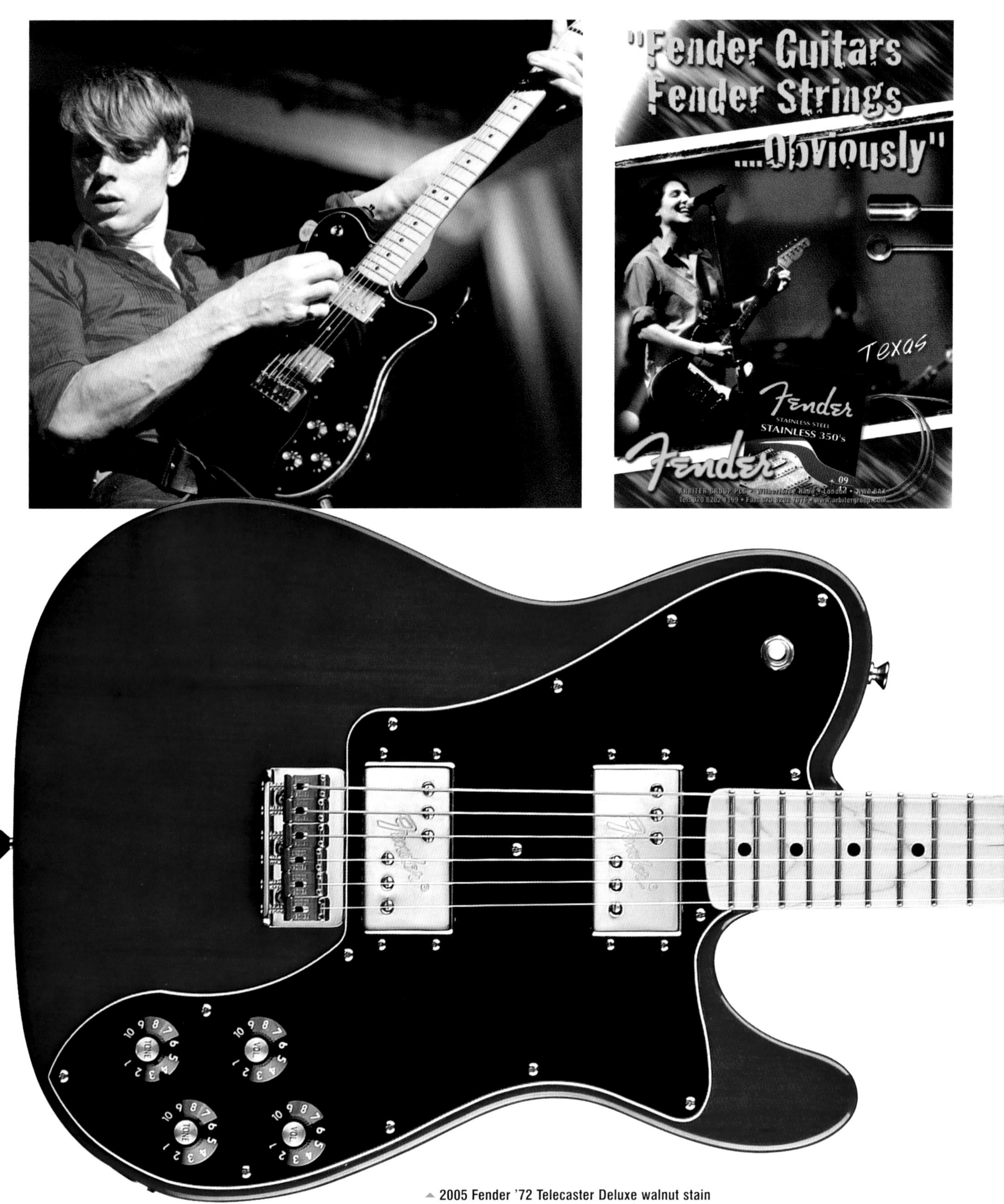

▲ 2005 Fender '72 Telecaster Deluxe walnut stain

◀ 2000 Leo Fender Broadcaster blond

The big news among some Tele players in the late 90s and early 00s came with their rediscovery of the humbucker-equipped models that originated in the 70s. Among the popular models was the Thinline, as played by Ian Ball of Gomez (above), who opted for the model's two-humbucker period, a style reissued by Fender in 1999 alongside the single-humbucker Custom. Franz Ferdinand's mainman Alex Kapranos (opposite, top left) opted for the Deluxe, also reissued in a Mexican version (main guitar) in 2004. Many still wanted the traditional single-coil Teles, including Sharleen Spiteri of Texas (strings ad, opposite). With the 50th anniversary in 2000 of the Broadcaster, the Telecaster's shortlived predecessor, Fender's Custom Shop produced a limited-edition run of just 50 Leo Fender Broadcasters, with Leo's signature emblazoned on the headstock in place of the usual Fender logo.

Fender-brand signature models from the Custom Shop since 2003 (with or without Bigsby) and from the Mexico factory since 2005 (with two or three pickups), and in 2009 he completed the set with the Squier J5 Tele, made in China.

John recalls walking around the NAMM show back around the turn of the millennium, when he was playing Ibanez guitars. "I've played Fender my whole life, but I was starting to do some big gigs, and I got an endorsement with Ibanez," John says. So, there he was at the Ibanez booth at the show, and there's no picture of him to be seen anywhere. "I was like: that's strange. But I didn't really care, because I wasn't a big Ibanez connoisseur. I loved Fender." Of course, he wandered to the Fender booth – where there was a picture of him. "Because when I played with Rob Halford and with David Lee Roth I played a Telecaster – which I wasn't supposed to, but I did." Fender welcomed John to the fold, and he says it was probably one of the greatest days of his life. He's been with them ever since.

As a collector, he's close to achieving his goal of owning a Fender Telecaster from every year, from the start in 1951 up to 1980. For his signature models, he chops in a distinctive three-tuners-a-side headstock, various humbuckers, and a black-and-chrome look, but they're still Teles at heart.

What he found peculiar at first, given the model's versatility, was that hardly anyone in heavy rock played a Tele. "What's the problem with these people, I wondered? I wanted my guitar to be able to scream through the loudest amps, and I wanted to be able to play country with it and jazz with it, to have it be an all-around guitar. The Les Pauls can do that, but they can't really get that twang, they can't get that *thing*. I really think my Tele can do that – and it's not because of me, I'm not taking credit for this at all – but I see a lot more heavy artists playing Telecasters now. After I started doing it, I saw Jim Root from Slipknot playing one, and I think I saw Tom Morello playing my signature model with Street Sweeper Social Club. It's like one of my kids, the Telecaster, you know? I'm passionate about it."[116]

It was Richard McDonald – senior vice president, marketing, of Fender brands – who started the company's relationship with John 5. "When I took over the line, there were a lot of similar-genre players, and I really wanted to shake it up a bit," McDonald says. "So I did the Tele with John – who just is Tele mad. He's one of the best examples of the versatility of the instrument, just in one person's hands. He dismantled a lot of misconceptions about it.

But really, says McDonald, what John 5 was doing was personifying all that's true about the Telecaster. "Which is that it's the one instrument with no place to hide. There's no whammy bar to hide behind. There's no place to hide when you find yourself lost in some corner. Technique-wise, it'll show every weakness you have, and yet whatever individual style you bring to the table, the Tele takes it and brings it to the forefront. I think that's why people just love it."[117]

Fender tried to trademark its three most famous body shapes, including the Telecaster, in legal action starting in 2003. The claims were opposed by 17 other makers, and pickup-maker Jason Lollar summed up the opposition when he said that industry-wide replication of the Fender shapes "has caused those body styles to become generic".[118] Fender's position was that it had established common-law trademark rights over the body shapes of the Telecaster, Stratocaster, and Precision

Bass, and that it was now seeking to obtain federal legal rights to those particular designs. The company already had federal trademark registrations for a number of its headstock shapes, but in 2009 the body-shape claims were rejected by the US Trademark Trial And Appeal Board. The Board concluded that Fender "failed to establish that the configurations involved in the applications before us have acquired distinctiveness".[119]

That must have been a blow to Fender's plans. But it certainly hasn't dented the popularity of the company's guitars, with the Telecaster more prominent than ever on stages, in bedrooms, in studios, and online. Leo Fender loved few things more than gadgets, and he would have been enthralled by the present-day Fender plant, with its unchanging functions at the root of guitar-making alongside its modern fixes and remedies. But also Leo would be looking beyond all that, to what tomorrow might bring. Fender now has no option but to acknowledge its rich history, full of great guitars and even greater players. And it must continue to find ways to attract the musicians of today and tomorrow.

Fender Japan was reorganised early in 2005 when a new company, Dyna Boeki, was formed to produce Fender's Japanese instruments. Fender said that this was simply a tidying-up of the business arrangements and that nothing about the physical production of the guitars changed. At the same time, distribution was simplified: all Japan-made instruments were distributed in Japan by Kanda Shokai, while the rest of the Fender and Squier catalogue made in the USA and elsewhere was distributed by Yamano Music. Meanwhile, fewer Japan-made Fenders have been sold outside Japan in recent years, indicating that Fender is content to rely on its two main sources, the US and Mexico factories, to provide instruments for Western markets.

Richard McDonald says it's possible that Japanese-made Fenders may return to play a bigger role outside Japan in the future. "When you look at all the places we've manufactured guitars over the years, we come back now to asking the fundamental question: why do people want a Fender? And then a Japanese Fender becomes attractive again, because it is a unique, highly-crafted, and respectable product. It's a bit of a different flavour, and there are enough people out there that dig it, so I could see that market growing in the future. I think Japan is going to come back on the map for Fender, because of our legacy there. We've been producing guitars there for a long time, and there are people who like them a lot."[120]

Upstairs in the boardroom, Bill Schultz stepped down as Fender CEO in 2005, staying on as chairman of the board of directors, and Bill Mendello became CEO. Sadly, Schultz died in September 2006. Mendello retired from Fender in 2010, and Larry Thomas took over as CEO. Dan Smith waved goodbye to Fender in 2006 after 25 remarkable years with the company, his era including the crucial management buy-out from CBS in 1985 and the creative struggle through the years immediately following. "Part of being able to retire," Smith says, "was that I knew we'd accomplished a lot. And the heart of the company is always the product. I could walk away proud, knowing Fender was so far ahead of where it had been, in terms of technology and training and people, and that it was going to continue and go way beyond that."[121]

More anniversaries lined up for celebration. In 2005 there was the 20th birthday of the revived Fender operation, while the following year marked the 60th anniversary of Leo's original Fender

Pulling strings, making Teles

John 5 (right) is not only the guitarist for Rob Zombie and an accomplished musician in his own right, but also a confirmed Telecaster fan and collector. His first Fender signature model appeared in 2003, from the Custom Shop, and two years later a Mexican-made version, the J5 (main guitar), retained John's novel headstock and black-and-chrome visuals. In 2007, a three-humbucker Strat-head version (ad, right) rounded out the John 5 models. Meanwhile, Fender continued to make guitars at its two American factories: in Corona, California (Teles and cases ready for shipping, opposite, top) and in Ensenada, Mexico (paint finishing, below). Offshore sources have included Japan, China, Korea (until 2008), and Indonesia, where this handsome dual-humbucker FMT model (opposite) was produced.

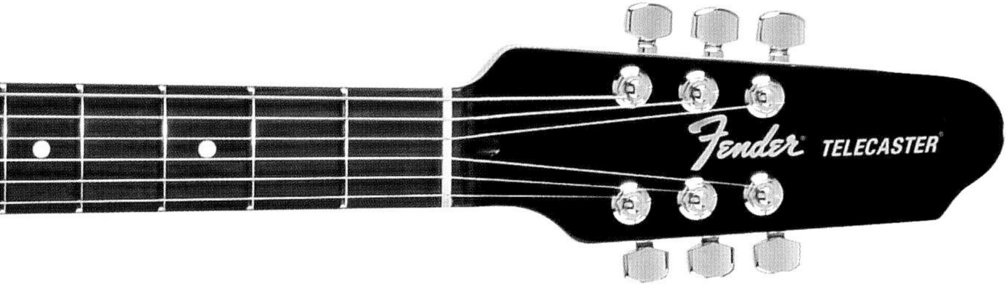

▲ 2005 Fender J5 Telecaster black

▶ 2005 Fender Custom Telecaster FMT HH black cherry burst

Manufacturing company. The modern Fender Musical Instruments Corporation (FMIC) took the opportunity to blow its own trumpet (or maybe that should be strum its own guitar). "Fender is now the single largest and most successful manufacturer of electric guitars, basses, and amplifiers in the world," the company's press material claimed. "In addition to the Fender brandname, FMIC markets under the brandnames Squier, Guild, Jackson, Charvel, SWR, Tacoma, Olympia, Orpheum, Gretsch, and Rodriguez. The company operates directly in more than 12 countries around the globe … and it maintains its own state-of-the-art manufacturing facilities in California, Washington, and Ensenada, Mexico."

The Classic Player series built on the growing idea at Fender of adding fashionable modern twists to a vintage-flavoured core, this time combining Custom Shop know-how with Mexican production skills. (The budget Squier brand's Vintage Modified series had similar intentions.) The Baja Telecaster, launched in 2006, was the first model – and, for a while, the only model – in the Classic Player series.

Fender had for a while been sending Master Builders from the Custom Shop to the Mexican factory to offer advice and guidance. One of those builders, Chris Fleming, decided to design a guitar for Mexican production. The result was the Baja, a vintage-style Tele but with modern appointments, such as a Twisted Tele neck pickup and S-1 switching. Fender was pleased, because it stretched the Mexico plant and justified recent refinements there. That single member of the Classic Player series was joined in 2010 by two more Teles: the Thinline Deluxe (chambered body, Deluxe features, with or without trem), and the Deluxe Black Dove (with a pair of Black Dove P90-like pickups).

The Twisted Tele pickup, first seen on the Baja and then the Custom Shop's Tele Pro, was the latest attempt to put a decent pickup in the Tele's neck position – which, as we've seen, is viewed by some as the guitar's weak link. Paul Waller, a Custom Shop Master Builder, decided to use taller bobbins under the nickel-alloy cover, providing a little more bass and midrange, taming the high-end somewhat, and arriving at something more of a Strat-like tone.

The Twisted Tele pickup turned up on other Custom Shop Teles such as the John 5 Signature, the Bent Top, the 2012 Custom Deluxe, and some Time Machines. In addition to the Baja model, the Mexico factory used it for 2010's Acoustasonic Tele (a modelling Tele that made for a surprisingly useful hybrid), and Corona added it to the American Standard Tele from 2012.

The US-made Vintage Hot Rod guitars, new for 2007, were based on vintage reissues but with thin-skin lacquer finishes, flatter fingerboards, bigger frets, modern pickups, and custom wiring. The series kicked off with a '52 Tele (as well as '57 and '62 Strats) with a Duncan mini-humbucker at the neck. In 2012, its vintage-style three-saddle bridge was upgraded with 'compensated' saddles, designed to improve intonation.

The original three-saddle bridge has always been a matter of interest to some Tele players. The guitar started life with that style of bridge at first, and had it for many years, with the Thinline of 1971 the first Tele to offer the wider adjustability of a six-saddle unit. Since that, quite a few Tele models have come as standard with a six-saddle bridge, particularly following the 80s American Standard model, which underlined the practical usefulness of more accurate intonation. The problem of the original bridge and its three brass saddles was that intonation adjustments were necessarily limited. Each saddle governed two strings, and that is a compromise. Some argue that the resulting not-quite-in-tuneness is one of the things that makes a vintage Tele sound like a vintage Tele, and that moving to six small saddles will always be accompanied by a loss when compared to the original bridge's tone. Others, most famously Danny Gatton, have compensated the angle of the three saddles by drilling the barrels off-camber to try to improve the intonation. The rest, meanwhile, are content with a modern six-saddle bridge. It's the Gatton approach that Fender applied to the Vintage Hot Rod '52 Tele and a few others.

Meanwhile, Fender was describing its new Tribute series as an "elite program" designed to offer the ultimate artist instrument. Each consists of a very limited run (usually 100) of an ultra-exact copy of a renowned artist's guitar. It's like an extreme, nitpicking version of the regular signature-model idea. The Tribute name has been around at Fender since at least 1997, when a Hendrix Strat appeared. But one of the first Teles was a re-creation of Andy Summers's careworn Custom, which appeared from the Custom Shop in a limited Tribute edition in 2007. "They took the original to pieces and photographed it," Summers said at the time, "and they made this map of where all the scratches and cracks are. It's like my guitar had babies."[122]

Fender managers realised they were a style short among the artist Telecasters. "In our signature line, everybody should see their style reflected back at them," says Justin Norvell, vice president of marketing at Fender. "So, if you're a blues player, you look and go OK: Albert Collins, Eric Clapton, Stevie Ray Vaughan; I get it. Same if you're a rock player. With punk, however, although Fender had a lot of ownership of that era, we felt that a kid might look at the Fender line and wonder if it was for him. We wanted something very representative of punk that gave instant recognition. And that's where the Strummer Telecaster fit."

We've seen how Joe Strummer's painted, stickered, and stencil'd Tele became a visible emblem throughout the story of The Clash. Norvell recalls that for the company's 2007 Strummer Tele, Fender decided to make a hybrid of that famous '66 Tele and a 70s maple-neck model that Strummer occasionally played.

Norvell brought in street artist Shepard Fairey to provide a kit of graphic material to go with the first 1,500 guitars. Some of these stencils and stickers were simply Strummer-themed, while others were replicas of his originals. "The whole spirit of punk isn't that you have a facsimile of something," Norvell says, "and the customisation kit gave you the option to do it in your own way, to be more individualistic. You could choose to collect the kit, which came in a 12-inch album cover, and put it away; you could choose to design it the way you wanted; or you could choose to do whatever you liked and be more in control of keeping it unique."

At first, the Fender team talked about making the Strummer guitar a fully-fledged Custom Shop Tribute model, in precise detail, but they figured that, again, was contrary to the spirit of the guitar's owner and his band. The resulting Mexico-made guitar was also significant for the catalogue name of its ravaged finish, described as Custom Road Worn. This was Mexico's new take on the Custom Shop's aged Relic finish. Norvell: "Joe's guitar was really, really rough and rusty. So we said to the Mexico factory: can you make it look like this, but dialled down and more refined? They absolutely

Birthday tributes and twisted pickups

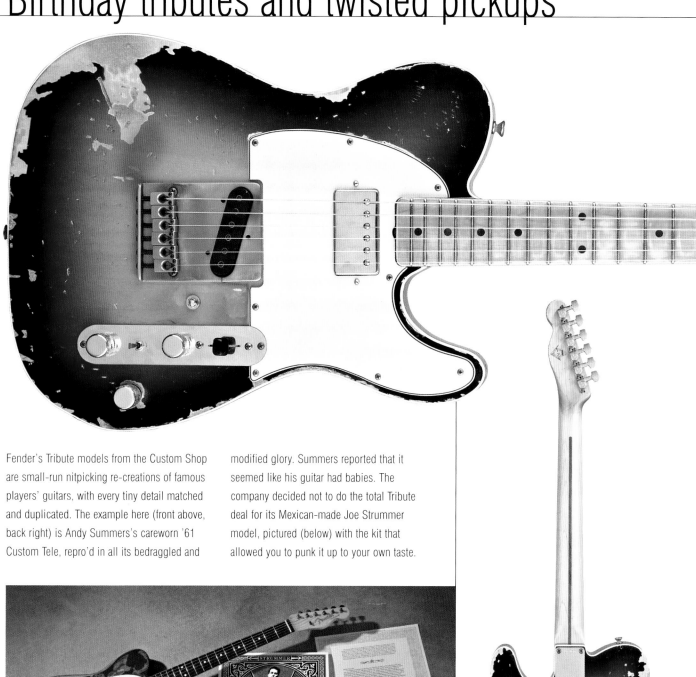

Fender's Tribute models from the Custom Shop are small-run nitpicking re-creations of famous players' guitars, with every tiny detail matched and duplicated. The example here (front above, back right) is Andy Summers's careworn '61 Custom Tele, repro'd in all its bedraggled and modified glory. Summers reported that it seemed like his guitar had babies. The company decided not to do the total Tribute deal for its Mexican-made Joe Strummer model, pictured (below) with the kit that allowed you to punk it up to your own taste.

The Fender company's diamond anniversary in 2006 generated a series of personalised 60th birthday ads, and here's a trio of the Tele-related treats (below, left to right): Maroon 5 and Deluxe; Bill Frisell and Thinline; Johnny Marr and Relic. Two popular recent models are the Baja Telecaster (bottom) and the Vintage Hot Rod '52 (ad, right). Both had a vintage vibe, but the Baja was Custom Shop-designed and made in Mexico, with a tweaked Twisted Tele neck pickup, while the Hot Rod '52 added a neck humbucker and intonatable bridge.

▲ 2007 Fender Andy Summers Tribute Series Telecaster

▼ 2012 Fender Classic Player Baja Telecaster 2-color sunburst

did that. A few years later, we came out with our Road Worn series from Mexico."[123] So far, there are two Road Worn Teles, both launched in 2011: the 50s Telecaster, a blond model with white 'guard and fairly obvious ageing, and the Player Telecaster, with neck humbucker and less overt wear.

The 2009 pricelist featured the following Teles: Standard, $690; Blackout Tele, $830; Deluxe Nashville Tele, $930; JA-90, $1,000; Muddy Waters, $1,090; James Burton Standard, $1,100; Highway One, $1,130; Classic 50s, $1,180; Classic '69 Thinline, $1,180; Classic '72 Thinline, $1,180; Classic 60s, $1,180; Road Worn 50s, $1,200; Deluxe Nashville Power Tele, $1,230; Classic '72 Custom, $1,240; Classic '72 Deluxe, $1,240; Acoustasonic, $1,250; Highway One Texas, $1,340; Classic Player Baja, $1,390; J5, $1,460; J5 Triple Tele, $1,500; Joe Strummer, $1,500; Jim Root, $1,500; Classic 60s w/Bigsby, $1,530; American Standard, $1,680; American Nashville B-Bender, $1,990; American Deluxe, $2,190; American Deluxe Ash, $2,300; American Vintage '52, $2,300; James Burton, $2,350; G.E. Smith, $2,350; American Vintage '62 Custom, $2,430; Vintage Hot Rod '52, $2,700. (As in every case in this book, these are list prices. Street prices are almost always less, of course, especially in recent years, and the official lists quoted here and throughout are intended simply to provide a historical guide to relative prices.)

It was probably hard to resist calling the Telecaster's 60th anniversary in 2011 a Tele-bration. Fender did not. There was, of course, a vintage-looking 60th Anniversary model (though it was closer in feel to a modern American Standard), but more interestingly, Fender also launched 12 different Tele-bration models, each in a year-long limited-edition run of 500 pieces. The press release outlined the idea, saying that they "stay inside the Telecaster's famously elegant lines while offering the finest and most unusual takes on the instrument's past, present, and future". The specs ranged from odd materials, such as laminated bamboo or hundred-year-old redwood, to fancy looks, like an Antique Burst flame-top model, and on to the Cabronita, which had TV Jones Filter'Tron pickups and a big slab body, or a Rosewood Tele with rosewood over a spruce heart. "Some of it was cool looking, some of it was really deep in there with new designs, and some of it was neat collectable stuff," Fender's Justin Norvell concludes.

There was some surprise when Fender launched its Modern Player models in 2011 because these were the first Fender-brand guitars to be made in China. The series included the Telecaster Plus, with pine body and three pickups (humbucker, Strat, and Tele), and the Tele Thinline Deluxe, with mahogany body and P90-style pickups. Both have distinct echoes of the carefree let's-mess-with-this attitude that has distinguished some Squier models in recent years.

"There's always been an area where Squier and Fender crossfade from one brand to the other," Norvell explains. "In the last few years, with things like the Classic Vibe series, Squier's quality level has come way up. We knew that most things in the world are continuing to get more expensive, and so we wanted to have a Fender-branded product that was at an entry-level price point."

The Modern Player guitars are made at the same Chinese factory that produces those classy Squier Classic Vibe models. "If you want a stock traditional Telecaster, you should still go to the Fender Standard series," says Norvell, "but we wanted to be a little more playful with the Modern Players, because at the entry level, people aren't quite as traditional."[124]

Meanwhile at the Custom Shop, in recent years there's been a shift in the way it presents its lines, now emphasising a unique collection of models that's refreshed each year. Where before models would come into the line and stay as long as they were popular, just as happens with the factory models, the scheme is now more focussed. The original idea for a set catalogue of Shop models dates back to 1992, but today, says Mike Eldred – Fender's director, marketing, at the Custom Shop – there's a move toward a catalogue that is anything but stagnant.

"We want an offering that's constantly changing," Eldred says, "and so we now have a custom collection for each specific year. For instance, the 2012 Custom Collection is all the models we're going to make that year. At the end of that year, we wipe the slate clean and do a whole other 2013 Custom Collection. That keeps everything fresh, it keeps our customers engaged and interested, and it really pushes us internally."

Within each annual collection there are four main categories: Time Machine, Custom Deluxe, Pro, and Limited Edition. "Every year we reload these four platforms," Eldred says. "Those are the ones we really focus on and move around each year." We met the aged and exacting Time Machine models – the Relics, Heavy Relics, N.O.S.s, and Closet Classics – earlier in the book. They remain popular, with Eldred estimating that they constitute maybe two-thirds of the Shop's business. Custom Deluxes use luscious materials for high-end treats, while the Pro collection is not, as many suspect, meant to imply *Pro*fessional, but *Pro*totype. It's where the Shop gets to tweak and experiment more, with different woods, neck shapes, fret sizes, and the rest. The Limited Editions tag provides a useful place for anything else – for example, 2012's Bent Top Tele.

In addition to Eldred's four platforms, there are three further categories of Shop guitars. There's the Artist line of upscale signature models, which remains relatively constant; the Dealer Select specials, made for specific retailers; and the Master Built guitars, which are exactly what most people would understand as the work of a custom shop. These are instruments made by a single person – one of Fender's Master Builders – with acute attention to detail and a price to match. "They're still extremely important to the Custom Shop," Eldred says. "This is where we get to push ourselves, and from these types of projects, newer designs emerge."

By 2012, the Shop had nine Master Builders who individually make the one-off Master Built instruments: John Cruz, Greg Fessler, Dennis Galuszka, Todd Krause, Yuriy Shishkov, Jason Smith, Stephen Stern, Paul Waller, and Dale Wilson.

At the time of writing, a problem facing the Custom Shop is a result of its own popularity. "We have a big back-order of something like 24 months," Mike Eldred explains. "It's crazy. We don't want people waiting that long. Some don't mind, but for the majority it's nuts. We deter people from ordering from certain builders who have a very long back-order. We say, why don't you go with this builder who doesn't have that much back-order? He doesn't get a Master Builder decal just for showing up to work – he has to go through a huge process to get that decal."

A further sub-division of the true one-offs is the Custom Shop's art guitars. Master Builder Fred Stuart made his Egyptian Telecaster in 1994, and it was the first Fender art guitar. It had pyramids, snakes, and runes hand-carved by George Amicay into a finish of Corian synthetic stone. Another example was Master Builder Chris Fleming's 2004 Leather Hula Esquire, covered in hand-tooled

Road worn but still Tele-brating

2011 Fender Tele-bration Lamboo Telecaster natural

▲ **2011 Fender Road Worn Player Telecaster candy apple red**

When the 60th birthday of the Telecaster arrived in 2011, Fender not only made exactly what you'd expect – a 60th anniversary model – but also produced an intriguing set of 12 Tele-bration models, a diverse bunch of Tele interpretations. Included was the Lamboo (top guitar), with laminated bamboo body, bamboo neck, and shell guard, as well as Teles in empress wood or ancient pine, with f-hole bodies, pearl-block inlays, and more. The Mexican factory moved on from the aged finish devised for the Strummer Tele and in 2009 started the Road Worn series, its own take on the Custom Shop's successful Relic idea. This Player model (main guitar) matches the aged look with a useful humbucker. Custom Shop worker Silverio Castillo is pictured (top) with the most expensive Tele on Fender's pricelist, the Merle Haggard model, and this page from a 2010 catalogue (above) details the Shop's top-materials model, the Custom Deluxe.

leather by Nevena Christi and intended to convey something of a surfing Hawaiian vibe. These are expensive items. The Shop apparently turned down $75,000 for an Aztec Telecaster and $50,000 for a Bird-o-Fire Strat some years ago. Meanwhile, the trend has developed. "We've worked with several artists," Eldred says, "in order to really make the art-guitar moniker more true. Shepard Fairey, Pamelina, Shag, and Crash are just some of the artists we work with, offering them a new and unique canvas."

Aside from the Master Built guitars, the Shop's day-to-day work is in the Custom Collection instruments. Part of the reason for moving to the new notion of an annual collection is to underline that, now, most Custom Shop models are unique and shortlived. Eldred offers the example of a guitarist who might have bought one of the Shop's guitars a year or two ago. He loves this guitar, has it for a while, and then decides he really needs, say, that Les Paul he's just seen.

"Immediately," Eldred smiles, "a guitar player starts going through what I call the mental inventory. What have I got at the house that I don't play any more? So maybe he goes to trade in this guitar. And because it was a limited edition, part of the 2012 Custom Collection, and that guitar now has some value to it." More value, Eldred insists, than a model you could still buy. "We're trying to make instruments that retain value."

The Shop's team are also keen to promote guitarists they like. Take the Jim Campilongo Telecaster, a Custom Shop Limited Edition in 2011. Campilongo is based in New York City and probably best known for working with Norah Jones in a part-time band, The Little Willies. "He's this quirky player dude," Eldred explains. "Hardly known outside the United States," he says, and then, laughing: "Hardly known inside, either. But an amazing musician."

Eldred suggested that the Shop make a run of 50 guitars based on Campilongo's '59 top-loader Tele. Campilongo was, as you might imagine, surprised, but Eldred told him Fender was looking at three things: he's a great player; his Tele is interesting; and a signature model will help promote him as a guitarist. As it turned out, it was one of the most difficult signature models the Shop has made, including a just-so neck tint, pickups wound very particularly, and oil-and-foil capacitors that had to be sourced from Jensen in Italy. "He's closest to Roy Buchanan, if you're going to compare him to anybody," Eldred concludes, "but to me he's a much better guitar player and musician. He's just very musical."

Through all the recent changes of focus, the main aim of the Shop has not diminished. "We offer a unique experience for the end user," Eldred says, "whether that's John 5, Eric Clapton, Jeff Beck, or just a guy who likes a good guitar. They all have an opportunity to have a small team of builders make an instrument they have always dreamed of owning."[125]

Over at the main factory, meanwhile, in 2012 Fender organised its Telecaster models into 15 series: American Deluxe; American Special; American Standard; American Vintage; Artist; Blacktop; Classic; Classic Player; Deluxe; Modern Player; Road Worn; Select; Special Edition; Standard; and Vintage Hot Rod.

American Deluxe models first appeared in 1998, with two major upgrades since then. They're more or less deluxe versions of the American Standards, intended by Fender to attract contemporary players. They have S-1 switching (a push-pull volume knob that gives extra sound options), locking tuners, and impressive cosmetics. The last upgrade, in 2010, added N3 Noiseless pickups, a compound-radius fingerboard (nine-and-a-half inches at the nut to a flatter fourteen inches at the body), and new colours such as tungsten and olympic pearl.

The American Special Tele was launched in 2010, loosely based on Fender's long-held position as a maker of the workingman's guitar. It's US-made but relatively budget-priced – what guitar-makers like to call affordable – and features Texas pickups, jumbo frets, and a black pickguard.

The American Standard Tele first appeared back in 1988, as we've seen, and this is a relatively straightforward modern interpretation of the original Telecaster. The core American Standard Tele features modern fingerboard radiuses and modern hardware with an otherwise generally traditional vibe. Fender added Custom Shop pickups and a 'belly' body contour from 2012.

American Vintage models are what you'd expect: a variety of US-made period-style instruments. Artist guitars are star-specific signature models that reflect the sometimes idiosyncratic requirements of name players. The Blacktop Tele, new for 2010, is an aggressive two-humbucker model with top-loader bridge and 'reversed' control plate (selector at the back), aimed apparently at new players who might fall for this particular combination of specs.

The Classic models, first seen in 1998, are Mexico's versions of vintage-style guitars, while the Classic Player models, which first appeared in 2006, are upgraded Classics still made in Mexico but revamped by Custom Shop Master Builders. Deluxe models first began to appear on Fender pricelists in 1998. Today, the series seems ill-defined, although at first it was intended to include heavily upgraded versions of Mexico's basic Standard series, often with high-end electronics.

New in 2011 was the Modern Player series, the first Fender-brand models to be made in China, a source previously limited to Squier-brand guitars. They're curious experiments with a combination of features not usually available together, and it will be interesting to see if the feature sets and relatively low prices hit home with players.

The Road Worn series, new in 2009, offers a cheaper way for players to get the style of the Custom Shop's highly successful Relic-finish instruments. The Mexican factory applies the aged look to thin nitro finishes, assisted in this task, Fender says, by Custom Shop advisors.

The Fender Select series was launched in 2012 and marks a fresh attempt at high-end factory models, complete with fancy woods and pretty cosmetics. It's almost as if Fender needs to impress that flash is not limited to the Custom Shop. Special Edition is a series name used at the time of writing to round up a jumble of models still coming from Fender's Japanese factories.

Mexico's Standard model first appeared in 1991, and it is just that: a standard, unchanged, affordable Telecaster. The Vintage Hot Rod models, which appeared in 2007, are similar to Classic Players in that Fender intends them to be vintage-based instruments with player-friendly mods and upgrades.

With so many different series and models, it can be daunting these days trying to find your way around the Fender lines. At the time of writing, Fender had no fewer than 55 different Fender-brand Telecasters (including a few Esquires and Nocasters) and a further 15 Squier models. They ranged in list-price from a Squier Affinity Tele at $279.99 to a Fender Merle Haggard Signature

Brand new and sixty years old

▼ 2012 Fender Modern Player Telecaster Plus honey burst

▲ 2012 Fender Standard Telecaster lake placid blue

Sixty years old and more, the Telecaster shows no signs of grumpy old age. In fact, it's never been more popular, and its versatility puts it at home in a range of music other guitars might secretly covet. There it is (opposite) with Vince Gill, underlining the mainstream country appeal its enjoyed since birth; here it is (right) with Jim Root and Slipknot, an altogether more turbulent environment. The Tele can do it all, and it continues to adapt and prosper with no apparent loss of its original vitality.

▼ **2010 Damien Hirst Spot Fender Telecaster**

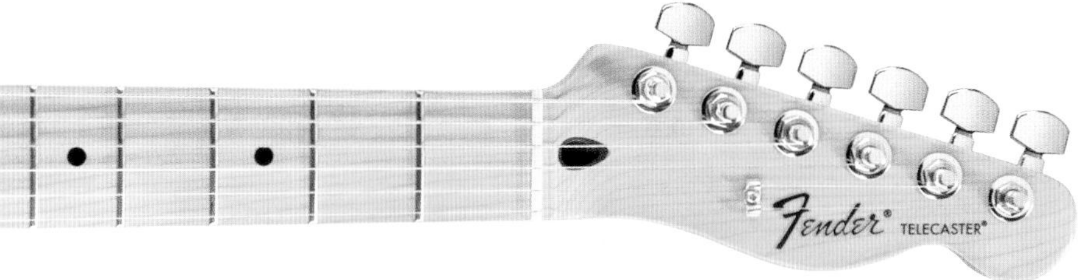

The Telecaster today can keep you close to the original or take you far, far away, all the while retaining enough Tele-centric properties that you won't doubt what you're playing. There's the old-style package updated, such as the Mexican-made born-in-1991 Standard model (main guitar). But it's pickups that have defined the Telecaster's moves from strict tradition, for example with this humbucker/Strat/Tele layout on the Chinese-made Plus (top), or that twin-humbucker Blacktop (catalogue, right). The Standard won't break the bank, but this one-off decorated by Damien Hirst (above) sold for £30,000 ($47,000). We're spoilt for choice.

Telecaster at $7,500. In a recent catalogue, Fender defended this apparently continually growing multitude. "So, why do we make so many models of Fender electric guitars? Because there are so many different styles of music, and even more individual artists playing them!"

Fair point: but with all that choice – and often with nothing more on the guitar than 'Fender' and 'Telecaster' – it can be tricky to know for sure what you're looking at. Is it a Standard or is it a Special Edition Custom Telecaster FMT HH? Perhaps you're buying a secondhand guitar, an activity where sellers have been known to blur the truth. This book tries hard to clarify the position, but Fender doesn't make it easy and shows no signs of addressing the problem.

Of course, Fender has to acknowledge its rich history, which as we've seen is just full to the brim with great guitars and even greater players. But perhaps even more importantly, Fender needs to keep an eye on you: the players of today and the players of tomorrow. And with the Telecaster, the history has twisted around on itself so that Fender's very first solidbody electric, the guitar that started almost everything, has never been more popular and never so diverse.

Today, Fender's factory in Corona, California, may be some 20 miles from Fullerton and Leo Fender's original workshops, but it's a universe away from the humble steel shacks that were the first home for Fender production and the birthplace of the earliest Esquires and Broadcasters and Telecasters, back at the turn of the 50s. At Corona, the business is to make great new guitars and to sell them. But that doesn't stop the bosses ruminating on the curious case of The Guitar That Came Back.

"You have everyone from Vince Gill, a smooth country guy who's as loyal to Telecasters as anybody that you'd ever meet, to Jim Root, of Slipknot, one of the heaviest bands out there," Richard McDonald says. "I can't think of any other guitar that's as accepted like that across such a wide range. Not only has it survived 60 years, it's flourishing."[126]

Justin Norvell contrasts the Tele against the slightly younger Stratocaster, which for years seemed like the Fender that had it all. "There's a person to whom a Strat is a little virtuosic," he suggests. "Something proceeds you when you pick up a Strat. A lot of modern players go for a Telecaster and use it as more of a paintbrush, for textural sonic palettes or savvy kind of punk. They don't want to be envisioned up there with a cowboy hat and a fan blowing on them while they're playing. It's taken 60 years or so, but today the Telecaster has become the equal of the Stratocaster. It was in the shadow of its larger sibling, but it seems that after all this time it's finally coming around."[127]

The last word goes to John 5, a great ambassador for the Tele. "I always think that the Telecaster, as our first solidbody electric guitar, is the greatest guitar in the world," he says. "They should stop making any other kind of guitar and just make the Telecaster. That's how strongly I feel about it."[128]

Endnotes

1 Author's interview February 6 1992
2 *Guitar Player* October 1982
3 Author's interview February 10 1992
4 *Bay Area Music* August 29 1980
5 Author's interview with Karl Olmsted February 5 1992
6 *Guitar Player* September 1971
7 Author's interview February 5 1992
8 Author's interview February 8 1992
9 Author's interview February 10 1992
10 Author's interview with Forrest White February 5 1992
11 Author's interview February 10 1992
12 Author's interview February 5 1992
13 *Daily News Tribune* November 8 1949
14 *Guitar Player* September 1971
15 *Washington Post* December 17 1972
16 Author's interview with Bill Carson September 6 1991
17 Author's interview February 8 1992
18 *Guitar World* September 1980
19 Smith *Fender: The Sound Heard 'Round The World*
20 Author's interview February 8 1992
21 *Fender Catalogue No.2* 1950
22 Author's interview February 10 1992
23 Author's interview February 10t 1992
24 *Guitar Player* December 1984
25 Author's interview February 10 1992
26 Author's interview February 8th 1992
27 Author's interview February 8th 1992
28 *Guitar Player* May 1978
29 Author's interview September 6 1991
30 Author's correspondence May 13 2010
31 *Guitar Player* July 1979
32 Author's interview with Bill Carson September 6 1991
33 Author's interview February 10 1992
34 *Los Angeles Times* April 3rd 1955
35 *The Music Trades* June 1953
36 Author's interview February 5 1992
37 Author's interview February 5 1992
38 Author's interview February 5 1992
39 Author's interview February 5 1992
40 *La Habra Journal* March 8 2001
41 Author's interview February 10 1992
42 Author's interview April 29 2005
43 *Melody Maker* September 8 1956
44 *Melody Maker* October 25 1958
45 *Guitar Player* August 1983
46 Author's interview February 8 1992
47 Author's interview February 10 1992
48 Author's interview February 5 1992
49 Author's interview February 10 1992
50 Author's interview February 10 1992
51 *The Music Trades* January 1965
52 *The Music Trades* January 1965
53 *International Musician* August 1978
54 Author's interview February 10 1992
55 Author's interview February 10 1992
56 Author's interview February 5 1992
57 Author's interview February 8 1992
58 Author's interview February 10 1992
59 Author's interview February 10 1992
60 Smith *Fender: The Sound Heard*
61 Author's interview February 5 1992
62 *Melody Maker* June 25th 1966
63 *Beat Instrumental* October 1967
64 Author's interview July 10 2003
65 Author's interview April 27 2005
66 Author's interview February 8 1992
67 Author's interview April 29 2005
68 Author's interview February 10 1992

69 Author's interview February 8 1992
70 *Guitar Player* April 1983
71 Author's interview April 27 2005
72 *Guitar Player* October 1976
73 Howe, Bacon *Steve Howe Guitar Collection*
74 Author's interview August 31 1981
75 Author's interview October 30 1992
76 *Guitar Player* October 1976
77 *Rolling Stone* April 1 1999
78 *Syracuse Herald* June 29th 1986
79 *The Guardian* July 4 2010
80 *Washington Post* December 17 1972
81 *Guitar Player* September 1983
82 *Rolling Stone* February 13 1975
83 *Guitar Player* December 1976
84 Author's correspondence May 13 2010
85 Author's interview February 5 1992
86 Author's interview February 4 1992
87 Author's interview June 2 2005
88 Author's interview June 2 2005
89 Author's interview February 4 1992
90 *Guitar Player* May 1978
91 Author's interview February 4 1992
92 Author's interview February 4 1992
93 *Guitar Trader Vintage Guitar Bulletin* Vol.2 No.7 July 1983
94 Author's interview February 4 1992
95 *Guitar Player* May 1981
96 Author's interview April 12 2005
97 *San Francisco Chronicle* January 15 1985
98 Author's interview May 11 2011
99 Author's interview June 3 2011
100 Author's interview May 11 2010
101 Author's interview February 11 1985
102 Author's interview May 11 2011
103 Author's interview February 4 1992
104 Author's interview June 2nd 2005
105 Author's interview April 29 2005
106 Author's interview April 27 2005
107 Author's interview with Dan Smith June 2 2005
108 *The Guardian* July 4 2010
109 Author's interview April 12 2005 & January 30 2012
110 Author's interview February 6 1992
111 *New York Times* January 16 1992
112 Author's interview December 2 1997
113 *The Guitar Magazine* April 2004
114 fender.com December 16 2011
115 Author's interview December 19 2011
116 Author's interview May 24 2011
117 Author's interview January 10 2012
118 forbes.com June 22 2004
119 United States Patent And Trademark Office, Trademark Trial And Appeal Board, Application serial no. 76516127, Opinion by Kuhlke, Administrative Trademark Judge, March 25 2009
120 Author's interview January 10 2012
121 Author's interview March 30 2007
122 *The Guardian* July 4 2010
123 Author's interview December 19 2011
124 Author's interview December 19 2011
125 Author's interviews March 27 2007, June 8 2010, January 6 2012
126 Author's interview January 10 2012
127 Author's interview December 19 2011
128 Author's interview March 24 2011

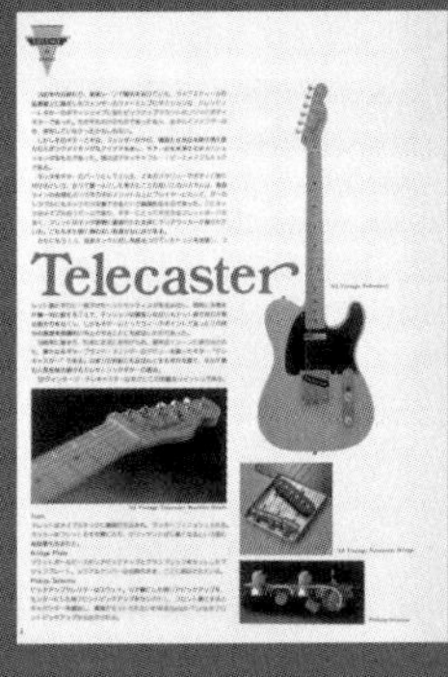

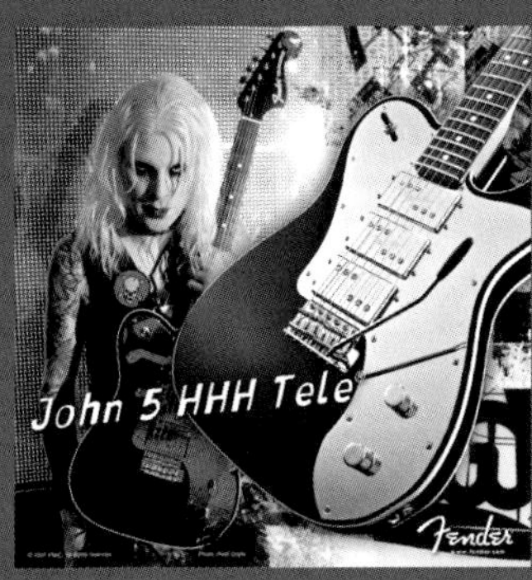

THE REFERENCE LISTING

HOW TO USE THE **REFERENCE LISTING**

We've designed this Reference Listing to make it easier to identify Fender Telecasters, Esquires, and related models made between 1950 and early 2012. The notes here should help you get the most from this unique inventory.

The list covers all the production Fender-brand Telecasters and related models made by Fender US between 1950 and early 2012, by Fender Mexico between 1991 and early 2012, the export models of Fender Japan issued from 1982 to early 2012, and the few Fender-brand models made in Korea from 1992 to 2008, in Indonesia from 2005 to early 2102, and in China from 2011 to early 2012.

Models by Squier and other Fender-related brands are beyond the detailed scope of this Reference Listing, although there is a brief summary of Squier guitars at the end. Most limited editions and other special runs from the Custom Shop issued in small numbers are also beyond the scope of this Listing.

Using the lists

The six main sections within the Reference Listing are ordered according to the year the country began making Fender Telecaster-related guitars:

US Models (began 1950)
Japanese Models (began 1985)
Mexican Models (began 1991)
Korean Models (began 1992)
Indonesian Models (began 2005)
Chinese Models (began 2011)
Also, a brief round-up of the Squier brand

Within the US section, we've grouped the models into what we term US Regular Models, US Replica Models, and US Revised Models, and in the Japanese and Mexican sections into Replica and Revised models. The Korean, Indonesian, and Chinese sections are each one simple list.

'Regular' models are what we determine as models with established normal-design specifications. If you're looking at a 'Regular' model – that's one with standard pickups and controls and nothing out of the ordinary – then there's not much more to be said. We've given some general clues to period and style, but generally what you see is what you've got.

'Replica' models reproduce relatively accurately a period look and vibe of one of the various standard-version US Regular Models.

'Revised' models are pretty much all the rest, and indeed make up the bulk here – in other words, the ones that depart in various significant ways from the Regular models.

In all these sections and sub-sections, each model is listed in alphabetical order of the model name, usually following published Fender catalogues and pricelists for style. Where a person's name is the model name, the forename, not the surname, determines the alphabetical order. For example, the Jerry Donahue Telecaster is under J, not D. The exception to alphabetical order is the US Regular Models, where the listings are in chronological order for ease of reference.

Understanding the data

At the head of each model entry is the model name in **bold type**. Next is a year or range of years indicating the production period of the particular model. It should be stressed that these dates are approximate, because it's not easy to pinpoint manufacturing spans with accuracy. The dates shown are based on our extensive research as well as official data supplied by Fender, and therefore they represent the best information available.

Following the year or years is a single sentence *in italic type* describing the specific model's most identifiable unique features. This brief summary is designed to help you to be able to recognise an instrument quickly.

For some models, below the heading is a sentence that starts "Similar to ... , except: ...". This is a reference to another model entry, and the specification points that follow indicate only the differences between the two.

Most guitar entries then include a list of bullet points below the heading that relate to the particular model's specifications and other features. In order, these points refer to the following components, where present or relevant:

- Neck, fingerboard; scale, frets; truss-rod adjuster; tuners; string-guide(s); headstock; neckplate.
- Body; finish colour(s).
- Pickup(s).
- Controls; output jack.
- Pickguard.
- Bridge.
- Metalwork finish.
- *Any other information, including model variations, Custom Shop origin, etc.*

To avoid needless repetition, we consider certain features as common to all models, and so these are not shown in the entries. Unless stated otherwise, you can always assume the following:

Bolt-on neck.
Fingerboard with dot position-markers.
Scale length of twenty-five-and-a-half inches.
Twenty-one frets.
Metal tuner buttons.
Familiar Fender headstock shape.
Four-screw neckplate.
Solid slab single-cutaway body.
Single-coil pickups.
Nickel or chrome-plated metalwork.

US MODELS

US-made models are divided into three sections: US Regular Models; US Replica Models; and US Revised Models.

US Regular Models

Listed here in chronological order are the models we regard as the original standard US-made versions of the Telecaster and Esquire.

ESQUIRE 1950–69 *Model name on headstock, slab single-cutaway body, one pickup.*

- Fretted maple neck (1950–59 and 1969), maple neck with rosewood fingerboard (1959–69), maple fingerboard official option (1967–69); truss-rod adjuster at body end; one string-guide.
- Solid slab single-cutaway body; originally blond only, later sunburst or colours.
- One black six-polepiece pickup (angled at bridge).
- Two controls (volume, tone) and three-way selector, all on metal plate adjoining pickguard; side-mounted output jack.
- Five-screw (eight-screw from 1959) black plastic pickguard (white plastic from 1954; white laminated-plastic from 1963).
- Three-saddle bridge with through-body stringing (strings anchored at bridgeplate not through body 1958–60).
- *Very few earliest pre-production examples without truss-rod, and some have second pickup at neck.*
- *Also* ***CUSTOM ESQUIRE*** *with bound body (1959–69).*

BROADCASTER 1950–51 *See following* ***TELECASTER*** *listing.*

TELECASTER 1951–83 *Twenty-one frets, slab single-cutaway body, two single-coils, three-saddle bridge.*

- Fretted maple neck (1951–59 and 1969–83), maple neck with rosewood fingerboard (1959–83), maple fingerboard official option (1967–69); truss-rod adjuster at body end; one string-guide (two from 1972).
- Solid slab single-cutaway body; originally blond only, later sunburst or colours.
- One plain metal-cover pickup (at neck) and one black six-polepiece pickup (angled at bridge).
- Two controls (volume, tone; but originally volume, pickup blender) and three-way selector, all on metal plate adjoining pickguard; side-mounted output jack.
- Five-screw (eight-screw from 1959) black plastic pickguard (white plastic from 1954; white laminated-plastic 1963–75 and 1981–83; black laminated-plastic 1975–81).
- Three-saddle raised-sides bridge with through-body stringing (strings anchored at bridgeplate and not through body 1958–60).
- *Previously known as* ***BROADCASTER*** *(1950–51), the forerunner of the Telecaster and very similar, but with 'Broadcaster' model name on headstock. A transitional type has no model name on the headstock, known (unofficially) as the* ***NOCASTER***.
- *Fender/Bigsby bridge and vibrato tailpiece option (1967–74), no through-body string holes if unit factory-fitted.*
- *Also* ***CUSTOM TELECASTER***, *with bound body (1959–72).*
- *Also* ***PAISLEY RED TELECASTER***, *with red paisley-pattern body finish and clear plastic pickguard (1968–69).*
- *Also* ***BLUE FLOWER TELECASTER***, *with blue floral-pattern body finish and clear plastic pickguard (1968–69).*
- *Also* ***ROSEWOOD TELECASTER***, *with fretted rosewood neck, solid (later semi-solid) rosewood body, and black laminated-plastic pickguard (1969–72).*
- *Also* ***ANTIGUA TELECASTER***, *with white/brown shaded body finish and matching-colour laminated-plastic pickguard (1977–79).*
- *Also* ***INTERNATIONAL COLOR TELECASTER***, *with special colour finishes, white laminated-plastic pickguard, and black-plated pickguard screws (1981).*

THINLINE TELECASTER first version 1968–71 *F-hole body, two single-coils.*

- Maple neck with maple fingerboard (fretted maple neck, or maple neck with rosewood fingerboard, from 1969); truss-rod adjuster at body end; one string-guide.
- Semi-solid body with f-hole; sunburst or colours.
- One plain metal-cover pickup with visible height-adjustment screws (at neck) and one black six-polepiece pickup (angled at bridge).
- Two controls (volume, tone) and three-way selector, all on pickguard; side-mounted output jack.
- 12-screw pearl laminated-plastic pickguard.
- Three-saddle raised-sides bridge with through-body stringing.

THINLINE TELECASTER second version 1971–79 *F-hole body, two humbuckers.*

- Fretted maple neck; bullet truss-rod adjuster at headstock; one string-guide; three-screw neckplate.
- Semi-solid body with f-hole; sunburst or colours.
- Two metal-cover split-polepiece humbuckers.
- Two controls (volume, tone) and three-way selector, all on pickguard; side-mounted output jack.
- 12-screw black, white, or white pearl laminated-plastic re-styled pickguard.
- Six-saddle small bridge with through-body stringing.

TELECASTER CUSTOM 1972–81 *One humbucker and one single-coil, four controls.*

- Fretted maple neck, or maple neck with rosewood fingerboard; bullet truss-rod adjuster at headstock end; two string-guides; three-screw neckplate.
- Solid slab single-cutaway body; sunburst or colours.
- One metal-cover split-polepiece humbucker (at neck) and one black six-polepiece pickup (angled at bridge).
- Four controls (two volume, two tone) and three-way selector, all on pickguard; side-mounted output jack.
- 16-screw black laminated-plastic pickguard.
- Six-saddle raised-sides bridge with through-body stringing.
- *Earliest examples with 15-screw pickguard and/or three-saddle raised-sides bridge.*
- *Also* ***ANTIGUA TELECASTER CUSTOM***, *with white/brown shaded body finish and matching-colour laminated-plastic pickguard (1977–79).*
- *For Custom Telecaster model with bound body, see Custom Telecaster in* ***TELECASTER*** *listing (left).*

TELECASTER DELUXE 1973–81 *Two covered humbuckers, normal Tele body, Strat-style head.*

- Fretted maple neck; bullet truss-rod adjuster at headstock end; two string-guides; large Stratocaster-style headstock; three-screw neckplate.
- Solid contoured single-cutaway body; sunburst or colours.

- Two metal-cover split-polepiece humbuckers.
- Four controls (two volume, two tone) and three-way selector, all on pickguard; side-mounted output jack.
- 16-screw black laminated-plastic pickguard.
- Six-saddle small bridge with through-body stringing; some examples with Stratocaster-type six-pivot bridge/vibrato unit.
- *Also* ***ANTIGUA TELECASTER DELUXE****, with white/brown shaded body finish and matching-colour laminated-plastic pickguard (1977–79).*

TELECASTER STANDARD 1983–84 *21 frets, slab single-cutaway body, two single-coils, six-saddle bridge/tailpiece.*
- Fretted maple neck; truss-rod adjuster at headstock end; two string-guides.
- Solid slab single-cutaway body; sunburst or colours.
- One plain metal-cover pickup at neck and one black six-polepiece pickup (angled at bridge).
- Two controls (volume, tone) and three-way selector, all on metal plate adjoining pickguard; side-mounted output jack.
- Five-screw (originally eight-screw) white plastic pickguard.
- Six-saddle flat bridge/tailpiece (no through-body stringing).
- *Also in red, yellow or blue streaked finish, unofficially known as* ***BOWLING BALL*** *or* ***MARBLE TELECASTER*** *(1984).*

AMERICAN TELECASTER *See following* ***AMERICAN STANDARD*** *listing.*

AMERICAN STANDARD TELECASTER 1988–current *22 frets, slab single-cutaway body, two single-coils, six-saddle bridge.*
- Fretted maple neck or maple neck with rosewood fingerboard; 22 frets; truss-rod adjuster at headstock end; one string-guide.
- Solid slab single-cutaway body ('belly' contour from 2012); sunburst or colours.
- One plain metal-cover pickup with visible height-adjustment screws (at neck) and one black six-polepiece pickup (angled at bridge).
- Two controls (volume, tone) and three-way selector, all on metal plate adjoining pickguard; side-mounted output jack.
- Eight-screw laminated-plastic pickguard.
- Six-saddle flat bridge with through-body stringing (earliest examples with raised-sides type).
- *Anodised aluminium hollow-body option (1994–95).*
- *Known as* ***AMERICAN TELECASTER*** *(2001–07).*

US Replica Models

Listed here in alphanumerical order are the US-made models we regard as replicas of various standard-version US-made Regular Telecasters and Esquires.

RELIC NOCASTER 1995–98 *Aged-finish replica of 1950-period original with no model name on headstock (see Nocaster in* ***TELECASTER*** *listing in earlier US Regular Models section). Custom Shop production.*

'51 NOCASTER 1999–current *Replica of 1951-period original with no model name on headstock (see Broadcaster in* ***TELECASTER*** *listing in earlier US Regular Models section). Available with three levels of aged finish: N.O.S, Closet Classic, and Relic. Custom Shop production.*

'52 TELE SPECIAL 1999–2001 *Replica of 1952-period Telecaster original (see* ***TELECASTER*** *listing in earlier US Regular Models section). Body sunburst only, gold-plated hardware.*

'52 TELECASTER *See* ***AMERICAN VINTAGE '52 TELECASTER*** *or* ***VINTAGE HOT ROD '52 TELE*** *in later US Revised Models section.*

'53 HEAVY RELIC TELECASTER 2011 *Aged-finish replica of 1953-period original (see* ***TELECASTER*** *listing in earlier US Regular Models section). Custom Shop production.*

'59 ESQUIRE 2003–06 *Replica of 1959-period original (see* ***ESQUIRE*** *listing in earlier US Regular Models section). No through-body stringing. Available with three levels of aged finish: N.O.S, Closet Classic, and Relic. Custom Shop production.*

50s TELECASTER 1996–98 *Replica of 50s-period original (see* ***TELECASTER*** *listing in earlier US Regular Models section). Gold-plated hardware option. Custom Shop production.*

'60 TELECASTER CUSTOM 2003–04 *Replica of 1960-period original (see Custom Telecaster in* ***TELECASTER*** *listing in earlier US Regular Models section). Available with three levels of aged finish: N.O.S, Closet Classic, and Relic. Custom Shop production.*

'61 RELIC TELECASTER CUSTOM 2012 *Replica of 1961-period original (see Custom Telecaster in* ***TELECASTER*** *listing in earlier US Regular Models section) with aged black or sunburst Relic finish. Custom Shop production.*

'62 CUSTOM TELECASTER *See* ***AMERICAN VINTAGE '62 CUSTOM TELECASTER*** *in later US Revised Models section.*

'63 HEAVY RELIC TELECASTER CUSTOM 2011 *Aged-finish replica of 1963-period original (see Custom Telecaster in* ***TELECASTER*** *listing in earlier US Regular Models section). Custom Shop production.*

'63 TELECASTER 1999–2009 *Replica of 1963-period original (see* ***TELECASTER*** *listing in earlier US Regular Models section). Available with three levels of aged finish: N.O.S., Closet Classic, and Relic. Custom Shop production.*

'64 RELIC TELECASTER 2009 *Aged-finish replica of 1964-period original (see* ***TELECASTER*** *listing in earlier US Regular Models section). Custom Shop production.*

'67 TELECASTER 2005–08, 2011 *Replica of 1967-period original (see* ***TELECASTER*** *listing in earlier US Regular Models section). Available with three levels of aged finish: N.O.S., Closet Classic, and Relic. Custom Shop production.*

60s TELECASTER CUSTOM 1996–98 *Replica of 60s-period original (see Custom Telecaster in* ***TELECASTER*** *listing in earlier US Regular Models section). Gold-plated hardware option. Custom Shop production.*

US Revised Models

Listed here in alphabetical order are the US-made models we regard as revised and adapted versions of the standard-version US-made Regular Telecasters and Esquires.

ALBERT COLLINS TELECASTER 1990–current *Signature on headstock.*

- Maple neck with maple fingerboard; truss-rod adjuster at body end; one string-guide; Albert Collins signature on headstock.
- Bound body; natural only.
- One metal-cover six-polepiece humbucker (at neck) and one black six-polepiece pickup (angled at bridge).
- Two controls (volume, tone) and three-way selector, all on metal plate adjoining pickguard; side-mounted output jack.
- Eight-screw white laminated-plastic pickguard.
- Six-saddle raised-sides bridge with through-body stringing.
- *Also known as* ***ALBERT COLLINS SIGNATURE TELECASTER****.*
- *Custom Shop production.*

ALUMINUM-BODY TELECASTER 1994–95 *Anodised aluminium hollow-body option on* ***AMERICAN STANDARD TELECASTER*** *(see listing in earlier US Regular Models section).*

AMERICAN ASH TELECASTER 2003–07 *Five-screw pickguard, 22 frets.*

Similar to **AMERICAN TELECASTER** (see listing in earlier US Regular Models section), except:

- Fretted maple neck only.
- Body sunburst or blond.
- Five-screw white or black plastic pickguard.

AMERICAN CLASSIC TELECASTER first version 1995–99 *Three pickups (two white, one black), reversed control plate, five-way selector.*

Similar to AMERICAN STANDARD TELECASTER (see listing in earlier US Regular Models section), except:

- Two white six-polepiece pickups and one black six-polepiece pickup (angled at bridge).
- Two controls (volume, tone) and five-way selector (at rear), all on metal plate adjoining pickguard.
- Eight-screw white pearl or tortoiseshell laminated-plastic pickguard.

Gold-plated hardware option.

- *Custom Shop production.*

AMERICAN CLASSIC TELECASTER second version 1999–2000 *Two single-coils, reversed control plate, three-way selector.*

Similar to AMERICAN CLASSIC TELECASTER first version (see previous listing), except:

- One plain metal-cover pickup with visible height-adjustment screws (at neck) and one black six-polepiece pickup (angled at bridge).
- Two controls (volume, tone) and three-way selector (at rear), all on metal plate adjoining pickguard.
- Eight-screw white laminated-plastic pickguard.
- *Custom Shop production.*

AMERICAN DELUXE ASH TELECASTER 2004–current *Ash body, 22 frets, volume control with push-switch.*

Similar to AMERICAN DELUXE TELECASTER third version (see later listing), except:

- Fretted maple neck only.
- Unbound ash body; sunburst or blond.
- Eight-screw black plastic pickguard.

AMERICAN DELUXE POWER TELE 1999–2001 *Contoured bound body, two dual-concentric controls.*

Similar to AMERICAN DELUXE TELECASTER second version (see later listing), except:

- Two dual-concentric controls (volume, tone for magnetic and piezo pickups), three-way selector and mini-switch, all on metal plate adjoining pickguard.
- Fishman Power Bridge with six piezo-pickup saddles.

AMERICAN DELUXE TELECASTER first version 1998–99 *Contoured bound body, 22 frets, additional centre pickup.*

Similar to AMERICAN STANDARD TELECASTER (see listing in earlier US Regular Models section), except:

- Contoured single-cutaway bound body.
- One plain metal-cover pickup with visible height-adjustment screws (at neck), one white six-polepiece pickup (in centre), and one black six-polepiece pickup (angled at bridge).
- Two controls (volume, tone), five-way selector and mini-switch, all on metal plate adjoining pickguard.
- Eight-screw white or tortoiseshell laminated-plastic pickguard.

AMERICAN DELUXE TELECASTER second version 1999–2003 *Contoured bound body, 22 frets, two single-coils.*

Similar to AMERICAN DELUXE TELECASTER first version (see earlier listing), except:

- One plain metal-cover pickup with visible height-adjustment screws (at neck) and one black six-polepiece pickup (angled at bridge).
- Two controls (volume, tone) and three-way selector, all on metal plate adjoining pickguard.

AMERICAN DELUXE TELECASTER third version 2004–current *Contoured bound body, 22 frets, volume control with push-switch.*

Similar to AMERICAN DELUXE TELECASTER second version (see previous listing), except:

- One plain metal-cover pickup with visible height-adjustment screws (at neck) and one black six-polepiece pickup (angled at bridge).
- Two controls (volume with push-switch, tone) and three-way selector, all on metal plate adjoining pickguard.
- Eight-screw white or tortoiseshell laminated-plastic pickguard, or gold plastic pickguard.

AMERICAN DELUXE TELECASTER FMT 2004–06 *Figured top body, two humbuckers, no pickguard.*

- Maple neck with ebony fingerboard; 22 frets; truss-rod adjuster at headstock end; one string-guide.
- Body with figured top; sunburst or colours.
- Two black coverless humbuckers.
- Two controls (volume with push-switch, tone) and three-way selector, all on body; side-mounted output jack.
- No pickguard.
- Six-saddle small bridge with through-body stringing.

- *Also* ***AMERICAN DELUXE TELECASTER QMT****, with quilted maple top (2004–06).*

AMERICAN DELUXE TELECASTER QMT *See previous listing.*

AMERICAN FAT TELE *See later* ***U.S. FAT TELE*** *listing.*

AMERICAN NASHVILLE B-BENDER TELE 1998–current
Additional centre pickup, B-Bender string-bending device installed.
Similar to AMERICAN STANDARD B-BENDER TELECASTER (see later listing), except:
- One plain metal-cover pickup with visible height-adjustment screws (at neck), one white six-polepiece pickup (in centre) and one black six-polepiece pickup (angled at bridge).
- Two controls (volume, tone) and five-way selector, all on metal plate adjoining pickguard.
- Eight-screw white pearloid laminated-plastic pickguard.
- *Known as* ***NASHVILLE B-BENDER TELE*** *(1998–99).*

AMERICAN SPECIAL TELECASTER 2010–current *Three bridge-saddles, 22 frets.*
- Fretted maple neck; 22 frets; truss-rod adjuster at headstock end; one string-guide.
- Body sunburst or white.
- One plain metal-cover pickup (at neck) and one black six-polepiece pickup (angled at bridge).
- Two controls (volume, tone) and three-way selector, all on metal plate adjoining pickguard; side-mounted output jack.
- Eight-screw black laminated-plastic pickguard.
- Three-saddle raised-sides bridge with through-body stringing.

AMERICAN STANDARD B-BENDER TELECASTER 1995–97
Standard Tele pickup layout, 22 frets, B-Bender string-bending device installed.
Similar to AMERICAN STANDARD TELECASTER (see listing in earlier US Regular Models section), except:
- Fretted maple neck only.
- Factory-fitted B-Bender built-in bending device for 2nd string.

AMERICAN STANDARD TELECASTER *See listing in earlier US Regular models section.*

AMERICAN TELECASTER HH first version 2003–04 *Two black coverless humbuckers, no pickguard.*
Similar to AMERICAN TELECASTER HS first version (see later listing), except:
- Two black coverless humbuckers.
- Six-saddle small bridge with through-body stringing.

AMERICAN TELECASTER HH second version 2004–06 *Two black coverless humbuckers, black pickguard.*
Similar to AMERICAN TELECASTER HS second version (see later listing), except:
- Two black coverless humbuckers.
- Six-saddle small bridge with through-body stringing.

AMERICAN TELECASTER HS first version 2003–04 *Coverless black humbucker at neck, no pickguard.*
- Fretted maple neck, or maple neck with rosewood fingerboard; 22 frets; truss-rod adjuster at headstock end; one string-guide.
- Body various colours.
- One black coverless humbucker (at neck) and one black six-polepiece pickup (angled at bridge).
- Two controls (volume, tone) and three-way selector, all on metal plate; side-mounted output jack.
- No pickguard.
- Six-saddle flat bridge with through-body stringing.

AMERICAN TELECASTER HS second version 2004–06
Coverless black humbucker at neck, black pickguard.
Similar to AMERICAN TELECASTER HS first version (see previous listing), except:
- Two controls (volume with push-switch, tone) and three-way selector, all on metal plate.
- Eight-screw black plastic pickguard.

AMERICAN VINTAGE '52 TELECASTER 1982–84 and 1986–current *Replica of 1952-period original (see* ***TELECASTER*** *listing in earlier US Regular Models section). Also known as* ***VINTAGE '52 TELECASTER*** *(1982–87) and* ***US VINTAGE '52 TELECASTER*** *(1988–97).*

AMERICAN VINTAGE '62 CUSTOM TELECASTER
1999–current *Replica of 1962-period original (see Custom Telecaster in* ***TELECASTER*** *listing in earlier US Regular Models section).*

AMERICAN VINTAGE '69 TELECASTER THINLINE
2011–current *Replica of 1969-period original (see* ***THINLINE TELECASTER first version*** *listing in earlier US Regular Models section).*

AMERICAN VINTAGE '72 TELECASTER CUSTOM
2011–current *Replica of 1972-period original (see* ***TELECASTER CUSTOM*** *listing in earlier US Regular Models secrtion).*

AMERICAN VINTAGE '72 TELECASTER THINLINE
2011–current *Replica of 1972-period original (see* ***THINLINE TELECASTER second version*** *listing in earlier US Regular Models section).*

AMERICAN 60th ANNIVERSARY TELECASTER 2006
Commemorative neckplate, maple neck with rosewood fingerboard.
Similar to AMERICAN STANDARD TELECASTER (see listing in earlier US Regular Models section), except:
- Maple neck with rosewood fingerboard only; commemorative headstock logo with jewel inlay; commemorative neckplate.

ANTIGUA TELECASTER *See Antigua Telecaster in* ***TELECASTER*** *listing in earlier US Regular Models section.*

ANTIGUA TELECASTER CUSTOM *See* ***TELECASTER CUSTOM*** *listing in earlier US Regular Models section.*

ANTIGUA TELECASTER DELUXE *See* ***TELECASTER DELUXE*** *listing in earlier US Regular Models section.*

BAJO SEXTO TELECASTER 1992–98 *Model name on headstock, long-scale neck.*
- Fretted maple neck; 30.2-inch scale, 24 frets; truss-rod adjuster at body end; one string-guide; 'Bajo Sexto' on headstock.
- Body sunburst or blond.
- One plain metal-cover pickup (at neck) and one black six-polepiece pickup (angled at bridge).
- Two controls (volume, tone) and three-way selector, all on metal plate adjoining pickguard; side-mounted output jack.
- Five-screw black plastic pickguard.
- Three-saddle raised-sides bridge with through-body stringing.
- *Custom Shop production.*

B-BENDER TELECASTER *See earlier AMERICAN STANDARD B-BENDER TELECASTER listing.*

BENT TOP TELECASTER 2012 *Filter'Tron-style pickup at bridge, quilted maple top.*
Similar to CUSTOM DELUXE TELECASTER (see later listing), except:
- Body with figured maple-veneer top 'bent' over contour; sunburst only.
- One plain metal-cover pickup with visible height-adjustment screws (at neck) and one metal-cover humbucker with 12 screws (at bridge).
- Six-saddle flat bridge with through-body stringing.
- *Custom Shop production.*

BLACK & GOLD TELECASTER 1981–83 *Normal Tele pickup layout, 21 frets, black body, gold hardware.*
Similar to 1981-period TELECASTER (see listing in earlier US Regular Models section), except:
- Black-face headstock.
- Body black only.
- Black laminated-plastic pickguard.
- Six-saddle heavy-duty small bridge with through-body stringing.
- Gold-plated brass hardware.

BLUE FLOWER TELECASTER *See Blue Flower Telecaster in TELECASTER listing in earlier US Regular Models section.*

BOWLING BALL TELECASTER (also unofficially known as Marble Telecaster) *See TELECASTER STANDARD listing in earlier US Regular Models section.*

BROADCASTER *See Broadcaster in TELECASTER listing in earlier US Regular Models section.*

BROWN'S CANYON TELECASTER *See later TELE-BRATION SERIES listing.*

CABRONITA TELECASTER *See later TELE-BRATION SERIES listing.*

CALIFORNIA FAT TELE 1997–98 *'California Series' on headstock, one humbucker and one single-coil.*
- Fretted maple neck; truss-rod adjuster at headstock end; one string-guide; 'California Series' on headstock.
- Body sunburst or colours.
- One metal-cover six-polepiece humbucker (at neck) and one black six-polepiece pickup (angled at bridge).
- Two controls (volume, tone) and three-way selector, all on metal plate adjoining pickguard; side-mounted output jack.
- Eight-screw white laminated-plastic pickguard.
- Six-saddle raised-sides bridge with through-body stringing.

CALIFORNIA TELE 1997–98 *'California Series' on headstock, two single-coils.*
Similar to CALIFORNIA FAT TELE (see previous listing), except:
- Fretted maple neck, or maple neck with rosewood fingerboard.
- One white six-polepiece pickup (at neck) and one black six-polepiece pickup (angled at bridge).

CLARENCE WHITE TELECASTER 1993–2001 *Signature on headstock.*
- Fretted maple neck; truss-rod adjuster at body end; Scruggs Peg banjo-style de-tuners for 1st and 6th strings; Clarence White signature on headstock.
- Body sunburst only.
- One white six-polepiece pickup (at neck) and one black six-polepiece pickup (angled at bridge).
- Two controls (volume, tone) and three-way selector, all on metal plate adjoining pickguard; side-mounted output jack.
- Eight-screw tortoiseshell laminated-plastic pickguard.
- Three-saddle raised-sides bridge with through-body stringing; factory-fitted B-Bender built-in bending device for 2nd string.
- *Custom Shop production.*

CLASSIC S-1 TELECASTER 2009 *Aged finish, 22 frets, volume control with push-switch.*
- Fretted maple neck; 22 frets; truss-rod adjuster at body end; one string-guide.
- Body black or sunburst, available with two levels of aged finish: N.O.S. or Relic.
- One plain metal-cover pickup (at neck) and one black six-polepiece pickup (angled at bridge).
- Two controls (volume with push-switch, tone) and three-way selector, all on metal plate adjoining pickguard; side-mounted output jack.
- Eight-screw mint green laminated-plastic pickguard.
- Three-saddle raised-sides bridge with through-body stringing.
- *Custom Shop production.*

CLOSET CLASSIC PINE TELECASTER PRO *See later TELE PRO listing.*

CLOSET CLASSIC TELECASTER PRO *See later TELE PRO listing.*

CUSTOM CLASSIC TELECASTER 2000–08 *Two single-coils, reversed control plate, four-way selector.*
Similar to AMERICAN CLASSIC TELECASTER second version (see earlier listing), except:
- Two controls (volume, tone) and four-way selector (at rear), all on metal plate adjoining pickguard.
- *Custom Shop production.*

CUSTOM DELUXE TELECASTER 2009–current *Quilted-maple top.*

- Flame-maple neck with rosewood or maple fingerboard; 22 frets; truss-rod adjuster at headstock end; one string-guide; contoured heel.
- Body with figured maple-veneer top; sunbursts or red.
- One plain metal-cover pickup with visible height-adjustment screws (at neck) and one black six-polepiece pickup (angled at bridge).
- Two controls (volume, tone) and three-way selector, all on metal plate adjoining pickguard; side-mounted output jack.
- Eight-screw white plastic pickguard.
- *Custom Shop production.*

CUSTOM ESQUIRE *See Custom Esquire in* ESQUIRE *listing in earlier US Regular Models section.*

CUSTOM SHOP *Established in 1987, Fender's Custom Shop soon began producing a fixed catalogue of general models, which are noted in the main US listing and indicated as 'Custom Shop production', and from 2009 the line-up of models has changed annually. The Shop also makes limited-edition instruments, which over the years have variously been called Builder Select, Custom Team Built, Dealer Select, Limited Edition, Limited Release, Master Builder, Master Built, Master Design Limited Edition, Stock Team Built, Tribute Series, and probably more besides. These limited editions are clearly still big business, with the majority ordered by distributors or stores worldwide. Quantities of each item can range from tens to hundreds, and the number of models so far is considerable – making it impossible to identify and itemise all of them here, especially as Fender does not have complete records. Regardless of order size, all official Custom Shop instruments carry an identifying logo on the rear of the headstock. The logo was originally oval, and later it was amended to the current 'V' shape.*

CUSTOM TELECASTER *See Custom Telecaster in* TELECASTER *listing in earlier US Regular Models section.*

DANNY GATTON TELECASTER 1990–current *Signature on headstock.*

- Fretted maple neck; 22 frets; truss-rod adjuster at body end; one string-guide; Danny Gatton signature on headstock.
- Body blond or gold.
- Two black twin-blade pickups (bridge pickup angled).
- Two controls (volume, tone) and three-way selector, all on metal plate adjoining pickguard; side-mounted output jack.
- Five-screw cream plastic pickguard.
- Modified three-saddle raised-sides bridge with through-body stringing.
- *Also known as* DANNY GATTON SIGNATURE TELECASTER.
- *Custom Shop production.*

DELUXE TELECASTER PLUS *See later* TELECASTER PLUS *listing.*

ELITE TELECASTER 1983–84 *Two white plain-top pickups.*

- Fretted maple neck, or maple neck with rosewood fingerboard; truss-rod adjuster at headstock end; two string-guides.
- Bound body; sunburst or colours.
- Two white plain-top humbuckers.
- Four controls (two volume, two tone) and three-way selector, all on body; side-mounted output jack; active circuit.
- White laminated-plastic optional mini pickguard.
- Re-designed six-saddle bridge/tailpiece.
- *Also* GOLD ELITE TELECASTER, *with pearl tuner buttons and gold-plated hardware (1983–84).*
- *Also* WALNUT ELITE TELECASTER, *with walnut neck and ebony fingerboard, walnut body, pearl tuner buttons, and gold-plated hardware (1983–84).*

EMPRESS TELECASTER *See later* TELE-BRATION SERIES *listing.*

ESQUIRE *See* ESQUIRE *listing in earlier US Regular Models section.*

FLAME TOP TELECASTER *See later* TELE-BRATION SERIES *listing.*

FLAT HEAD TELECASTER 2003–04 *Name on headstock, 22 frets, one humbucker, single-cutaway body.*

- Maple neck with ebony fingerboard; 22 frets; truss-rod adjuster at headstock end; staggered height locking tuners; no position markers except crossed-pistons inlay at 12th fret; 'Flat Head' on headstock.
- Body various colours.
- One black coverless humbucker.
- One control (volume) on body; side-mounted output jack.
- No pickguard.
- Six-saddle small bridge with through-body stringing.
- Black-plated hardware.
- *Custom Shop production.*

FLAT HEAD TELECASTER HH 2004–06 *Name on headstock, 22 frets, two black plain-top humbuckers, single-cutaway body.*

Similar to FLAT HEAD TELECASTER (see previous listing), except:

- Two black plain-top active humbuckers.
- One control (volume) and three-way selector, both on body.
- *Custom Shop production.*

G.E. SMITH TELECASTER 2007–current *Various black position markers, cut-down bridge, body-mounted bridge pickup.*

- Fretted maple neck, various-pattern black position markers; truss-rod adjuster at body end; one string-guide.
- Body red or blond.
- One plain metal-cover pickup (at neck) and one black six-polepiece pickup (angled at bridge).
- Two controls (volume, tone) and three-way selector, all on metal plate adjoining pickguard; side-mounted output jack.
- Five-screw white or black plastic pickguard.
- Three-saddle raised-sides cut-down bridge with through-body stringing.

GOLD ELITE TELECASTER *See earlier* ELITE TELECASTER *listing.*

HIGHWAY ONE TELECASTER first version 2002–06 *Satin finish, 22 frets, five-screw pickguard.*

- Fretted maple neck, or maple neck with rosewood fingerboard; 22 frets; truss-rod adjuster at headstock end; one string-guide.
- Body sunburst or colours, satin finish.
- One plain metal-cover pickup (at neck) and one black six-polepiece pickup (angled at bridge).
- Two controls (volume, tone) and three-way selector, all on metal plate adjoining pickguard; side-mounted output jack.

- Five-screw white plastic pickguard.
- Three-saddle raised-sides bridge with through-body stringing.

HIGHWAY ONE TELECASTER second version 2006–11 *Satin finish, 22 frets, eight-screw pickguard.*
Similar to HIGHWAY ONE TELECASTER first version (see previous listing), except:
- Eight-screw white laminate plastic pickguard.

HIGHWAY ONE TEXAS TELECASTER 2003–09 *Satin finish, 21 frets.*
Similar to HIGHWAY ONE TELECASTER (see previous listing), except:
- Fretted maple neck only; 21 frets.
- Body sunburst or blond, satin finish.

INDIANA BARN '52 TELECASTER *See later TELE-BRATION SERIES listing.*

INTERNATIONAL COLOR TELECASTER *See International Color Telecaster in TELECASTER listing in earlier US Regular Models section.*

J5:BIGSBY *See later JOHN 5 BIGSBY SIGNATURE TELECASTER listing.*

J5:HB TELECASTER *See later JOHN 5 SIGNATURE TELECASTER listing.*

J5 TELECASTER *See later JOHN 5 SIGNATURE TELECASTER listing.*

JAMES BURTON TELECASTER first version 1990–2005 *Signature on headstock.*
- Fretted maple neck; truss-rod adjuster at body end; one string-guide; pearl tuner buttons; James Burton signature on headstock.
- Body black with gold or red paisley-pattern, red or white.
- Three black plain-top Lace Sensor pickups (bridge pickup angled).
- Two controls (volume, tone) and five-way selector, all on metal plate; side-mounted output jack.
- No pickguard.
- Six-saddle small bridge with through-body stringing.
- Black-plated or gold-plated hardware.

JAMES BURTON TELECASTER second version 2006–current
Similar to JAMES BURTON TELECASTER first version (see previous listing), except:
- Body black with blue or red paisley flame pattern, white.
- Three black plain-top pickups.

JERRY DONAHUE TELECASTER 1992–2001 *Signature on headstock.*
- Fretted maple neck; truss-rod adjuster at body end; one string-guide; Jerry Donahue signature on headstock.
- Body sunburst, blue, or red.
- Two black six-polepiece pickups (bridgeplate pickup angled).
- Two controls (volume, tone) and five-way selector, all on metal plate adjoining pickguard; side-mounted output jack.
- Five-screw black laminated-plastic pickguard.
- Three-saddle raised-sides bridge with through-body stringing.
- Gold-plated hardware.
- *Custom Shop production.*

JIM CAMPILONGO TELECASTER 2012–current *Signature on headstock rear, no through-body stringing.*
- Fretted maple neck; truss-rod adjuster at body end; one string-guide; signature on headstock rear.
- Body white blond only.
- One plain metal-cover pickup (at neck) and one black six-polepiece pickup (angled at bridge).
- Two controls (volume, tone) and three-way selector, all on metal plate adjoining pickguard.
- Five-screw white plastic pickguard.
- Three-saddle lipped-sides bridge without through-body stringing.
- *Custom Shop production.*

JIMMY BRYANT TELECASTER 2003–05 *Decorative tooled leather pickguard overlay.*
- Fretted maple neck; truss-rod adjuster at body end; one string-guide.
- Body blond only.
- One plain metal-cover pickup (at neck) and one black six-polepiece pickup (angled at bridge).
- Two controls (volume, tone) and three-way selector, all on metal plate adjoining pickguard; side-mounted output jack.
- Five-screw black plastic pickguard with decorative tooled leather overlay.
- Three-saddle raised-sides bridge with through-body stringing.
- *Custom Shop production.*

JOHN JORGENSON TELECASTER 1998–2001 *Signature on headstock.*
- Maple neck, rosewood or ebony fingerboard; 22 frets; truss-rod adjuster at headstock; no string-guide; John Jorgenson signature on headstock.
- Bound body; black or sparkle colours.
- Two plain metal-cover pickups (at neck) and two black six-polepiece pickups (angled at bridge).
- Two controls (volume, tone) and five-way selector, all on metal plate adjoining pickguard; side-mounted output jack.
- Eight-screw clear plastic pickguard.
- Three-saddle raised-sides bridge with through-body stringing.
- *Custom Shop production.*

JOHN 5 BIGSBY SIGNATURE TELECASTER 2003–current *Headstock with three tuners each side, Bigsby vibrato tailpiece.*
Similar to JOHN 5 SIGNATURE TELECASTER (see following listing), except:
- One plain metal-cover pickup with visible height-adjustment screws (at neck) and one black six-polepiece pickup (angled at bridge).
- Two controls (volume, tone) on metal plate adjoining pickguard.
- Six-saddle bridge, 'F'-logo Bigsby vibrato tailpiece.
- *Also known as J5:BIGSBY.*
- *Custom Shop production.*

JOHN 5 SIGNATURE TELECASTER 2003–current *Headstock with three tuners each side, humbucker at bridge.*
- Maple neck with rosewood fingerboard; 22 frets; truss-rod adjuster at headstock end; no string-guide; black-face three-tuners-each-side headstock.

- Bound body; black only.
- One plain metal-cover pickup with visible height-adjustment screws (at neck) and one black coverless humbucker (in bridgeplate).
- Two controls (both volume) on metal plate adjoining pickguard, three-way selector on body; side-mounted output jack.
- Eight-screw chromed pickguard.
- Six-saddle flat bridge with through-body stringing.
- *Also known as* J5 TELECASTER *and* J5:HB TELECASTER.
- *Custom Shop production.*

LAMBOO TELECASTER *See later TELE-BRATION SERIES listing.*

LITE ROSEWOOD TELECASTER *See later TELE-BRATION SERIES listing.*

MAHOGANY TELECASTER *See later TELE-BRATION SERIES listing.*

MARBLE TELECASTER (also unofficially known as Bowling Ball Telecaster) *See TELECASTER STANDARD listing in earlier US Regular Models section.*

MERLE HAGGARD SIGNATURE TELECASTER 1997–current *Signature on headstock.*

- Glued-in fretted maple neck; 22 frets; truss-rod adjuster at body end; one string-guide; pearl tuner buttons; 'Tuff Dog Tele' inlay and Merle Haggard signature on headstock.
- Semi-solid bound body; sunburst only.
- One plain metal-cover pickup (at neck) and one black six-polepiece pickup (angled at bridge).
- Two controls (volume, tone) and four-way selector, all on metal plate adjoining pickguard; side-mounted output jack.
- Seven-screw cream plastic re-styled pickguard.
- Six-saddle flat bridge with through-body stringing.
- Gold-plated hardware.
- *Custom Shop production.*
- *Catalogue name varies: Merle Haggard Tribute Tuff Dog Tele (1997–2000); Merle Haggard Tribute Tele (2001–2003); Merle Haggard Signature Telecaster (2004–current).*

MODERN THINLINE TELE *See later TELE-BRATION SERIES listing.*

NASHVILLE B-BENDER TELE *See earlier AMERICAN NASHVILLE B-BENDER TELE listing.*

NOCASTER *See TELECASTER in earlier US Regular Models section.*

PAISLEY RED TELECASTER *See Paisley Red Telecaster in TELECASTER listing in earlier US Regular Models section.*

RELIC BIGSBY TELECASTER 2011 *Blue body, Bigsby vibrato.*

- Fretted maple neck; truss-rod adjuster at body end; one string-guide.
- Body blue aged Relic finish only.
- One plain metal-cover pickup (at neck) and one black six-polepiece pickup (angled at bridge).
- Two controls (volume, tone) and three-way selector, all on metal plate adjoining pickguard; side-mounted output jack.
- Eight-screw white laminated-plastic pickguard.
- Six-saddle bridge, 'F'-logo Bigsby vibrato tailpiece.
- *Custom Shop production.*

RELIC PINSTRIPE ESQUIRE 2012 *Pinstriping decoration on body.*
Similar to 50s-period **ESQUIRE** (see listing in earlier US Regular Models section), except:

- Body white blond with custom pinstriping.
- *Custom Shop production.*

ROSEWOOD TELECASTER *See Rosewood Telecaster in TELECASTER listing in earlier US Regular Models section, and Lite Rosewood Telecaster in later TELE-BRATION listing.*

SELECT CARVED KOA TOP TELECASTER 2012–current *Bound body with carved figured-koa top, no pickguard.*
Similar to **SELECT CARVED MAPLE TOP TELECASTER** (see following listing), except:

- Figured maple neck with rosewood fingerboard.
- Bound contoured body with carved figured koa top; sunburst only.

SELECT CARVED MAPLE TOP TELECASTER 2012–current *Bound body with carved flame-maple top, no pickguard.*
Similar to **SELECT TELECASTER** (see following listing), except:

- Bound contoured body with carved figured maple top; amber only.
- No pickguard.
- Hardware nickel/chrome only.

SELECT TELECASTER 2012–current *Semi-solid bound body with flame-maple top.*

- Figured maple neck with figured maple fingerboard; 22 frets; truss-rod adjuster at headstock end; one string-guide; 'Fender Select' logo on headstock rear.
- Semi-solid bound contoured body with figured maple top; sunburst only.
- One plain metal-cover pickup with visible height-adjustment screws (at neck) and one black six-polepiece pickup (angled at bridge).
- Two controls (volume, tone) and three-way selector, all on metal plate adjoining pickguard.
- Eight-screw white laminated-plastic pickguard.
- Six-saddle flat bridge with through-body stringing.
- Gold-plated hardware option.

SET NECK TELECASTER 1991–95 *Two coverless humbuckers, glued-in neck.*

- Mahogany glued-in neck with rosewood fingerboard (pao ferro from 1993); 22 frets; truss-rod adjuster at headstock end; two string-guides; neck and headstock face match body colour.
- Semi-solid bound body; various colours.
- Two black coverless humbuckers.
- Two controls (volume, tone), three-way selector and coil-tap, all on body; side-mounted output jack.
- No pickguard.
- Six-saddle small bridge with through-body stringing.
- *Custom Shop production.*

SET NECK TELECASTER COUNTRY ARTIST 1992–95 *One humbucker and one single-coil, glued-in neck.*
Similar to SET NECK TELECASTER (see previous listing), except:
- One black coverless humbucker (at neck) and one black six-polepiece pickup (angled at bridge).
- Five-screw tortoiseshell laminated-plastic small pickguard.
- Six-saddle flat bridge with through-body stringing.
- Gold-plated hardware.
- *Custom Shop production.*

SET NECK TELECASTER FLOYD ROSE 1991–92 *Two coverless humbuckers and one single-coil, glued-in neck, locking vibrato system.*
Similar to SET NECK TELECASTER (see earlier listing), except:
- Ebony fingerboard; locking nut.
- Two black coverless humbuckers and one black six-polepiece pickup (in centre).
- Two controls (volume, tone), five-way selector and coil-tap, all on body; side-mounted output jack.
- Twin-pivot locking bridge/vibrato unit.
- *Custom Shop production.*

SET NECK TELECASTER PLUS 1991–92 *Two coverless humbuckers, glued-in neck, vibrato.*
Similar to SET NECK TELECASTER (see earlier listing), except:
- Ebony fingerboard; locking tuners; roller nut.
- Twin-pivot bridge/vibrato unit.
- *Custom Shop production.*

SEYMOUR DUNCAN SIGNATURE ESQUIRE 2003–08 *Signature on headstock.*
- Fretted maple neck; truss-rod adjuster at body end; one string-guide; Seymour Duncan signature on headstock.
- Body sunburst only.
- One black six-polepiece pickup (angled at bridge).
- Two controls (volume, tone) and three-way selector, all on metal plate adjoining pickguard; side-mounted output jack.
- Five-screw white plastic pickguard.
- Three-saddle bridge with through-body stringing.
- *Custom Shop production.*

SPARKLE TELECASTER 1992–95 *Coloured sparkle finish on body.*
- Fretted maple neck, or maple neck with rosewood fingerboard; truss-rod adjuster at body end; one string-guide.
- Body sparkle colours.
- One plain metal-cover pickup (at neck) and one black six-polepiece pickup (angled at bridge).
- Two controls (volume, tone) and three-way selector, all on metal plate adjoining pickguard; side-mounted output jack.
- Eight-screw white laminated-plastic pickguard.
- Three-saddle raised-sides bridge with through-body stringing.
- *Custom Shop production.*

SPECIAL EDITION 1994 TELECASTER 1994 *Commemorative neckplate.*
Similar to AMERICAN STANDARD TELECASTER (see listing in earlier US Regular Models section), except:
- Body black or blond; commemorative neckplate.
- Eight-screw grey pearl or tortoiseshell laminated-plastic pickguard.

SUB-SONIC TELE baritone 2001–05 *'Sub-Sonic' on headstock, long-scale neck.*
- Fretted maple neck; 27-inch scale, 22 frets; truss-rod adjuster at body end; one string-guide; 'Sub-Sonic' on headstock.
- Body sunburst or colours.
- One plain metal cover pickup (at neck) and one black six-polepiece pickup (angled at bridge).
- Two controls (volume, tone) and four-way selector, all on metal plate adjoining pickguard; side-mounted output jack.
- Eight-screw white laminated-plastic pickguard.
- Six-saddle bridge with through-body stringing.
- *Custom Shop production.*

TELE JNR 1995–2000 *Two large black rectangular pickups.*
- Mahogany glued-in neck with pao ferro fingerboard; 22 frets; truss-rod adjuster at headstock end; one string-guide; neck and headstock face match body colour.
- Semi-solid body; sunburst or colours.
- Two large black six-polepiece pickups.
- Two controls (volume, tone) and three-way selector (at rear), all on metal plate adjoining pickguard; side-mounted output jack.
- Small tortoiseshell plastic, or white pearl, tortoiseshell or black laminated-plastic pickguard.
- Six-saddle small bridge with through-body stringing.
- *Custom Shop production.*

TELE PLUS first version 1990–95 *Three Lace Sensor pickups (two at bridge).*
- Fretted maple neck or maple neck with rosewood fingerboard; 22 frets; truss-rod adjuster at headstock end; one string-guide.
- Body sunburst or colours.
- Three black plain-top Lace Sensor pickups (two in single separate surround at bridge).
- Two controls (volume, tone), three-way selector and coil-switch, all on metal plate adjoining pickguard; side-mounted output jack.
- Eight-screw white laminated-plastic pickguard.
- Six-saddle small bridge with through-body stringing.

TELE PLUS second version 1995–98 *Three Lace Sensor pickups (one angled at bridge).*
- Fretted maple neck or maple neck with rosewood fingerboard; 22 frets; truss-rod adjuster at headstock end; one string-guide.
- Bound body; sunburst or colours.
- Three plain-top Lace Sensor pickups (bridgeplate pickup angled).
- Two controls (volume, tone) and three-way selector, all on metal plate adjoining pickguard; side-mounted output jack.
- Eight-screw white pearl or tortoiseshell laminated-plastic pickguard.
- Six-saddle flat bridge with through-body stringing.

TELE PLUS DELUXE 1991–92 *Three Lace Sensor pickups (two at bridge), vibrato.*
Similar to TELE PLUS first version (see earlier listing), except:
- No string-guide; locking tuners; roller nut.
- Twin-pivot bridge/vibrato unit.

TELE PRO 2007–08 *Five-screw pickguard, 22 frets, four-way selector.*
- Fretted maple neck, or maple neck with rosewood fingerboard; 22 frets; truss-rod adjuster at headstock end; one string-guide.
- Body black or blond.
- One plain metal-cover pickup (at neck) and one black six-polepiece pickup (angled at bridge).
- Two controls (volume, tone) and four-way selector, all on metal plate adjoining pickguard; side-mounted output jack.
- Five-screw white plastic pickguard.
- Three-saddle raised-sides bridge with through-body stringing.
- *Custom Shop production.*
- *Also* ***TELE PRO RELIC*** *with aged Relic finish in sunburst, white, or blue (2009). Custom Shop Production.*
- *Also* ***TELECASTER PRO RELIC*** *with aged Relic finish in blond, black, or white (2010). Custom Shop production.*
- *Also* ***CLOSET CLASSIC PINE TELECASTER PRO*** *with aged 100-year-old pine body in blond, black, or copper, three-way selector (2011). Custom Shop production.*
- *Also* ***CLOSET CLASSIC TELECASTER PRO*** *with aged body various colours, three-way selector, flat bridge (2012). Custom Shop production.*

TELE THINLINE 2006–08 *F-hole body, two single-coils, 12-screw white or black pickguard.*
- Fretted maple neck; truss-rod adjuster at body end; one string-guide.
- Semi-solid body with f-hole; black or blond, available with three levels of aged finish: N.O.S., Closet Classic, and Relic.
- One plain metal-cover pickup (at neck) and one black six-polepiece pickup (angled at bridge).
- Two controls (volume, tone) and three-way selector, all on pickguard; side-mounted output jack.
- 12-screw white or black plastic pickguard.
- Three-saddle raised-sides bridge with through-body stringing.
- *Custom Shop production.*

TELE-BRATION SERIES 2011 *Twelve models celebrating Telecaster's 60th anniversary; limited run 500 each; commemorative neckplate.*
BROWN'S CANYON TELECASTER *Oiled redwood body from 1890s California railway bridge.*
CABRONITA TELECASTER *Two TV Jones Filter'Tron pickups, single control and selector, two-tone sunburst or black.*
EMPRESS TELECASTER *Lightweight empress-wood body, sunburst or white.*
FLAME TOP TELECASTER *Figured maple top, gold hardware.*
INDIANA BARN '52 TELECASTER *Ancient pine body from Indiana barn, oiled white finish.*
LAMBOO TELECASTER *Laminated bamboo natural body with brown binding, bamboo neck, shell pickguard.*
LITE ROSEWOOD TELECASTER *Spruce-core rosewood body.*
MAHOGANY TELECASTER *Natural oiled mahogany body, bamboo board, humbucker at bridge.*
MODERN THINLINE TELE *White f-hole body, regular pickups.*
VINTAGE HOT ROD '52 TELECASTER *As the regular version.*
'62 TELECASTER CUSTOM *White body with black binding, pearl-block inlays.*
'75 TELECASTER *70s Custom look with natural body, black block markers on maple board.*

TELECASTER CUSTOM *See* ***TELECASTER CUSTOM*** *listing in earlier US Regular Models section.*

TELECASTER DELUXE *See* ***TELECASTER DELUXE*** *listing in earlier US Regular Models section.*

TELECASTER PRO RELIC *See earlier* ***TELE PRO*** *listing.*

TELECASTER XII 12-string 1995–98 *Model name on 12-string headstock.*
- Fretted maple neck, or maple neck with rosewood fingerboard; truss-rod adjuster at headstock end; one bracket-style string-guide; six-tuners-each-side headstock.
- Body sunburst or colours.
- One plain metal-cover pickup (at neck) and one black six-polepiece pickup (angled at bridge).
- Two controls (volume, tone) and three-way selector, all on metal plate adjoining pickguard; side-mounted output jack.
- Five-screw black or white plastic, or white pearl laminated-plastic pickguard.
- Twelve-saddle bridge with through-body stringing.
- *Custom Shop production.*

TELE-SONIC 1998–2004 *Model name on headstock.*
- Maple neck with rosewood fingerboard, 24.75-inch scale, 22 frets; truss-rod adjuster at headstock end; one string-guide; black-face headstock.
- Semi-solid body; sunburst or red.
- Two black-top six-polepiece pickups.
- Four controls (two volume, two tone) and three-way selector, all on body; side-mounted output jack.
- Six-screw black laminated-plastic pickguard.
- Two-section wrapover bridge/tailpiece (six-saddle wrapover bridge/tailpiece from 2003).

THINLINE TELECASTER *See* ***THINLINE TELECASTER first version*** *and* ***THINLINE TELECASTER second version*** *in earlier US Regular models section.*

U.S. FAT TELE 1998–2000 *One humbucker and one single-coil, five-way selector.*
Similar to AMERICAN STANDARD TELECASTER (see listing in earlier US Regular Models section), except:
- One metal-cover humbucker (at neck) and one black six-polepiece pickup (angled at bridge).
- Two controls (volume, tone) and four-way selector, all on metal plate adjoining pickguard.
- *Known as* ***AMERICAN FAT TELE*** *(2001–03).*

VINTAGE HOT ROD '52 TELE 2007–current *Metal-cover small humbucker at neck.*
Similar to AMERICAN VINTAGE '52 TELECASTER (see earlier listing), except:
- One plain metal-cover small humbucker (at neck) and one black six-polepiece pickup (angled at bridge).
- *See also* ***TELE-BRATION SERIES*** *listing (left).*

WALNUT ELITE TELECASTER *See earlier* ***ELITE TELECASTER*** *listing.*

WAYLON JENNINGS TRIBUTE TELECASTER 1995–2003
Signature on headstock.
- Fretted maple neck; truss-rod adjuster at body end; one string-guide; pearl tuner buttons; Scruggs Peg banjo-style de-tuner for 6th string; 'W' inlay at 12th fret and Waylon Jennings signature on headstock.
- Bound body; black only with white leather inlay.
- One plain metal-cover pickup with visible height-adjustment screws (at neck) and one black six-polepiece pickup (angled at bridge).
- Two controls (volume, tone) and three-way selector, all on metal plate adjoining pickguard; side-mounted output jack.
- Eight-screw white laminated-plastic pickguard.
- Six-saddle flat bridge with through-body stringing.
- *Custom Shop production.*

WILL RAY TELECASTER 1998–2001 *Signature on headstock, skull markers.*
- Maple neck with rosewood fingerboard, skull markers; 22 frets; truss-rod adjuster at headstock end; one string-guide; locking tuners; Will Ray signature on small Stratocaster-style headstock.
- Body gold foil leaf on various colours.
- Two large rectangular white six-polepiece pickups (bridge pickup angled).
- Three controls (volume, two tone) and three-way selector, all on metal plate adjoining pickguard; side-mounted output jack.
- Eight-screw white pearl laminated-plastic re-styled pickguard.
- Modified three-saddle bridge with through-body stringing; optional Hipshot bending device for 2nd string.
- *Custom Shop production.*

'51 NOCASTER *See listing in earlier US Replica Models section.*

'52 TELECASTER *See earlier* ***AMERICAN VINTAGE '52 TELECASTER*** *listing.*

'52 TELECASTER HB 2010 *Metal-cover humbucker at neck, black pickguard.*
Similar to AMERICAN VINTAGE '52 TELECASTER (see earlier listing), except:
- Body with aged Relic sunburst or blond finish.
- One six-polepiece metal-cover humbucker (at neck) and one black six-polepiece pickup (angled at bridge).
- Five-screw black pickguard.
- *Custom Shop production.*

'59 ESQUIRE *See listing in earlier US Replica Models section.*

50s TELECASTER THINLINE 2009 *Aged-finish replica of late-60s-period original with 50s vibe (see* ***THINLINE TELECASTER first version*** *listing in earlier US Regular Models section). Available with two levels of aged finish: N.O.S. or Relic. Custom Shop production.*

50th ANNIVERSARY TELECASTER 1996 *Commemorative neckplate.*
Similar to AMERICAN STANDARD TELECASTER (see listing in earlier US Regular Models section), except:
- Fretted maple neck only; commemorative neckplate.
- Body sunburst only.
- Gold-plated hardware.
- *Numbered factory production run of 1,250.*

'62 CUSTOM TELECASTER *See earlier* ***AMERICAN VINTAGE '62 CUSTOM TELECASTER*** *listing.*

'62 TELECASTER CUSTOM *See earlier* ***TELE-BRATION SERIES*** *listing.*

'69 RELIC TELECASTER THINLINE 2011 *Aged-finish replica of 1969-period original (see* ***THINLINE TELECASTER first version*** *listing in earlier US Regular Models section). Custom Shop production.*

'69 TELECASTER THINLINE *See earlier* ***AMERICAN VINTAGE '69 TELECASTER THINLINE*** *listing.*

60th ANNIVERSARY TELECASTER 2011 *Commemorative neckplate.*
Similar to AMERICAN STANDARD TELECASTER (see listing in earlier US Regular Models section), except:
- Fretted maple neck only; commemorative neckplate.
- Body blond only.
- Eight-screw black laminated-plastic pickguard.
- *See also earlier* ***TELE-BRATION SERIES*** *listing.*
- *See also earlier* ***AMERICAN 60th ANNIVERSARY TELECASTER*** *listing.*
- *Note that almost all regular US-made Telecaster models produced during 2011 also have a 60th anniversary neckplate.*

'72 TELECASTER CUSTOM *See earlier* ***AMERICAN VINTAGE '72 TELECASTER CUSTOM*** *listing.*

'72 TELECASTER THINLINE *See earlier* ***AMERICAN VINTAGE '72 TELECASTER THINLINE*** *listing.*

'75 TELECASTER *See earlier* ***TELE-BRATION SERIES*** *listing.*

'98 COLLECTORS EDITION TELECASTER 1998
Commemorative fingerboard inlay and neckplate.
Similar to 50s TELECASTER (see listing in earlier Replica Telecasters section), except:
- Fretted maple neck with commemorative inlay at 12th fret; commemorative neckplate.
- Body sunburst only.
- Five-screw white plastic pickguard.
- Gold-plated hardware.
- *Numbered factory production run of 1,998.*

90s TELE THINLINE 1997–2000 *F-hole body, 22 frets.*
- Fretted maple neck, or maple neck with rosewood fingerboard; 22 frets; truss-rod adjuster at headstock end; one string-guide.
- Semi-solid bound body with f-hole; sunburst or colours.
- One plain metal-cover pickup with visible height-adjustment screws (at neck) and one black six-polepiece pickup (angled at bridge).
- Two controls (volume, tone) and three-way selector, all on pickguard; side-mounted output jack.
- 12-screw white pearl or tortoiseshell laminated-plastic pickguard.
- Six-saddle flat bridge with through-body stringing.

JAPANESE MODELS

This section lists only the models marketed outside of Japan, all of which have 'Made In Japan' or 'Crafted in Japan' somewhere on the instrument. It does not cover the guitars produced solely for the Japanese market, which include numerous interpretations of Fender's established designs and many combinations of construction, components, and cosmetics.

The periods of availability for models sold in Japan often differ greatly to those of the same models officially sold outside Japan. These export models, listed here, often appear to come and go in the line, usually because demand from a particular distributor fluctuates. For that reason, certain Japanese models are irregularly removed from and then replaced in Fender's catalogues in the USA and Europe – while manufacture of the model in Japan might well remain continuous.

This interrupted availability is confusing, from a Western point of view, and makes it difficult to accurately pin down the true periods of production. We have reflected this in the listing here, where relevant, by simply showing a start date followed by 'onward'.

Japanese-made models are divided into two sections: Japanese Replica Models; and Japanese Revised Models.

Japanese Replica Models

Listed here in alphabetical order are the Japanese-made models, offered for sale outside Japan, that we regard as replicas of various standard-version US-made Regular Telecasters and Esquires (see earlier US Regular Models section).

ANTIGUA TELECASTER 2004 *Replica of 1977-period US original with white/brown shaded body finish and matching pickguard (see* ***TELECASTER*** *listing in earlier US Regular Models section).*

BLUE FLOWER TELECASTER 1986–onward *Replica of 1969-period US original with blue floral pattern-finish body (see* ***TELECASTER*** *listing in earlier US Regular Models section).*

CUSTOM ESQUIRE 1986–onward *Replica of 1962-period US original with bound body (see* ***ESQUIRE*** *listing in earlier US Regular Models section).*

CUSTOM TELECASTER '62 1985–onward *Replica of 1962-period US original with bound-body (see* ***TELECASTER*** *listing in earlier US Regular Models section). Foto Flame fake figured wood finish option (1994–96).*

ESQUIRE 1986–onward *Replica of 1954-period US original (see* ***ESQUIRE*** *listing in earlier US Regular Models section).*

PAISLEY TELECASTER 1986–onward *Replica of 1969-period US original with paisley-pattern body finish (see* ***TELECASTER*** *listing in earlier US Regular Models section).*

ROSEWOOD TELECASTER 1986–onward *Replica of 1969-period US original with rosewood neck and body (see* ***TELECASTER*** *listing in earlier US Regular Models section).*

TELECASTER CUSTOM '72 1986–onward *Replica of 1972-period US original with humbucker and single-coil (see* ***TELECASTER CUSTOM*** *listing in earlier US Regular Models section).*

THINLINE TELECASTER '69 1986–onward *Replica of 1969-period US original with two single-coils (see* ***THINLINE TELECASTER first version*** *listing in earlier US Regular Models section).*

THINLINE TELECASTER '72 1986–onward *Replica of 1972-period US original with two humbuckers (see* ***THINLINE TELECASTER second version*** *listing in earlier US Regular Models section).*

50s TELECASTER 1990–onward *Replica of 1952-period US original (see* ***TELECASTER*** *listing in earlier US Regular Models section). Previously known in UK as* ***SQUIER SERIES '52 TELECASTER****, with small 'Squier Series' logo on headstock (1982). Sold under actual Squier brandname (1983–84) and new Fender version introduced in 1990, although Japanese-market manufacture continuous since 1982. Foto Flame fake-figured-wood-finish option (1994).*

Japanese Revised Models

Listed here in alphabetical order are the Japanese-made models, offered for sale outside Japan, that we regard as revised and adapted versions of the standard-version US-made Regular Telecasters (see earlier US Regular Models section).

AERODYNE TELE 2004–06 *'Aerodyne Series' on headstock, two pickups.*

- Maple neck with rosewood fingerboard; 22 frets; truss-rod adjuster at headstock end; one string guide; 'Aerodyne Series' on black-face headstock.
- Bound body with carved top; black only.
- One large black rectangular six-polepiece pickup (at neck) and one black six-polepiece pickup (angled at bridge).
- Two controls (volume, tone) and three-way selector, all on body; side-mounted output jack.
- No pickguard.
- Six-saddle flat bridge with through-body stringing.

BUCK OWENS TELECASTER 1998 *Signature on headstock, red-silver-and-blue sparkle striped body front.*

- Maple neck with rosewood fingerboard; truss-rod adjuster at body end; one string-guide; red-silver-and-blue sparkle striped headstock face; Buck Owens signature on headstock.
- Bound body; red-silver-and-blue sparkle striped front.
- One plain metal-cover pickup (at neck) and one black six-polepiece pickup (angled at bridge).
- Two controls (volume, tone) and three-way selector, all on metal plate adjoining pickguard; side-mounted output jack.
- Eight-screw gold pickguard.
- Three-saddle raised-sides bridge with through-body stringing.
- Gold-plated hardware.

CONTEMPORARY TELECASTER first type 1985–87 *Black neck, two humbuckers.*

- Maple neck with rosewood fingerboard; 22 frets; truss-rod adjuster at headstock end; string clamp; black neck.
- Body various colours.
- Two black coverless humbuckers.
- Two controls (volume, tone), three-way selector and coil-switch, all on body; side-mounted output jack.

- No pickguard.
- Two-pivot bridge/vibrato unit.
- Black-plated hardware.

CONTEMPORARY TELECASTER second type 1985–87 *Black neck, two single-coils and one humbucker.*
Similar to CONTEMPORARY TELECASTER first type (see previous listing), except:
- Two black six-polepiece pickups and one black coverless humbucker (at bridge).
- Two controls (volume, tone) and three mini-switches, all on body.

FOTO FLAME TELECASTER 1995–96 *Fake figured wood finish on neck and body; two single-coils.*
Similar to 60s TELECASTER (see later listing), except:
- Foto Flame fake-figured-wood-finish body; sunbursts or natural.

FRANCIS ROSSI SIGNATURE TELECASTER 2003–04
Signature on headstock.
- Fretted maple neck; truss-rod adjuster at body end; one string-guide; Francis Rossi signature on headstock.
- Body with circular hole; black with green front only, satin finish.
- Three white plain-top pickups (bridge pickup angled in cut-down bridgeplate).
- Two controls (volume, tone) and five-way selector, all on metal plate adjoining pickguard; side-mounted output jack.
- Eight-screw white laminated-plastic pickguard.
- Six-saddle small bridge with through-body stringing.

HMT ACOUSTIC-ELECTRIC first version 1991–94 *Stratocaster-style headstock, wooden-base bridge.*
- Maple neck with rosewood fingerboard; 25-inch scale, 22 frets; truss-rod adjuster at headstock end; one string-guide; Stratocaster-style black-face headstock.
- Larger semi-solid bound body with f-hole; sunburst or colours.
- One black plain-top Lace Sensor (angled at neck) and piezo pickup (in bridge).
- Three controls (volume, tone, pan) all on body; side-mounted output jack; active circuit.
- No pickguard.
- Single-saddle wooden-base bridge.

HMT ACOUSTIC-ELECTRIC second version 1995–97
Telecaster headstock, wooden-base bridge.
Similar to HMT ACOUSTIC-ELECTRIC first version (see previous entry), except:
- Telecaster headstock.
- Body sunburst or black.
- One black plain-top pickup (angled at neck) and piezo pickup (in bridge).

HMT TELECASTER first type 1991–92 *Stratocaster-style headstock, f-hole body, two humbuckers.*
- Maple neck with rosewood fingerboard; 25-inch scale, 22 frets; truss-rod adjuster at headstock end; Stratocaster-style black-face headstock.
- Larger semi-solid bound body with f-hole; sunburst or colours.
- Two black coverless humbuckers.
- Two controls (volume, tone), three-way selector, and coil-switch, all on body; side-mounted output jack.
- No pickguard.
- Six-saddle small bridge with through-body stringing.

HMT TELECASTER second type 1991–92 *Drooped headstock with long streamlined-style Fender logo, f-hole body, angled Lace Sensor and humbucker.*
Similar to HMT TELECASTER first version (see previous listing), except:
- Split-triangle markers; locking nut; long streamlined-style Fender logo on drooped black-face headstock.
- One black plain-top Lace Sensor pickup (angled at neck) and one black coverless humbucker (at bridge).
- Two-pivot locking bridge/vibrato unit.

J.D. TELECASTER 1992–99 *'JD' on headstock, black six-polepiece pickup at neck.*
- Fretted maple neck; truss-rod adjuster at body end; one string-guide; Jerry Donahue initials on headstock.
- Bound body; sunburst or colours.
- Two black six-polepiece pickups (bridgeplate pickup angled).
- Two controls (volume, tone) and five-way selector, all on metal plate adjoining pickguard; side-mounted output jack.
- Eight-screw black laminated-plastic pickguard.
- Three-saddle raised-sides bridge with through-body stringing.
- *Based on signature model of US Custom Shop.*

NOKIE EDWARDS TELECASTER 1996 *Signature on headstock, two twin-blade humbuckers.*
- Maple neck with ebony fingerboard; 22 frets; truss-rod adjuster at body end; brass nut; optional Scruggs Peg banjo-style de-tuner for 6th string; Nokie Edwards signature on headstock.
- Body with figured front; natural only.
- Two black twin-blade humbuckers.
- Two controls (volume, tone) and three-way selector, all on body; side-mounted output jack.
- No pickguard.
- Six-saddle small bridge with through-body stringing.
- Gold-plated hardware.
- *Optional Nokie Edwards logo for body.*

RICHIE KOTZEN SIGNATURE TELECASTER 2005–06
Signature on headstock.
- Fretted maple neck; truss-rod adjuster at headstock end; one string-guide; Richie Kotzen signature on headstock.
- Contoured bound body; sunburst or green.
- One plain metal-cover pickup with visible height-adjustment screws (at neck) and one black twin-blade humbucker (angled at bridge).
- One control (volume), pickup-mode rotary switch and three-way selector, all on metal plate adjoining pickguard; side-mounted output jack.
- Eight-screw white plastic or white pearl laminated-plastic pickguard.
- Six-saddle flat bridge with through-body stringing.
- Gold-plated hardware.

RICK PARFITT SIGNATURE TELECASTER 2003–04 *Signature on headstock.*
- Maple neck with rosewood fingerboard; truss-rod adjuster at body end; one string-guide; Rick Parfitt signature on headstock.
- Body white only, satin finish.
- One plain metal-cover pickup (at neck) and one black six-polepiece pickup (angled in cut-down bridgeplate).
- Two controls (volume, tone) and three-way selector, all on metal plate adjoining pickguard; side-mounted output jack.
- Eight-screw black plastic pickguard.
- Four-saddle wrapover bridge/tailpiece with through-body stringing.
- Some hardware gold-plated.

SPECIAL TELECASTER *UK designation for STANDARD TELECASTER (see later listing).*

SQUIER SERIES '52 TELECASTER *See earlier 50s TELECASTER listing in Japanese Replica Models section.*

STANDARD TELECASTER 1988–91 *Two string-guides, five-screw pickguard, six-saddle bridge/tailpiece with no through-body stringing.*
- Fretted maple neck; truss-rod adjuster at body end; two string-guides.
- Body black or blond.
- One plain metal cover pickup (at neck) and one black six-polepiece pickup (angled at bridge).
- Two controls (volume, tone) and three-way selector, all on metal plate adjoining pickguard; side-mounted output jack.
- Five-screw white plastic pickguard.
- Six-saddle flat bridge/tailpiece with no through-body stringing.
- *Previously marketed under the Squier brandname (1985–88). Production moved to Mexico from 1991 (see STANDARD TELECASTER listing in later Mexican Revised Models section). Known as SPECIAL TELECASTER in UK.*

WILL RAY JAZZ-A-CASTER 1997–98 *Signature and model name on headstock, two large white pickups.*
- Maple neck with rosewood fingerboard, triangle markers; 22 frets; truss-rod adjuster at headstock end; one string guide; locking tuners; 'Hellecasters' inlay at 12th fret; Will Ray signature on small Stratocaster-style headstock.
- Body gold foil leaf only.
- Two large white rectangular six-polepiece pickups (bridge pickup angled).
- Two controls (volume, tone) and four-way selector, all on metal plate adjoining pickguard; side-mounted output jack.
- Eight-screw white pearl laminated-plastic pickguard.
- Modified six-saddle bridge with through-body stringing; Hipshot bending device for 2nd string.

50s TELECASTER WITH BIGSBY 2005–06 *Fretted maple neck, 'F'-logo Bigsby vibrato tailpiece*
Similar to **50s TELECASTER** (see listing in earlier Japanese Replica Models section), except:
- Body natural or blond.
- Six-saddle bridge, 'F'-logo Bigsby vibrato tailpiece.

60s TELECASTER 1994 *Fake figured wood finish on neck and body, two single-coils.*
- Foto flame fake-figured-wood-finish neck with rosewood fingerboard; truss-rod adjuster at body end; one string-guide.
- Foto Flame fake-figured-wood-finish body; natural only.
- One plain metal-cover pickup (at neck) and one black six-polepiece pickup (angled at bridge).
- Two controls (volume, tone) and three-way selector, all on metal plate adjoining pickguard; side-mounted output jack.
- Eight-screw white or white pearl laminated-plastic pickguard.
- Three-saddle raised-sides bridge with through-body stringing.
- *Known as FOTO FLAME TELECASTER (1995–96); see earlier listing.*

60s TELECASTER WITH BIGSBY 2005–09 *Bound body, rosewood fingerboard, 'F'-logo Bigsby vibrato tailpiece.*
Similar to **60s TELECASTER** (see previous listing), except:
- Bound body; sunburst or red.?
- Six-saddle bridge, 'F'-logo Bigsby vibrato tailpiece.

90s TELECASTER CUSTOM 1995–98 *Black or white bound body with matching headstock face, pearl pickguard, gold-plated hardware.*
- Maple neck with rosewood fingerboard; truss-rod adjuster at body end; one string-guide; black or white-face headstock.
- Bound body; black or white.
- One plain metal-cover pickup (at neck) and one black six-polepiece pickup (angled at bridge).
- Two controls (volume, tone) and three-way selector, all on metal plate adjoining pickguard; side-mounted output jack.
- Eight-screw grey or white pearl laminated-plastic pickguard.
- Six-saddle flat bridge with through-body stringing.
- Gold-plated hardware.

90s TELECASTER DELUXE 1995–98 *Contoured body, three six-polepiece pickups, reversed control plate.*
- Maple neck with rosewood fingerboard; truss-rod adjuster at body end; one string-guide.
- Body sunburst or colours.
- Two white six-polepiece pickups (neck and centre) and one black six-polepiece pickup (angled at bridge).
- Two controls (volume, tone) and five-way selector (at rear), all on metal plate adjoining pickguard; side-mounted output jack.
- Eight-screw white pearl laminated-plastic pickguard.
- Six-saddle flat bridge with through-body stringing.
- *Foto Flame fake-figured-wood-finish option (1995–96).*

MEXICAN MODELS

Mexican-made models are divided into two sections: Mexican Replica Models; and Mexican Revised Models.

Mexican Replica Models

Listed here in alphabetical order are the Mexican-made models we regard as replicas of various standard-version US-made Telecasters and Esquires (see earlier US Regular Models section).

CLASSIC 50s ESQUIRE 2005–current *Replica of 50s-period US original (see ESQUIRE listing in earlier US Regular Models section).*

CLASSIC 50s TELECASTER 1999–current *Replica of 50s-period original (see TELECASTER listing in earlier US Regular Models section).*

CLASSIC '69 TELECASTER THINLINE 1998–current *Replica of 1969-period original (see TELECASTER THINLINE first version listing in earlier US Regular Models section).*

CLASSIC 60s TELECASTER 2001–current *Replica of 60s-period original (see TELECASTER listing in earlier US Regular Models section).*

CLASSIC '72 TELECASTER CUSTOM 1999–current *Replica of 1972-period original (see TELECASTER CUSTOM listing in earlier US Regular Models section).*

CLASSIC '72 TELECASTER DELUXE 2004–current *Replica of 1972-period original (see TELECASTER DELUXE listing in earlier US Regular Models section).*

CLASSIC '72 TELECASTER THINLINE 1999–current *Replica of 1972-period original (see TELECASTER THINLINE second version listing in earlier US Regular Models section).*

Mexican Revised Models

Listed here in alphabetical order are the Mexican-made models we regard as revised and adapted versions of the standard-version US-made Regular Telecasters (see earlier US Regular Models section).

ACOUSTASONIC TELE 2010–current *Wooden bridge with no visible pickup.*

- Maple neck with rosewood fingerboard; truss-rod adjuster at headstock end; one string-guide.
- Semi-solid body; sunburst or white.
- One plain metal-cover pickup (at neck), Fishman piezo pickup under saddle (at bridge).
- One dual-concentric control (volume, tone for neck pickup), one control (master volume), three-way selector, all on metal plate adjoining pickguard; two controls (volume, tone for bridge pickup), switch for four modelling presets, all on plastic plate on body top; side-mounted output jack.
- Eight-screw laminated-tortoiseshell pickguard.
- Single-saddle flat wooden bridge with through-body stringing.

BAJA TELCASTER *See later CLASSIC PLAYER BAJA TELECASTER listing.*

BLACKOUT TELECASTER second version 2008–current *Three pickups, regular scale.*

- Maple neck with maple fingerboard; truss-rod adjuster at headstock end; one string-guide.
- Body black only.
- Two plain metal-cover pickups and one black six-polepiece pickup (angled at bridge).
- Two controls (volume, tone) and five-way selector, all on body; side-mounted output jack.
- Eight-screw black laminated-plastic pickguard.
- Six-saddle flat bridge with through-body stringing.
- *See later Korean Models section for first version listing.*

BLACKTOP BARITONE TELECASTER 2012–current *Three pickups, long scale, reversed control plate.*

- Maple neck with rosewood fingerboard; 27-inch scale, 22 frets; truss-rod adjuster at headstock end; one string-guide.
- Body sunburst, silver, or copper.
- Two plain metal-cover pickups with visible height-adjustment screws and one six-polepiece metal-cover humbucker with black surround (at bridge).
- Two controls (volume, tone) and five-way selector (at rear), all on metal plate adjoining pickguard.
- Eight-screw black laminated-plastic pickguard.
- Six-saddle small bridge with through-body stringing.

BLACKTOP TELECASTER HH 2011–current *Two humbuckers, reversed control plate.*

- Maple neck with maple or rosewood fingerboard; 22 frets; truss-rod adjuster at headstock end; one string-guide.
- Body black, red, or silver.
- Two metal-cover six-polepiece humbuckers.
- Two controls (volume, tone) and three-way selector (at rear), all on metal plate adjoining pickguard.
- Eight-screw black laminated-plastic pickguard.
- Six-saddle small bridge with through-body stringing.

CLASSIC PLAYER BAJA TELECASTER 2006–current Similar to CLASSIC 50s TELECASTER (see listing in earlier Mexican Replica Models section), except:

- Neckplate with 'Custom Shop designed' logo.
- Body blond, sunburst, or colours.
- Two controls (volume with push-switch, tone) and four-way selector, all on metal plate adjoining pickguard.

CLASSIC PLAYER TELE DELUXE BLACK DOVE 2010–current *Large headstock, two black six-polepiece pickups.*

- Fretted maple neck; bullet truss-rod adjuster at headstock end; two string-guides; large Stratocaster-style headstock.
- Contoured body; red or black.
- Two black six-polepiece pickups.
- Four controls (two volume, two tone) and three-way selector, all on pickguard; side-mounted output jack.
- 15-screw black laminated-plastic pickguard.
- Six-saddle small bridge with through-body stringing.

CLASSIC PLAYER TELE DELUXE W/TREMOLO 2010–current *Large headstock, vibrato bridge.*
Similar to CLASSIC PLAYER TELE DELUXE BLACK DOVE (see previous listing), except:
- Contoured body; sunburst or black.
- Two metal-cover split-polepiece humbuckers.
- 14-screw black laminated-plastic pickguard.
- Six-pivot bridge/vibrato unit.

CLASSIC PLAYER TELE THINLINE DELUXE 2010–current *F-hole body, selector on body.*
- Fretted maple neck; bullet truss-rod adjuster at headstock end; one string-guide.
- Semi-solid body with f-hole; sunburst or black.
- Two metal-cover split-polepiece humbuckers.
- Four controls (two volume, two tone) on pickguard; three-way selector on body; side-mounted output jack.
- 13-screw white laminated-plastic pickguard.
- Six-saddle small bridge with through-body stringing.

CONTEMPORARY TELECASTER *See later TELE SPECIAL listing.*

DELUXE BIG BLOCK TELECASTER 2005–06 *Block markers, black headstock face, chrome pickguard.*
- Maple neck with rosewood fingerboard, block markers; truss-rod adjuster at headstock end; one string-guide; black-face headstock.
- Body black only.
- Two plain metal-cover pickups with visible height-adjustment screws (at neck and in centre) and one black six-polepiece pickup (angled at bridge).
- Two controls (volume, tone) and five-way selector, all on metal plate adjoining pickguard; side-mounted output jack.
- Eight-screw chrome plastic pickguard.
- Six-saddle flat bridge with through-body stringing.

DELUXE NASHVILLE POWER TELE 1999–current *White six-polepiece pickup in centre position, one dual-concentric control.*
Similar to DELUXE NASHVILLE TELE (see following listing), except:
- One dual-concentric control (volume, tone for magnetic pickups), one control (volume for piezo pickups), and five-way selector.
- Eight-screw tortoiseshell laminated-plastic pickguard.
- Fishman Power Bridge with six piezo-pickup saddles.

DELUXE NASHVILLE TELE 1997–current *White six-polepiece pickup in centre position.*
Similar to STANDARD TELECASTER (see later listing), except:
- Fretted maple neck, or maple neck with rosewood fingerboard.
- Body sunburst or colours.
- One plain metal-cover pickup with visible height-adjustment screws (at neck), one white six-polepiece pickup (in centre), and one black six-polepiece pickup (angled at bridge).
- Two controls (volume, tone) and five-way selector.
- Eight-screw tortoiseshell laminated-plastic pickguard.
- Six-saddle raised-sides bridge with through-body stringing.
- *Known as DELUXE NASHVILLE TELE ASH (2005–06).*

DELUXE NASHVILLE TELE ASH *See previous listing.*

GRAHAM COXON TELECASTER 2011 *Signature on headstock rear, metal-cover humbucker in black surround at neck.*
- Maple neck with rosewood fingerboard; truss-rod adjuster at body end; one string-guide; signature on headstock (rear).
- Body blond only.
- One six-polepiece metal-cover small humbucker with black surround (at neck) and one black six-polepiece pickup (angled at bridge).
- Two controls (volume, tone) and three-way selector, all on metal plate adjoining pickguard.
- Eight-screw tortoiseshell laminated-plastic pickguard.
- Three-saddle raised-sides bridge with through-body stringing.

J5 TELECASTER 2005–09 *Headstock with three tuners each side, humbucker at bridge.*
- Maple neck with rosewood fingerboard; 22 frets; truss-rod adjuster at headstock end; no string-guide; black-face three-tuners-each-side headstock.
- Bound body; black only.
- One plain metal-cover pickup with visible height-adjustment screws (at neck) and one black coverless humbucker (in bridgeplate).
- Two controls (volume, tone) on metal plate adjoining pickguard, three-way selector on body; side-mounted output jack.
- Eight-screw chromed pickguard.
- Six-saddle flat bridge with through-body stringing.

J5 TRIPLE TELE DELUXE 2007–current *Three split-polepiece humbuckers.*
- Maple neck with rosewood fingerboard; 22 frets; truss-rod adjuster at headstock end; no string-guide; black-face large Stratocaster-style headstock.
- Contoured bound body; black only.
- Three metal-cover split-polepiece humbuckers.
- Two controls (volume, tone) and three-way selector, all on pickguard; side-mounted output jack.
- 13-screw chromed pickguard.
- Six-pivot bridge/vibrato unit.
- *Also known as JOHN 5 HHH TELE.*

JAMES BURTON STANDARD TELECASTER 1995–current *Signature on headstock.*
Similar to STANDARD TELECASTER (see later listing), except:
- James Burton signature on headstock.
- Eight-screw white plastic pickguard.
- Six-saddle raised-sides bridge with through-body stringing.

JIM ROOT TELECASTER 2007–current *One control, two black-cover pickups.*
- Maple neck with ebony or maple fingerboard; 22 frets; truss-rod adjuster at headstock end; one string-guide.
- Body white or black.
- One EMG-logo black-cover pickup (neck) and one EMG-logo black covered humbucker (at bridge).
- One control (volume) and three-way selector on body; side-mounted output jack.
- Eight-screw black or white plastic pickguard.
- Six-saddle small bridge with through-body stringing.
- Black-plated hardware.

JOE STRUMMER TELECASTER 2007–09 *Road Worn aged body, 'Revolution Rock' neckplate.*
- Maple neck with rosewood fingerboard; truss-rod adjuster at body end; one string-guide; 'Revolution Rock' neckplate.
- Body black over grey aged Custom Road Worn finish.
- One plain metal-cover pickup (at neck) and one black six-polepiece pickup (angled at bridge).
- Two controls (volume, tone) and three-way selector, all on metal plate adjoining pickguard; side-mounted output jack.
- Eight-screw white laminated-plastic pickguard.
- Aged three-saddle raised-sides bridge with through-body stringing.
- *First 1,500 with kit of stickers and stencils.*

MUDDY WATERS TELECASTER 2001–09 *'Custom Telecaster' on headstock, amplifier-type black plastic control knobs.*
Similar to CLASSIC 60s TELECASTER (see listing in earlier Mexican Replica Models section), except:
- 'Custom Telecaster' on headstock.
- Body red only.
- Nine-screw white plastic pickguard.
- Amplifier-type black plastic control knobs.

ROAD WORN PLAYER TELECASTER 2011–current *Humbucker at neck, reversed control plate.*
- Fretted maple neck; truss-rod adjuster at headstock end; one string-guide.
- Body black or red, lightly aged Road Worn finish.
- One metal-cover six-polepiece small humbucker in black surround (at neck) and one black six-polepiece pickup (angled at bridge).
- Two controls (volume, tone) and three-way selector (at rear), all on metal plate adjoining pickguard.
- Eight-screw black laminated-plastic pickguard.
- Six-saddle flat bridge with through-body stringing.
- Aged hardware.
- *Some early examples with regular control layout, not reversed.*

ROAD WORN 50s TELECASTER 2009–current *Vintage 50s-style features, aged finish, aged hardware.*
- Fretted maple neck; truss-rod adjuster at body end; one string-guide.
- Body sunburst or blond, aged Road Worn finish.
- One plain metal-cover pickup (at neck) and one black six-polepiece pickup (angled at bridge).
- Two controls (volume, tone) and three-way selector, all on metal plate adjoining pickguard.
- Five-screw white plastic pickguard.
- Three-saddle raised-sides bridge with through-body stringing.
- Aged hardware.

SPECIAL TELECASTER *See later STANDARD TELECASTER listing.*

SQUIER SERIES STANDARD TELECASTER *See later TRADITIONAL TELECASTER listing.*

STANDARD TELECASTER 1991–current *Modern-style chunky Fender headstock logo in silver, two single-coils.*
- Fretted maple neck; truss-rod adjuster at headstock end; one string-guide.
- Body sunburst or colours.
- One plain metal-cover pickup with visible height-adjustment screws (at neck) and one black six-polepiece pickup (angled at bridge).
- Two controls (volume, tone) and three-way selector, all on metal plate adjoining pickguard; side-mounted output jack.
- Eight-screw white laminated-plastic pickguard.
- Six-saddle flat bridge/tailpiece (no through-body stringing).
- *Originally known as SPECIAL TELECASTER in UK.*

TELE SPECIAL 1994–96 *Humbucker at neck, black pickguard.*
Similar to STANDARD TELECASTER (see previous listing), except:
- One metal-cover six-polepiece humbucker (at neck) and one black six-polepiece pickup (angled at bridge).
- Two controls (volume, tone) and five-way selector.
- Eight-screw black laminated-plastic pickguard.
- Six-saddle raised-sides bridge with through-body stringing.
- *Known as CONTEMPORARY TELECASTER in UK.*

TEX-MEX TELE SPECIAL 1997 *Humbucker at neck, white pickguard.*
Similar to STANDARD TELECASTER (see earlier listing), except:
- One metal-cover six-polepiece humbucker (at neck) and one black six-polepiece pickup (angled at bridge).
- Two controls (volume, tone) and five-way selector.
- Six-saddle raised-sides bridge with through-body stringing.

TRADITIONAL TELECASTER 1996 *Modern-style chunky Fender headstock logo in black, two single-coils.*
Similar to vintage-style Telecaster, except:
- Fretted maple neck; truss-rod adjuster at headstock end; one string-guide.
- Body various colours.
- One plain metal-cover pickup with visible height-adjustment screws (at neck) and one black six-polepiece pickup (angled at bridge).
- Two controls (volume, tone) and three-way selector, all on metal plate adjoining pickguard; side-mounted output jack.
- Eight-screw white laminated-plastic pickguard.
- Six-saddle flat bridge/tailpiece (no through-body stringing).
- *Previously known as SQUIER SERIES STANDARD TELECASTER, with small 'Squier Series' logo on headstock (1994–96).*

KOREAN MODELS

Many models made in Korea for Fender bear the Squier brandname and so are beyond the scope of this reference section. However, some have prominently featured the Fender logo, and these are listed here, in alphabetical order. All have 'Made in Korea' or 'Crafted in Korea' somewhere on the instrument.

ASH TELECASTER *See later LITE ASH TELECASTER.*

BLACKOUT TELECASTER first version 2004–05 *Glued-in neck, no front markers, two Seymour Duncan humbuckers.*
- Maple glued-in neck with rosewood fingerboard, no front markers; 22 frets; truss-rod adjuster at headstock end; two string-guides.
- Body black or blue.
- Two Seymour Duncan-logo black coverless humbuckers.
- Two controls (volume, tone) and three-way selector, all on body; side-mounted output jack.

- No pickguard.
- Six-saddle small bridge with through-body stringing.
- Black-plated hardware.
- *See earlier Mexican Revised Models listing for second version listing.*

CUSTOM TELECASTER FMT HH first version 2003–04
Glued-in neck, bound body with figured top.
- Maple glued-in neck with bound rosewood fingerboard; 22 frets; truss-rod adjuster at headstock end; two string-guides.
- Bound body with figured carved top; various colours.
- Two black coverless humbuckers.
- Two controls (volume, tone) and three-way selector, all on body; side-mounted output jack.
- No pickguard.
- Six-saddle small bridge with through-body stringing.
- Smoked chrome-plated hardware.
- *See Indonesian Models section (below) for second version listing.*

ESQUIRE CUSTOM CELTIC 2003 *Celtic-design inlay at 12th fret, single-cutaway body.*
- Mahogany glued-in neck with rosewood fingerboard; 22 frets; truss-rod adjuster at headstock end; two string-guides; no front markers; Celtic-design inlay at 12th fret.
- Contoured body; silver only, satin finish.
- One black coverless humbucker (at bridge).
- One control (volume) on body; side-mounted output jack.
- No pickguard.
- Six-saddle small bridge with through-body stringing.
- Black-plated hardware.

ESQUIRE CUSTOM GT 2003 *Centre-striped single-cutaway body.*
- Mahogany glued-in neck with bound rosewood fingerboard; 22 frets; truss-rod adjuster at headstock end; two string-guides.
- Contoured bound body; blue, red, or silver, with centre stripes.
- One black coverless humbucker (at bridge).
- One control (volume) on body; side-mounted output jack.
- No pickguard.
- Six-saddle small bridge with through-body stringing.
- Black-plated hardware.

ESQUIRE CUSTOM SCORPION 2003 *Scorpion inlay at 12th fret.*
- Mahogany glued-in neck with bound rosewood fingerboard; 22 frets; truss-rod adjuster at headstock end; two string-guides; no front markers except scorpion inlay at 12th fret.
- Contoured bound body; black only.
- One black coverless humbucker (at bridge).
- One control (volume) on body; side-mounted output jack.
- No pickguard.
- Six-saddle small bridge with through-body stringing.
- Black-plated hardware.

KOA TELECASTER 2006–08 *Rosewood fingerboard, white pearl pickguard.*
- Maple neck with rosewood fingerboard; 22 frets; truss-rod adjuster at headstock end; two string-guides.
- Body with koa veneer top; sunburst only.
- One plain metal-cover pickup (at neck) and one Seymour Duncan-logo black six-polepiece pickup (angled at bridge).
- Two controls (volume, tone) and three-way selector, all on metal plate adjoining pickguard; side-mounted output jack.
- Eight-screw white pearl laminated-plastic pickguard.
- Three-saddle raised-sides bridge/tailpiece with through-body stringing.

LITE ASH TELECASTER 2004–08 *Maple neck with maple fingerboard, black pickguard.*
- Maple neck with maple fingerboard; 22 frets; truss-rod adjuster at headstock end; two string-guides.
- Body natural, black, or white.
- One plain metal-cover pickup (at neck) and one Seymour Ducan-logo six-polepiece pickup (angled at bridge).
- Two controls (volume, tone) and three-way selector, all on metal plate adjoining pickguard; side-mounted output jack.
- Eight-screw black plastic pickguard.
- Three-saddle raised-sides bridge/tailpiece, some with no through-body stringing.
- *Also known as* ASH TELECASTER.

SQUIER SERIES STANDARD TELECASTER 1992–94 *Small 'Squier Series' logo on headstock.*
- Fretted maple neck; 21 frets; truss-rod adjuster at headstock end; one string-guide; small 'Squier Series' logo on headstock.
- Body black, blue, red, or white.
- One plain metal-cover pickup with visible height-adjustment screws (at neck) and one black six-polepiece pickup (angled at bridge).
- Two controls (volume, tone) and three-way selector, all on metal plate adjoining pickguard; side-mounted output jack.
- Eight-screw white plastic pickguard.
- Six-saddle flat bridge/tailpiece with no through-body stringing.
- *Replaced by Mexican-made version in 1994 (see* TRADITIONAL TELECASTER *in earlier Mexican Revised Models section).*

INDONESIAN MODELS

Many models made in Indonesia for Fender bear the Squier brandname and so are beyond the scope of this reference section. However, some have prominently featured the Fender logo, and these are listed here, in alphabetical order. All have 'Crafted in Indonesia' somewhere on the instrument.

CUSTOM SPALTED MAPLE TELE 2008–current *Body with spalted (black-line-figured) maple top veneer.*
Similar to CUSTOM TELECASTER FMT HH second version (see following listing), except:
- Mahogany glued-in neck with bound rosewood fingerboard.
- Bound body with figured spalted-maple-veneer carved top.
- Chrome-plated hardware.

CUSTOM TELECASTER FMT HH second version
2005–current *Glued-in neck, bound body with figured top.*
- Mahogany glued-in neck with bound rosewood fingerboard; 22 frets; truss-rod adjuster at headstock end; two string-guides.
- Bound body with figured carved top; various colours.
- Two black coverless humbuckers.

- Two controls (volume, tone with push-switch) and three-way selector, all on body; side-mounted output jack.
- No pickguard.
- Six-saddle small bridge with through-body stringing.
- Smoked-chrome-plated hardware.
- *See earlier Korean Models section for first version listing.*

JA-90 TELECASTER *See following JIM ADKINS JA-90 TELECASTER THINLINE listing.*

JIM ADKINS JA-90 TELECASTER THINLINE 2009–current *F-hole body, controls and selector on body, signature on headstock rear.*

- Mahogany neck with rosewood fingerboard; 22 frets; truss-rod adjuster at headstock end; two string-guides; neck and headstock face match body colour; signature on headstock (rear).
- Semi-solid body with f-hole; red, black, or natural.
- Two Seymour Duncan-logo black six-polepiece pickups.
- Four controls (two volume, two tone) and three-way selector, all on body; side-mounted output jack.
- Seven-screw black laminated-plastic pickguard.
- Six-saddle bridge, bar tailpiece.
- *Also known as JA-90 TELECASTER.*

CHINESE MODELS

Many models made in China for Fender bear the Squier brandname and so are beyond the scope of this reference section. However, two recent models have prominently featured the Fender logo, and these are listed here, just about in alphabetical order. Both have the legend 'Crafted in China' somewhere on the instrument.

MODERN PLAYER TELECASTER PLUS 2011–current *Three pickups, coil-split switch.*

- Fretted maple neck; 22 frets; truss-rod adjuster at headstock end; two string-guides.
- Body sunburst or brown.
- One plain metal-cover pickup (at neck), one black six-polepiece pickup with visible height-adjustment screws (centre), one black humbucker with metal surround (at bridge).
- Two controls (volume, tone), mini-switch (bridge pickup coil-split), and five-way selector, all on metal plate adjoining pickguard.
- Eight-screw black laminated-plastic pickguard.
- Six-saddle small bridge with through-body stringing.

MODERN PLAYER TELECASTER THINLINE DELUXE 2011–current *F-hole body, two black six-polepiece pickups.*

- Fretted maple neck; 22 frets; truss-rod adjuster at headstock end; two string-guides.
- Semi-solid body with f-hole; sunburst or 'black transparent'.
- Two black six-polepiece pickups.
- Four controls (two volume, two tone) on pickguard, three-way selector on body; side-mounted output jack.
- 13-screw white or back laminated-plastic pickguard.
- Six-saddle small bridge with through-body stringing.

SQUIER-BRAND MODELS

Fender launched its Squier brand in 1982, using it at first for Japan-made instruments exported into Europe, and soon elsewhere. The name was borrowed from the US Fender-owned V.C. Squier string company. Fender intended the Squier line to cater for lower-price instruments, maintaining the company's ever-expanding market coverage – but not by cheapening the Fender name itself.

The Squier logo, supported by a small but important 'by Fender' line, appeared on an increasing number of models during the 80s. At first, these came from Japan, but escalating production costs led to a move to cheaper manufacturing sources. Korea came on line in 1988, and India made a brief contribution around the same time for a few early and ill-fated Squier II and Sunn-branded guitars.

Fender's facility in Mexico helped out, too, in the 90s, and more recently China, India, and Indonesia have entered the picture, providing entry-level electrics with the kudos of a Fender connection. Periodic returns to Japanese production have yielded impressive results, such as the Silver and Vista series, while the Pro Tone line from Korea and recent Chinese efforts such as the Classic Vibe and Vintage Modified series have offered good quality at competitive prices.

The continuing success story of Squier makes this a very important support brand for Fender, with a level of design and build quality that often exceeds its apparent status as a second-string line.

DATING CLUES

Finding a method to date a guitar is important. Not only can it help satisfy our natural curiosity about the origins of a guitar, but also, in the case of desirable instruments, the vintage can have a great bearing on the guitar's value. The Fender brand has its fair share of collectables, and with high prices for the more sought-after models, any corroboratory clues that indicate the year of production become ever more useful.

Changes specific to each Fender model appear in the main listings in the previous pages. Although the respective features for some individual models can provide dating clues, comparatively few of them are consistent across all Fender models, and fewer still have chronological significance. We've brought together here some of these few general pointers that are relevant to the period of production of US-made models, but even these should be regarded as fallible.

Neckplate

Fender's standard method to fix a guitar neck to the body is with four screws – often erroneously called bolts in Fenderspeak – together with a metal neckplate to reinforce the joint. Fender used a rectangular four-screw neckplate from its earliest days, and it provides a simple and secure foundation for the neck. From 1971 to 1981, a restyled three-screw version (actually two screws and one bolt) was used on three Telecaster models –

Custom, Deluxe, and Thinline – as well as on the Stratocaster and Starcaster. After 1981, Fender reverted to using the four-screw type for most instruments (excluding any set-neck models, of course), although as usual there are exceptions.

From 1954 to 1976, the neckplate carried a stamped serial number. (From 1976 onward, the serial appears on the headstock face, save for various exceptions, including Custom Shop models, vintage reissues, and some limited editions.)

From 1965 to 1983, the neckplate (both four and three-screw types) was stamped with a large, reversed 'F'.

Tuners

It was not easy at first for Fender to find tuners to suit Leo's ideal of a small, neat headstock with straight string-pull. The problem was solved, with influence from Bigsby guitars, by using products supplied by the Chicago-based Kluson company, cut down by Race & Olmsted to squeeze them into the minimal length available. The Klusons that Fender used each had a safety string post, which is a slotted shaft with a central vertical hole designed to take the end of the string – and thus eliminate the unsightly and dangerous length of protruding string. These tuners were used from 1950 to 1966, and the following variations of the markings on their metal covers can provide an indication of date.

Version 1, used in 1950 and 1951, has 'Kluson Deluxe' and 'Pat. Appld' stamped on the cover.
Version 2, used from 1951 to 1957, has no markings on the cover.
Version 3, used from 1957 to 1964, has 'Kluson Deluxe' stamped in a single, central, vertical line on the cover.
Version 4, used from 1964 to 1966, has 'Kluson' and 'Deluxe' stamped in two parallel, vertical lines on the cover.

Due to supply and quality problems with Kluson, Fender wanted to make a tuner of its own, and in 1965 it contracted Race & Olmsted to supply a revised, cheaper design. The result was a tuner with an angled baseplate, 'F'-stamped cover, and a less rounded button. It was used on Fender instruments until 1976, when it was replaced by a more competitively-priced version made by the German Schaller company, until 1983. Although ostensibly very similar in appearance, the Schaller unit has a different construction and can be distinguished by its closed cover, with no visible axle-end on the side. A number of variations on these designs have been used since.

Neck and fingerboard construction

From 1950 to 1959, Fender used a fretted one-piece maple neck, with no separate fingerboard.

From 1959 to 1962, the top of the maple neck was planed flat and fitted with a rosewood fingerboard, flat on the base and cambered on top. It is known as a slab board because of the appearance of the straight join between fingerboard and neck when viewed from the body end of the neck.

From 1962 to 1983, the top of the maple neck itself was cambered and then fitted with a thin-section rosewood fingerboard that followed the same curve. This is known as a laminate board, because of the appearance of the curved join at the end of the neck. The board was made even thinner from around 1963.

A maple fingerboard was offered as an option, officially from 1967 but in practice earlier. Around 1970, the fretted one-piece maple neck was reinstated as an alternative to the rosewood fingerboard. Since 1983, Fender has offered various options on different models.

Neck date

During production, Fender marks dates on some components, and one of the most consistent and obvious is the neck. The date can be found on the body-end, either written or stamped. There have been periods when the neck did not carry this useful information – the longest was between 1973 and 1981 – and for these instruments other dating clues must suffice.

Serial numbers

A guitar's serial number should be regarded merely as a guide to dating, and ideally the production year of a guitar should be confirmed by other age-related aspects. As is usual with a mass-manufacturer, Fender has not always assigned serial numbers in exact chronological order, and number-bearing components such as neckplates have rarely been used in strict rotation. As a result, apparent discrepancies and contradictions of as much as several years can and do occur. Depending on the production period, serial numbers are located on the guitar's bridgeplate, or neckplate, or on the front or rear of the headstock.

The numbers shown here represent the bulk of Fender's US and Mexican production. There have been and continue to be various anomalies, odd series, special prefixes, and the like, but these have no overall dating relevance and are not listed. Also excluded are the series used on Vintage replica reissues, limited editions, signature instruments, and so on, as these are often specific to the series or models and do not relate directly to production year. The late-90s Fender California models, for example, featured AMXN serial prefixes, reflecting their mix of American and Mexican manufacture.

The listing here does not apply to Fenders which originate from countries other than the US and Mexico (and, later, Japan); these (and Squier-brand instruments) have their own various number series, which do sometimes duplicate those in the US system. Prefixes include C, CY, and YN for China, CN, VN, and NK for Korea, and IC, ICS, and IS for Indonesia, but there are many more. Any confusion has to be resolved by studying other aspects of an instrument to determine its correct origin (often simply determined by a 'Made In...' or 'Crafted In ...' stamp) and its production year.

Starting in 2010, Fender introduced a clear new serial-numbering system for instruments made in its US and Mexican factories. It consists of a two-letter prefix followed by eight or nine numbers. The two-letter prefix denotes the country of manufacture, with 'US' indicating US-made and 'MX' indicating Mexican-made. The first two digits of the number denote the year of manufacture, as shown in the listings, while the remaining numbers identify the individual instrument.

Fender Japan's production started in 1982, and the company has used a series of prefixes to indicate the year of manufacture. The data shown here is approximate and, again, should be used only as a general guide.

Some Japanese serial series have been used beyond the production spans listed here, in particular the original A-, C-, and G-prefix numbers. Somewhere on the guitar there should be a tag indicating 'Made In Japan' or 'Crafted In Japan'. Check the table nearby, and note the change from 'MADE IN JAPAN' to 'Crafted In Japan' and then back to 'Made in Japan' – this helps to differentiate between the sets of numbers.

Once again, all this underlines the need for caution when dating a Fender – and indeed most other guitars – by using a serial number alone.

Part numbers

Since the 70s, many Fender catalogues and pricelists and websites have used part numbers to make the process of ordering and stock-keeping easier for distributors and dealers. Each version and variation of a model is

US number series	Approximate year(s)
Up to 6,000	1950–54
Up to 10,000 (4 or 5 digits, inc 0 or - prefix)	1954–56
10,000s (4 or 5 digits, inc 0 or - prefix)	1955–56
10,000s to 20,000s (5 or 6 digits, inc 0 or - prefix)	1957
20,000s to 30,000s (5 or 6 digits, inc 0 or - prefix)	1958
30,000s to 40,000s	1959
40,000s to 50,000s	1960
50,000s to 70,000s	1961
60,000s to 90,000s	1962
80,000s to 90,000s	1963
Up to L10,000 (L + 5 digits)	1963
L10,000s to L20,000s (L + 5 digits)	1963
L20,000s to L50,000s (L + 5 digits)	1964
L50,000s to L90,000s (L + 5 digits)	1965
100,000s	1965
100,000s to 200,000s	1966–67
200,000s	1968
200,000s to 300,000s	1969–70
300,000s	1971–72
300,000s to 500,000s	1973
400,000s to 500,000s	1974–75
500,000s to 700,000s	1976
800,000s to 900,000s	1979–81
76 or S6 + 5 digits	1976
S7 or S8 + 5 digits	1977
S7, S8 or S9 + 5 digits	1978
S9 or E0 + 5 digits	1979
S9, E0, or E1 + 5 digits	1980–81
E1, E2, or E3 + 5 digits	1982
E2 or E3 + 5 digits	1983
E3 or E4 + 5 digits	1984–87
E4 + 5 digits	1987
E4 or E8 + 5 digits	1988
E8 or E9 + 5 digits	1989–90
E9 or N9 + 5 digits	1990–91
N0 + 5 digits	1990–91
N1 + 5/6 digits	1991–92
N2 + 5/6 digits	1992–93
N3 + 5/6 digits	1993–94
N4 + 5/6 digits	1994–95
N5 + 5/6 digits	1995–96
N6 + 5/6 digits	1996–97
N7 + 5/6 digits	1997–98
N8 + 5/6 digits	1998–99
N9 + 5/6 digits	1999–2000
DZ0 + 5/6 digits	2000
Z0 + 5/6 digits	2000–01
DZ1 + 5/6 digits	2001
Z1 + 5/6 digits	2001–02
DZ2 + 5/6 digits	2002
Z2 + 5/6 digits	2002–03
DZ3 + 5/6 digits	2003
Z3 + 5/6 digits	2003–04
DZ4 + 5/6 digits	2004
Z4 + 5/6 digits	2004–05
DZ5 + 5/6 digits	2005
Z5 + 5/6 digits	2005–06
DZ6 + 5/6 digits	2006
Z6 + 5/6 digits	2006–07
DZ7 + 5/6 digits	2007
Z7 + 5/6 digits	2007–08
DZ8 + 5/6 digits	2008
Z8 + 5/6 digits	2008–09
DZ9 + 5/6 digits	2009
Z9 + 5/6 digits	2009–10
10 + 5/6/7 digits	2009–10
US10 + 6/7 digits	2010
US11 + 6/7 digits	2011
US12 + 6/7 digits	2012

Mexico number series	Approximate years
MN1 + 5/6 digits	1991–92
MN2 + 5/6 digits	1992–93
MN3 + 5/6 digits	1993–94
MN4 + 5/6 digits	1994–95
MN5 + 5/6 digits	1995–96
MN6 + 5/6 digits	1996–97
MN7 + 5/6 digits	1997–98
MN8 + 5/6 digits	1998–99
MN9 + 5/6 digits	1999–2000
MZ0 + 5/6 digits	2001–02
MZ2 + 5/6 digits	2002–03
MZ3 + 5/6 digits	2003–04
MZ4 + 5/6 digits	2004–05
MZ5 + 5/6 digits	2005–06
MZ6 + 5/6 digits	2006–07
MZ7 + 5/6 digits	2007–08
MZ8 + 5/6 digits	2008–09
MZ9 + 5/6 digits	2009–10
10 + 5/6/7 digits	2009–10
MX10 + 6/7 digits	2010
MX11 + 6/7 digits	2011
MX12 + 6/7 digits	2012

'MADE IN JAPAN' number series	Approximate years
JV + 5 digits	1982–84
SQ + 5 digits	1983–84
E + 6 digits	1984–87
A + 6 digits	1985–86, 1997–98
B + 6 digits	1985–86, 1998–99
C + 6 digits	1985–86
F + 6 digits	1986–87
G + 6 digits	1987–88
H + 6 digits	1988–89
I + 6 digits	1989–90
J + 6 digits	1989–90
K + 6 digits	1990–91
L + 6 digits	1991–92
M + 6 digits	1992–93
N + 6 digits	1993–94
O + 6 digits	1993–94
P + 6 digits	1993–94
Q + 6 digits	1993–94
S + 6 digits	1994–95
T + 6 digits	1994–95
U + 6 digits	1995–96
V + 6 digits	1996–97

'Crafted in Japan' number series	Approximate years
A + 6 digits	1997–98
B + 6 digits	1998–99
N + 5 digits	1995–96
O + 0 [zero] + 5 digits	1997–2000
P + 0 [zero] + 5 digits	1999–2002
Q + 0 [zero] + 5 digits	2002–04
R + 0 [zero] + 5 digits	2004–06
S + 0 [zero] + 5 digits	2006–08
T + 0 [zero] + 5 digits	2007–08

'Made In Japan' number series	Approximate year(s)
T + 0 [zero] + 5 digits	2007–10
U + 0 [zero] + 5 digits	2010–

allocated a specific number. For instance, at the time of writing, a current (early 2012) natural-finish maple-board Fender American Standard Telecaster had the part number 011-0502-721. The digits provide various pieces of information such as model type, fingerboard wood, hardware options, finish colour, and if a case is included in the price. For our purposes, it's the first three digits (011 in the example) that are particularly useful, because they indicate the instrument's country of origin. The list below reveals the manufacturing country and brand that each code indicated in early 2012. Some codes have indicated a number of manufacturing countries over the years, and many of these obsolete sources are also shown here, marked as 'formerly'.

010 US factory, US Custom Shop (Fender)
011 US factory (Fender)
012 formerly US factory (Fender)
013 Mexico factory (Fender); formerly Mexico factory (Squier)
014 US factory, Mexico factory (Fender); formerly US factory (Squier)
015 US Custom Shop (Fender)
017 US factory (mostly special runs and Fender Select)
018 formerly US factory (Fender)
019 US factory, US Custom Shop (Fender)
024 China (Fender)
025 Japan (Fender)
026 Indonesia (Fender); formerly Korea (Fender); formerly Japan, China (Squier)
027 Japan (Fender); formerly Japan, Korea (Squier); formerly Japan (D'Aquisto)
028 China (Squier); China, Korea, Indonesia (Starcaster brand); formerly Japan (Fender), then India (Squier II, Sunn)
029 formerly India, Korea (Squier II, Sunn)
030 Indonesia, India, China (Squier)
031 China, Indonesia (Squier); formerly Japan (Heartfield)
032 Indonesia, China (Squier); formerly Japan (Squier); formerly Korea (Squier)
033 formerly India (Squier II); formerly Korea (Squier); formerly Japan (Squier); formerly China (Squier); formerly Indonesia (Squier)
034 Korea, China, Indonesia (Squier)
055 formerly US Custom Sho (Fender)
056 formerly US Custom Shop (Fender)
057 formerly US Custom Shop (Fender)
095 formerly US Custom Shop (Fender)
110 formerly US factory (Fender w/ Floyd Rose Tremolo)
111 formerly US factory (Fender w/ Floyd Rose Tremolo)
113 formerly Mexico factory (Fender w/ Floyd Rose Tremolo); formerly Mexico factory (Squier w/ Floyd Rose Tremolo)
114 Mexico factory (Fender w/ Floyd Rose Tremolo)
125 formerly Japan (Fender w/ or w/out Floyd Rose Tremolo); formerly Japan (Heartfield w/ Floyd Rose Tremolo); formerly Japan (Squier w/ Floyd Rose Tremolo)
132 formerly China, Indonesia (Squier w/ Floyd Rose Tremolo)
133 formerly Korea (Squier w/ Floyd Rose Tremolo)
150 US Custom Shop (Fender)
151 US Custom Shop (Fender)
152 formerly US Custom Shop (Fender)
155 US Custom Shop (Fender)
156 formerly US Custom Shop (Fender)
157 formerly US Custom Shop (Fender)
632 formerly China (Squier)
633 formerly China (Squier)
921 US Custom Shop (mostly Masterbuilt Fender)
923 US Custom Shop (mostly Custombuilt/Limited Fender); formerly US Custom Shop (mostly Teambuilt Fender)
927 US Custom Shop (Fender)

MODEL TIMELINE

All the models featured in the earlier parts of the Reference Listing are arranged here by year of first appearance.

- Models are US factory production except where marked (C) for China, (CS) for US Custom Shop, (I) for Indonesia, (J) for Japan, (M) for Mexico, or (K) for Korea.
- 1st version, 2nd type, etc indicate distinct model variations, reflecting the styles used in the Reference Listing.
- Japanese-made models sometimes have irregular availability outside Japan, and this is reflected in a date range here ending with '–onward'. For more information on this, see the Japanese Models heading on page 144.

1950
Broadcaster 1950–51
Esquire 1950–69

1951
Telecaster 1951–83

1959
Custom Esquire 1959–69
Custom Telecaster 1959–72

1968
Blue Flower Telecaster 1968–69
Paisley Red Telecaster 1968–69
Thinline Telecaster 1st version 1968–71

1969
Rosewood Telecaster 1969–72

1971
Thinline Telecaster 2nd version 1971–79

1972
Telecaster Custom 1972–81

1973
Telecaster Deluxe 1973–81

1977
Antigua Telecaster 1977–79
Antigua Telecaster Custom 1977–79
Antigua Telecaster Deluxe 1977–79

1981
Black & Gold Telecaster 1981–83
International Colour Telecaster 1981

1982
American Vintage '52 Telecaster 1982–84, 1986–current

1983
Elite Telecaster 1983–84
Gold Elite Telecaster 1983–84
Telecaster Standard 1983–84
Walnut Elite Telecaster 1983–84

1984
Bowling Ball/Marble Telecaster 1984

1985
Contemporary Telecaster 1st type (J) 1985–87
Contemporary Telecaster 2nd type (J) 1985–87
Custom Telecaster '62 (J) 1985–onward
Foto Flame Telecaster (J) 1995–96

1986
Blue Flower Telecaster (J) 1986–onward
Custom Esquire (J) 1986–onward
Esquire (J) 1986–onward
Paisley Telecaster (J) 1986–onward
Rosewood Telecaster (J) 1986–onward
Telecaster Custom '72 (J) 1986–onward
Thinline Telecaster '69 (J) 1986–onward
Thinline Telecaster '72 (J) 1986–onward

1988
American Standard Telecaster 1988–current
Standard Telecaster (J) 1988–91

1990
Albert Collins Telecaster 1990–current
Danny Gatton Telecaster 1990–current
James Burton Telecaster 1st version 1990–2005
Tele Plus 1st version 1990–95
50s Telecaster (J) 1990–onward

1991
HMT Acoustic-Electric 1st version (J) 1991–94
HMT Telecaster 1st type (J) 1991–92
HMT Telecaster 2nd type (J) 1991–92
Set Neck Telecaster 1991–95
Set Neck Telecaster Floyd Rose 1991–92
Set Neck Telecaster Plus 1991–92
Standard Telecaster (M) 1991–current
Tele Plus Deluxe 1991–92

1992
Bajo Sexto Telecaster 1992–98
JD Telecaster (J) 1992–99
Jerry Donahue Telecaster 1992–2001
Set Neck Telecaster Country Artist 1992–95
Sparkle Telecaster 1992–95
Squier Series Standard Telecaster (K) 1992–94

1993
Clarence White Telecaster 1993–2001

1994
Aluminum-Body Telecaster 1994–95
Special Edition 1994 Telecaster 1994
Tele Special (M) 1994–96
60s Telecaster (J) 1994

1995
American Classic Telecaster 1st version 1995–99
American Standard B-Bender Telecaster 1995–97
HMT Acoustic-Electric 2nd version (J) 1995–97
James Burton Standard Telecaster (M) 1995–current
Relic Nocaster (CS) 1995–98
Tele Jnr 1995–2000
Tele Plus 2nd version 1995–98
Telecaster XII 12-string 1995–98
Waylon Jennings Tribute Telecaster 1995–2003
90s Telecaster Custom (J) 1995–98
90s Telecaster Deluxe (J) 1995–98

1996
Nokie Edwards Telecaster (J) 1996
Traditional Telecaster (M) 1996
50s Telecaster 1996–98
50th Anniversary Telecaster 1996
60s Telecaster Custom 1996–98

1997
California Fat Tele 1997–98
California Tele 1997–98
Deluxe Nashville Tele (M) 1997–current
Merle Haggard Signature Telecaster 1997–current
Tex-Mex Tele Special (M) 1997
Will Ray Jazz-A-Caster (J) 1997–98
90s Tele Thinline 1997–2000

1998
American Deluxe Telecaster 1st version 1998–99
American Nashville B-Bender Tele 1998–current
Buck Owens Telecaster (J) 1998
Classic '69 Telecaster Thinline (M) 1998–current
John Jorgenson Telecaster 1998–2001
Tele-Sonic 1998–2004
U.S. Fat Tele 1998–2000
Will Ray Telecaster 1998–2001
'98 Collectors Edition Telecaster 1998

1999
American Classic Telecaster 2nd version 1999–2000
American Deluxe Power Tele 1999–2001
American Deluxe Telecaster 2nd version 1999–2003
American Vintage '62 Custom Telecaster 1999–current
Classic 50s Telecaster (M) 1999–current
Classic '72 Telecaster Custom (M) 1999–current
Classic '72 Telecaster Thinline (M) 1999–current
Deluxe Nashville Power Tele (M) 1999–current
'51 Nocaster (CS) 1999–current
'52 Tele Special 1999–2001
'63 Telecaster (CS) 1999–2009

2000
Custom Classic Telecaster (CS) 2000–08

2001
Classic 60s Telecaster (M) 2001–current
Muddy Waters Telecaster (M) 2001–09
Sub-Sonic Tele baritone 2001–05

2002
Highway One Telecaster 1st version 2002–06

2003
American Ash Telecaster 2003–07
American Telecaster HH 1st version 2003–04
American Telecaster HS 1st version 2003–04
Custom Telecaster FMT HH 1st version (K) 2003–04
Esquire Custom Celtic (K) 2003
Esquire Custom GT (K) 2003
Esquire Custom Scorpion (K) 2003
Flat Head Telecaster 2003–04
Francis Rossi Signature Telecaster (J) 2003–04
Highway One Texas Telecaster 2003–09
Jimmy Bryant Telecaster (CS) 2003–05
John 5 Bigsby Signature Telecaster (CS) 2003–current
John 5 Signature Telecaster (CS) 2003–current
Rick Parfitt Signature Telecaster (J) 2003–04
Seymour Duncan Signature Esquire (CS) 2003–08
'59 Esquire (CS) 2003–06
'60 Telecaster Custom (CS) 2003–04

2004
Aerodyne Tele (J) 2004–06
American Deluxe Ash Telecaster 2004–current
American Deluxe Telecaster 3rd version 2004–current
American Deluxe Telecaster FMT/QMT 2004–06
American Telecaster HH 2nd version 2004–06
American Telecaster HS 2nd version 2004–06
Antigua Telecaster (J) 2004
Blackout Telecaster 1st version (K) 2004–05
Classic '72 Telecaster Deluxe (M) 2004–current
Flat Head Telecaster HH 2004–06
Lite Ash Telecaster (K) 2004–08

2005
Classic 50s Esquire (M) 2005–current
Custom Telecaster FMT HH 2nd version (I) 2005–current
Deluxe Big Block Telecaster (M) 2005–06
J5 Telecaster (M) 2005–09
Richie Kotzen Signature Telecaster (J) 2005–06
50s Telecaster With Bigsby (J) 2005–06
'67 Telecaster (CS) 2005–08, 2011
60s Telecaster With Bigsby (J) 2005–09

2006
American 60th Anniversary Telecaster 2006

Classic Player Baja Telecaster (M) 2006–current
Highway One Telecaster 2nd version 2006–11
James Burton Telecaster 2nd version 2006–current
Koa Telecaster (K) 2006–08
Tele Thinline (CS) 2006–08

2007
G.E. Smith Telecaster 2007–current
J5 Triple Tele Deluxe (M)
Jim Root Telecaster (M) 2007–current
Joe Strummer Telecaster 2007–09 (M)
Tele Pro 2007–08
Vintage Hot Rod '52 Tele 2007–current

2008
Blackout Telecaster 2nd version (M) 2008–current
Custom Spalted Maple Tele (I) 2008–current

2009
Classic S-1 Telecaster (CS) 2009
Custom Deluxe Telecaster (CS) 2009–current
Jim Adkins JA-90 Telecaster Thinline (I) 2009–current
Road Worn 50s Telecaster (M) 2009–current
Tele Pro Relic (CS) 2009
50s Telecaster Thinline (CS) 2009
'64 Relic Telecaster (CS) 2009

2010
Acoustasonic Tele (M) 2010–current
American Special Telecaster 2010–current
Classic Player Tele Deluxe Black Dove (M) 2010–current
Classic Player Tele Deluxe w/Tremolo (M) 2010–current
Classic Player Tele Thinline Deluxe (M) 2010–current
Telecaster Pro Relic (CS) 2010
'52 Telecaster HB Relic (CS) 2010

2011
American Vintage '69 Telecaster Thinline 2011–current
American Vintage '72 Telecaster Custom 2011–current
American Vintage '72 Telecaster Thinline 2011–current
Blacktop Telecaster HH (M) 2011–current
Closet Classic Pine Telecaster Pro (CS) 2011
Graham Coxon Telecaster (M) 2011
Modern Player Telecaster Plus (C) 2011–current
Modern Player Telecaster Thinline Deluxe (C) 2011–current
Relic Bigsby Telecaster (CS) 2011
Road Worn Player Telecaster (M) 2011–current
Tele-bration Brown's Canyon Telecaster 2011
Tele-bration Cabronita Telecaster 2011
Tele-bration Empress Telecaster 2011
Tele-bration Flame Top Telecaster 2011
Tele-bration Indiana Barn '52 Telecaster 2011
Tele-bration Lamboo Telecaster 2011
Tele-bration Lite Rosewood Telecaster 2011
Tele-bration Mahogany Telecaster 2011
Tele-bration Modern Thinline Telecaster 2011
Tele-bration Vintage Hot Rod '52 Telecaster 2011
Tele-bration '62 Telecaster Custom 2011
Tele-bration '75 Telecaster 2011
'53 Heavy Relic Telecaster (CS) 2011
'63 Heavy Relic Telecaster Custom (CS) 2011
'67 NOS/Relic Telecaster (CS) 2011
'69 Relic Telecaster Thinline (CS) 2011
60th Anniversary Telecaster 2011

2012
Bent Top Telecaster (CS) 2012
Blacktop Baritone Telecaster (M) 2012–current
Closet Classic Telecaster Pro (CS) 2012
Jim Campilongo Telecaster (CS) 2012–current
Relic Pinstripe Esquire (CS) 2012
Select Carved Koa Top Telecaster 2012–current
Select Carved Maple Top Telecaster 2012–current
Select Telecaster 2012–current
'61 Relic Telecaster Custom (CS) 2012

INDEX

A page number in *italic type* indicates an illustration. A page number in the range 133–151 indicates an entry in the Reference Listing. Signature models are indexed by the first word of the name, not the surname; for example, the Clarence White Telecaster model is found under C, not W.

ACKNOWLEDGEMENTS

INSTRUMENT PICTURES

OWNERS KEY

The guitars we've photographed came from the collections of the following individuals and organisations, and we are most grateful for their help. The owners are listed here in the alphabetical order of the code that is used to identify their instruments in the Instruments Key below.

AG Arbiter Group; **AH** Adrian Hornbrook; **AO** Alex Osborne; **BF** Brian Fischer; **CC** Chinery Collection; **CH** Christie's; **CM** Country Music Hall Of Fame; **DG** David Gilmour; **FE** Fender Musical Instruments Corp; **GR** Gruhn Guitars; **JD** Jerry Donahue; **JE** John Entwistle; **MB** Mark Brend; **PD** Paul Day; **PM** Paul Midgley; **SA** Scot Arch.

INSTRUMENTS KEY

This key identifies who owned which guitars at the time they were photographed. After the relevant **bold-type** page number(s) there is a model identifier followed by the owner's initials (see the alphabetical list in the Owners Key above).

14–15 Bigsby CM. **22–23** Broadcaster DG. **23** Nocaster JE. **26–27** Telecaster GR. **30–31** Esquire BF. **34** '56 Telecaster BF. **34–35** '57 Telecaster BF. **42–43** Esquire BF. **46** Custom Telecaster AH. **50–51** Telecaster SA. **54** both Telecasters BF. **58–59** Thinline Telecaster BF. **62** Paisley Red Telecaster AH. **63** B-Bender Telecaster CC. **66–67** Rosewood Telecaster AH. **67** Thinline Telecasters both BF. **70** Telecaster Deluxe PM. **70–71** Telecaster Custom BF. **74** Telecaster BF. **78–79** Telecaster BF. **82–83** Telecaster Standards all BF. **86–87** '52 Telecaster DG. **90–91** Gold Elite Telecaster PM. **91** Gold Elite Telecaster PD. **94–95** American Standard Telecaster FE. **95** Contemporary Telecaster MB; Jerry Donahue Telecaster prototype JD. **98** Egyptian Telecaster FE. **98–99** James Burton Telecaster PM; Telecaster 40th Anniversary PM. **102–103** Clarence White Telecaster FE. **103** Set Neck FE; American Classic AG; 50s Telecaster AO. **106** HMT Acoustic-Electric FE. **106–107** '60 Telecaster Custom Relic FE. **110–111** '72 Telecaster Deluxe FE. **111** Leo Fender Broadcaster AG. **114–115** '05 J5 Telecaster FE. **115** '05 Custom Telecaster FE. **118–119** '07 Andy Summers Telecaster FE. **119** '12 Baja Telecaster FE. **122–123** '11 Tele-bration Lamboo Telecaster FE; '11 Road Worn Player Telecaster FE. **126–127** '12 Modern Player Telecaster Plus FE; '12 Standard Telecaster FE. **127** '10 Damien Hirst Telecaster CH.

Guitar photography for Backbeat UK was by William Taylor and Miki Slingsby. Other photography was by Garth Blore and Matthew Chattle, with further images supplied by FMIC.

ARTIST PICTURES

Images are identified by bold-type page number, subject, and photographer and/or collection and agency. **2–3** Waters, Richard E. Aaron/Redferns/Getty Images. **18** Aldrich, Richard Smith; Cooley, Michael Ochs Archive/Getty Images. **22** Kauffman, Richard Smith. **31** King, Michael Ochs Archive/Getty Images. **34** Brown, Michael Ochs Archive/Getty Images. **38** Waters, Michael Ochs Archive/Getty Images. **46** Cropper, Michael Ochs Archive/Getty Images. **47** Owens, EMI Archives/Redferns. **50** Bloomfield, Michael Ochs Archive/Getty Images. **55** Townshend, K&K Studios/Redferns/Getty Images. **58** Clapton, Jeremy Fletcher/Redferns/Getty Images; Beck, Petra Neimeier/Redferns. **59** Barrett, Andrew Whittuck/Redferns/Getty Images. **62** Burton, Sue Bradshaw/Redferns. **66** Harrison, Michael Ochs Archive/Getty Images. **71** Richards, Richard E. Aaron/Redferns/Getty Images; Dias, David Ellis/Redferns. **74** Harkleroad, Fin Costello/Redferns. **75** Robertson, Elliott Landy/Redferns; Buchanan, Michael Ochs Archive/Redferns. **78** Johnson, Colin Fuller/Redferns. **79** Strummer, Erica Echenberg/Redferns/Getty Images. **82** Gatton, Michael Ochs Archive/Getty Images. **83** Summers, Jorgen Angel/Redferns/Getty Images. **87** Stern, Tim Hall/Redferns. **90** Lee, Phil Dent/Redferns. **91** Hynde, Ian Dickson/Redferns. **95** Donahue, Roberta Parkin/Redferns. **102** Black, Paul Bergen/Redferns. **107** Yorke, Peter Pakvis/Redferns. **110** Kapranos, Peter Pakvis/Redferns. **111** Ball, Jill Douglas/Redferns. **126** Gill, Ethan Miller/Getty Images. **127** Root, Christie Goodwin/Redferns/Getty Images.

MEMORABILIA

Other items illustrated in this book – including advertisements, brochures, catalogues, and photographs (in fact anything that isn't a guitar or an artist shot) – came from the collections of Tony Bacon, Balafon Image Bank, Paul Day, FMIC, *The Music Trades*, National Jazz Archive (Loughton), John Page, Alan Rogan, and Dan Smith.

INTERVIEWS
Original interviews used in this book were conducted by Tony Bacon as follows: **Jeff Beck** (April 2005); **George Blanda** (May 2010); **James Burton** (April 2005); **Joe Carducci** (November 1997); **Bill Carson** (September 1991); **Jerry Donahue** (April 2005); **Mike Eldred** (January 2012); **Phyllis Fender** (February 1992); **George Fullerton** (February 1992); **Bob Heinrich** (December 1997); **Dale Hyatt** (February 1992); **John 5** (May 2011); **Bill Kirchen** (April 2005, January 2012); **Mike Lewis** (December 1997); **Seth Lover** (October 1992); **Richard McDonald** (January 2012); **Bill Mendello** (June 2011); **Justin Norvell** (December 2011); **Karl Olmsted** (February 1992); **John Page** (February 1992, December 1997); **Don Randall** (February 1992); **Dan Smith** (February 1985, February 1992, December 1997, June 2005, April 2007, May 2011); **Andy Summers** (August 1981); **Terry Tavares** (May 2010); **Forrest White** (February 1992).

THANKS
In addition to those already namechecked in these acknowledgements, the author would like to thank: Ralph Baker; Brandy Barker (FMIC); Jeff Beck; Julie Bowie; Martin Brady (Fender Europe); Mark Brend; John Bryant; Dave Burrluck; James Burton; Louise Burton; Walter Carter (Gruhn Guitars); Paul Cooper; Paul Day; Jerry Donahue; Mike Eldred (FMIC); Jason Farrell (FMIC); Brian Fischer; flyingvintage.com; Dave Gregory; Yvonne Groenendijk; Johnny Harper; Christopher Hjort; Dave Hunter; Kerry Keane (Christie's); Bill Kirchen; John Morrish; Jun Nakabayashi (Dyna Boeki); Justin Norvell (FMIC); Martina Oliver (Getty); John Page (John Page Guitars); Sung-Hee Park (Christie's); Bill Penn; Julian Ridgway (Getty); Morgan Ringwald (FMIC); Alan Rogan; John Ryall; Chris Scapelliti (*Guitar Aficinado*); Rich Siegle (FMIC); Dan Smith; Richard Smith; Simon Smith; Will Taylor; Neil Whitcher (Fender Europe); Bob Willocks (FMIC); Michael Wright.

BOOKS
Andy Babiuk *The Story Of Paul Bigsby* (FG 2008).
Tony Bacon *The Fender Electric Guitar Book* (Backbeat 2007); *Six Decades Of The Fender Telecaster* (Backbeat 2005); *60 Years Of Fender* (Backbeat 2010); *Squier Electrics* (Backbeat 2012); *The Stratocaster Guitar Book* (Backbeat 2010).
Tony Bacon (ed) *Electric Guitars: The Illustrated Encyclopedia* (Thunder Bay 2000).
Paul Balmer *Fender Telecaster Manual* (Haynes 2009).
Bill Carson *My Life And Times With Fender Musical Instruments* (Hal Leonard 1999).
Phil Carson *Roy Buchanan: American Axe* (Backbeat 2001).
Walter Carter & George Gruhn *Gruhn's Guide To Vintage Guitars* (Backbeat 2010).
A.R. Duchossoir *The Fender Telecaster* (Hal Leonard 1991); *Guitar Identification* (Hal Leonard 1990).
George Fullerton *Guitar Legends* (Centerstream 1993).
Guitar Trader *Vintage Guitar Bulletin Vol.2* (Bold Strummer 1992).
Ralph Heibutzki *Unfinished Business: The Life & Times Of Danny Gatton* (Backbeat 2003).
Christopher Hjort & Doug Hinman *Jeff's Book* (Rock'n'Roll Research Press 2000).
Steve Howe & Tony Bacon *The Steve Howe Guitar Collection* (Balafon 1994).
Dave Hunter *Star Guitars* (Voyageur 2010).
Martin Kelly, Terry Foster, Paul Kelly *The Golden Age Of Fender 1946–1970* (Cassell 2010).
Richard R. Smith *Fender: The Sound Heard 'Round The World* (Hal Leonard 2009).
Andy Summers *One Train Later* (Thomas Dunne 2006).
Tom Wheeler *American Guitars* (HarperPerennial 1990); *The Dream Factory* (Hal Leonard 2011); *The Stratocaster Chronicles* (Hal Leonard 2004).
Forrest White *Fender: The Inside Story* (Miller Freeman 1994).

UPDATES?
The author and publisher welcome any new information for future editions. Write to: Telecaster, Backbeat & Jawbone, 2A Union Court, 20–22 Union Road, London SW4 6JP, England. Or you can email: telecaster@jawbonepress.com.

It's a piercing, whining sound that forces you to pay attention, and it's filled with clear high-range harmonics. What makes it so appealing is that it makes the average ear say, 'My god, what brilliance!' – Freddie Tavares, 1972